SIKHISM
CONTINUITY OF INDIAN CULTURE

SIKHISM

Continuity of Indian Culture

Professor Nirbhai Singh

KALPAZ

ISBN: 978-81-7835-942-7

Price : ₹ 950

First Published 2013

Published by

Kalpaz Publications
C-30, Satyawati Nagar,
Delhi - 110052
E-mail: kalpaz@hotmail.com Ph.: 9212142040

Laser Typesetting : Rajender Vashist, Delhi
Printed at : G. Print Process, Delhi

Cataloging in Publication Data--DK
Courtesy: D.K. Agencies (P) Ltd. <docinfo@dkagencies.com>

Nirbhai Singh, 1935-
Sikhism : continuity of Indian culture / Nirbhai Singh.
p. cm.
Includes bibliographical references (p.) and indexes.
ISBN 9788178359427

1. SIkhism--Social aspects--India. 2. Religion and culture--India. 3. India--Civilization. I. Title.

DDC 294.60954 23

CONTENTS

Preface

The present book focuses attention on the Indian culture that waded through chequered historical epochs retaining its dynamic ontic essence. It has been written from the Indian and philosophical standpoints which mirrors global cultures. Culture is, often, misunderstood and confused with its manifest forms of traditions, rituals, customs, etc. From the philosophical perspective it is concerned with consciousness (mind) that mirrors inner selfs of the persons. Culture is always concerned with societal life for the good of people. Thus, culture is mainly concerned with ideals and values which create their own space independent of the phenomenon world. The values are not God given gifts. These are created by the creative thinkers. Once they are created, they become eternal.

Indian culture is action oriented. The central value of Indian culture is enshrined in Dharma (righteous action). This idea we find in the Indian epics (the Ramayana and the Mahabharata). The concept was carried forth in the teachings of the Gurus which are found in the Sikh scriptures. An endeavour is made to work out that Sikhism is a continuity of Indian culture. There is no departure from the fundamental philosophical doctrines of Indian culture though some now dimensions are added to it. Indian culture has been philosophically reinterpreted in the medieval context. It is hoped that critical insights of the readers will appreciate the philosophical interpretations based on 'simultaneity of the non-contemporaneous'.

It follows that there is no absolute truth. It is relative to time and context. It is the modern meaning of truth. Modern Austrian philosopher Wittgenstein asserts that there is no Platonic ontological base of reality or truth. And there is no Kantian dichotomy between the transcendent and the phenomenon. It has been argued in the book *passim* that the time is stretched into eternity with spiritual discipline. Thus, the phenomenon and the transcendental realms are reconciled into non-dual. Truth is activity that is knitted into logical space. It goes on changing with the changing conditions. Hence thread of arguments in the book is that Sikhism in essence is Indian culture revivified in the medieval time. And the present work is presented in modern idioms of philosophical hermeneutics. Contributions of Sikhism to Indian culture have been highlighted.

Underlying concept of Indian culture is at once transcendence from entices of this-world and disinterestedly involve in it. India's cultural world view is built on myths and traditions or ethos. Our forefathers deified traditions and legends, but the Gurus demythicised the Indic and the Semitic religious traditions and historicized them with a view to reviving reality of human action. Notwithstanding, ancient rishis had historical sense, but they considered the empirical world delusive because it is short-lived/ephemeral albeit, there are references of the otherworld, but these erode their ontic existence. The Gurus did away the medieval prevalent concept of the otherworld and restored historicity of karmas dominated with spirituality. The undercurrent of historicity was crystallized. They reconciled theory and praxis. They lived unto this ideal. There is no contradiction in their saying and doing. Nevertheless, historical action necessarily follows from their dynamic onto-theology. Their central emphasis was discharging disinterested action (*nishkama karmas*) for restoring peace and justice in society. It was recycling of the central message of the Bhagavata Gita. Realization of Indian ideal was processed in history from Guru Nanak to Guru Gobind Singh It was consummated with the creation of the Khalsa, even though decadence dominated in the Misl (Sikh confederation) period. In the present scenario spiritual (*piri*) is overshadowed by temporality (*mire*). Simultaneity of spirituality and temporality with dominance of the former is the central linchpin of Indian and Sikh concept of culture. The Indic and the Semitic cultures are blended without suppressing ontic non-duality or identity and otherness of either one. The present book is logically articulated to synthesize identity and otherness.

Nirbhai Singh
Former Member of ICPR (New Delhi)
Senior Fellow, IIAS (Shimla), and
Senior Fellow, ICSSR (New Delhi)

1

Cultural Milieu

(i) Introductory

Rethinking or reinterpretation is an epistemic necessity. If it is not accepted, it will lead to deviation from the truth. Terrorism, fanaticism, bigotry and bloodshed will be the natural outcome of it. Interpretation should be coeval or contemporaneous and contextual.

India is a land of multiple cultures, civilisations, religions, and philosophies. The different communities had their own dietary habits of food, different dialects, dresses, and other cultural diversities. The dietary and food conventions were not matters of taste, but they represented their customs, conventions, religious beliefs, taboos, and other social considerations. These depended on availability of food articles as well. Every community has its own distinct cultural identity. It is natural that hatred is deeply ingrained in the social consciousness of each ethnic group for other cultural and religious communities. This is due to inherent sense of superiority and cultural ethnocentricity. Communal violence has been a common game of politics in the past. One point that is more significant is that in the Arabic countries lack of liberal and democratic cultures were wanting. The nomadic people lacked social niceties of civilised life. Atrocities and the tyranny were domineering features of the barbarian and tribal Turco-Mongol peoples. Beastly elements were more active and niceties of culture were alien to their ways of living and life-style. They lived heroic ways of living. It is, therefore, desirable to take cognizance of these aspects as well. The invaders who came to India were mainly concerned with wealth of India. Because of rich natural resources, India was considered a "golden sparrow". Their concern was for power and wealth. They were least concerned with understanding Indian culture in-depth. Alberuni tried to understand Indian culture, but he could not succeed in his mission. His understanding was based on the traditional exegetes' conventional explanations. Besides, it is very difficult to evince alien culture in a short span of time.

Many cultural invasions on India created composite culture of India. They had significant impacts on our lifestyles. Many good elements of culture came to India from Baghdad. Despite all these variant factors, the core of Indian spiritual culture assimilated the alien cultures into its deep-rooted fold of antiquity. It will be pertinent to point out that India did retain her distinct spiritual and cultural identity. Our spiritual culture is an admixture of spiritual and material values, but the former dominates it. It is full of vitality and energy. Our Indian culture is the culture of struggle in life. It is a dynamic culture. Our sages refined spiritual culture through the ages. They refined our beastly nature and fashioned human crudities into spiritual identity as an embodiment of Indian cultural identity.

It may be kept in mind that difference between facts and values always remains. Culture is an ideational category. If studying or thinking is inspired to think originally, it is doing philosophy. New culture, thus, is created with new values. Ought is inbuilt in the facts. For example, if I warn a person that he should not cut his hair and beard, and then ought is implied in it. The Akâla Takht at Amritsar (Punjab) is a monumental architectural fact. It inherits norms of moral conduct for every member of the Sikh community. The argument can be extended to philosophy of culture. Every philosophy is a critique of various types of cultural identities, religious traditions, disintegration and reintegration. For this purpose philosopher creates values, judgment, culture and moral philosophy.

The present book focuses on purpose and meaning of human life in connection with existential societal realities. Man and his relations with 'others' are real. Societal relations are necessarily derived from the dynamic metaphysical reality that is precondition of cultural life in the society. My concern is to delineate cultural phenomenon of India and Sikhism. Both mirror perspectives of global cultures without suppressing distinctive identities of other cultures. My endeavour is to rope in temporality within eternity for explaining pronounced non-dual reality. Those who think that the primordial Being is static, then the social relations become illusory. From this standpoint dynamic nature of the ultimate presupposed reality must be dynamic. The Indic and the Semitic, and Chinese cultures have dynamic foundations of their philosophical traditions. These are taken into consideration for having a holistic and global perspective of human life. The viewpoint of life is interpreted from the philosophical viewpoint, which rationally analyses existential human conditions. There is no static-eternal substance. All are 'becoming', cycling and recycling, within the gamut of the universal law which regulates all cosmic processes. Man is required to attune himself with it.

For understanding India's cultural history we need not fragment it into past, present and future epochs because cultural life is a continuous flow of ethos, ideas and beliefs in the lived experiences. Some elements are dropped from the traditions and others emerge in the cosmic process of the cultural phenomenon. For having in-depth understanding of culture one is required to have a lived experience of social relations. It is difficult for the person to come out of the cocoon of one's culture and understand alien culture of others' minds. The person who inhales fragrance of his native culture and makes attempts to interpret other cultures is a difficult phenomenon. However, it is possible to articulate ideal cultural ideology if objective rules of logic and hermeneutic are used. It will be a utopian concept if it is not successfully put to *use* in social life. Sikhism is a philosophical attempt to project rational picture of ancient Indian culture in the Gurus' contemporary period.

The purpose of human life in the Western and the Indian cultures is fundamentally peace and justice, equality and egalitarian social order, but means to realise the coveted goals are diametrically divergent. The differences are due to cultural and religious as well as regional diversities. When the Turks came to India, they tried to suppress and destroy Indian culture. They might have influenced external aspects of Indian culture, but the core identity of Indian culture escaped alien cultural invasions. The impacts of the Semitic and the Western cultures are conspicuous on Indian culture. Sikhism was a vigorous attempt for revivifying our culture and added some significant elements which speak of its singular contributions to Indian culture and the global ideologies.

The Indian perspective shall be compared with the Greek, the Chinese, the Western, and the Semitic world-views. Out of these world-views, new world-view of India has been formulated with art of hermeneutic interpretations. The Bhakti cult of the medieval India revived culture in the medieval devotional literature of the South, Maharashtra, North India (U.P., Gujarat, Rajasthan, and Punjab) and so on. The Tamil Siddhas were the Buddhists in their religious beliefs and practices. In the tenth century Christian Era, the Vitthala[1] Bhakti movement developed into the Vitthala cult, which is synthesis of Shaivism and Vaishnavism. The waive of the Vitthala Bhakti, further, spread to the North in U.P., Rajasthan, Punjab and other parts of India.

The foreigners tried to understand Indian culture. Their researches escaped objective insightful conceptual grasp of the Sanskrit texts. Oral traditions were alien to their comprehension. They, often, lack insightful peep into Indian culture. They, of course, could not go beyond philological level. It was a problem of the alien scholars to read the other mind which is private or personal and subjective. Unless the other person discloses his mind, it remains private. Then the question of linguistic barrier came in their way. Every world is coloured in its milieu. It emerges out of its environment and is learned through mother tongue. Language is a treasure of culture. Meanings are hidden in it. The Europeans interpreted Indian culture couched in Western thought and languages and, thus, presented caricatured picture of India.

It may be pinpointed that it is easy to craft alien culture when one inherits native culture since conception in the womb. It, thus, becomes difficult to project objective picture of others' culture. Thus, the foreigners see Indian culture through the coloured grooves of their own cultures. Indian culture is a complex phenomenon. It will be a lopsided presentation of Indian culture if we limit it to one exclusive Indic traditions. It has other cultural traditions as well. It has multi-dimensional facets which are split up into variant traditions. These traditions are mixed-up with alien and native traditions that have been flowering into our traditions since time immemorial. All traditions have their independent stances and have Indian impact on them. The underlying identity of 'India' continues though outer manifestations are apparent in rituals, custom, ceremonies, and so on. The ancient Indian sages expressed their ideas through myths which have their own logic. Natural language cannot go beyond the temporal or phenomenon level. Therefore, the sages adopted twilight language which at once expresses the empirical and the non-empirical levels. Consciousness is the foundation of Indian culture. The transcendental identity of consciousness is acosmic and beyond history and time. It is eternal and can't be reduced to the empirical world. It implies that consciousness (*chita*) as such can't be reduced to the empirical self because it is the transcendental precondition or foundation of all representations (knowledge/judgments) and pluralities. Nevertheless, it can be harnessed to time (history) for carrying out real historical actions as categorical imperatives. It will be voluntarism where cosmic will (*rita / hukam*) is active in history. This is the central concept of Indian culture. Sikhism continues this vision.

The medieval saints motivated regional Indian rulers of principalities for resisting alien invaders. In Maharashtra Samratha Guru Ramanatha guided Shivaji to resist Aurangzeb and his bigotry and atrocities. In Rajasthan Bhakta Ravidâsa was *raj-guru* of Rânâ Sanga of Citorh and in Madhya Pradesh Bhakta Sein was spiritual *raj-guru* of Bir Singh Baghela of Riva state (M.P.). Bir Singh Baghela was protector of the saints.

Similarly, the network of the saints was spread all over India. The Sikh Gurus made a radical departure from this practice.

In the ancient past civilisations of Harappa and Mohenjo-Daro had been cauldrons of trades and intercultural exchange of idea and philosophies. Indian culture has been looked upon as the precursor of other Asian cultures. India has been a meeting land of Greek, Egyptian, Mesopotamia (now Iraq), Arabian, Persian, Chinese cultures, civilisations, philosophies, etc. Indian spiritual civilisation and culture continue to exist, though Egyptian, Babylonian, Sumerian, Roman, Greek civilisations have disappeared from the map of the world. Ancient religious rituals, creeds, conventions, customs and traditions are undying relics of the primitive societies that are hovering over our collective antennae.

The medieval Indian scenes depicted unity-in-diversity in which the latter dominated. The cementing forces of culture and religion always played a significant role in unifying the Indian society, but the alien cultures have been disintegrating the unity. The medieval society was split up into small princely states and feudatories of the feudal chiefs. After fall of Harsha's Empire (CE 1089-101), the central rule was shaken.

Despite all these turmoils and terrors, India continued to retain her distinct spiritual and cultural identity. Virtually Indian culture never presented a historical continuity of progress because of intermittent repeated foreign invasions. D.D. Kosambi aptly comments that: "... India was never a nation that Indian culture and civilisation was a by-product of foreign conquests whether Muslim or British."[2]

After crumbling of the Gupta Empire, India ceased to be a united nation. Foreign invasions were a frequent feature of the medieval times. The invaders carried along with them their tribal cultures, languages, religious beliefs, myths, legends, and so on. Thus, the Indian culture is blending of the alien cultures. It has been expressing progression and retrogression owing to foreign travelers and conquerors. Purity of essential Indic culture is a myth. It is a complex phenomenon.

It may be pertinent to point out that India has been an arena for the persistent foreign invaders. Many alien people came to India and settled down here. They carried along with them their respective cultures. The present book concentrates on composite culture of India consisting of Greek, Persian, Arabic, and other cultures with which Indian culture and civilisation interacted. Indian culture absorbed alien cultures into its fold.

The medieval cultural milieu is determined by the geographical location of the country. Civilisations of the Indus Valley, the Mohenjo-Daro, and the Gangetic fertile land were influenced by the foreign invasions. India had trades with foreign countries: Sumerian, Egyptian, Persian, and other Arabian civilisations. The fluid political situation created a composite Indian culture.

At that time, there were no international boundaries to cross over to other lands. Any horde of tribal people under the leadership of any person could come, plunder, and return with booty to their countries. 'Might is right' was rule of those days. India consists of Greco-Buddhist, Chinese, Turco-Mongolian and Arabic pagan religion of the White Huns, Turks, and Mughals, and Zoroastrian (sun worship—Multan and Kashmir).[3] Impact of these cultures was conspicuous from 10th to 13th centuries. During these centuries, India experienced frequent invasions of the foreigners.

The Punjab was a meeting point of different cultures because of its unique geographical location, abundance of natural resources, network of trade routes through passes with Central Asia, West-East countries, like Egypt, Mesopotamia. It has close proximity to internal borders of Afghanistan, China, etc. It, therefore, acquired a distinct character of its own. It was considered as the gateway to Central Asia and West-Asian countries. The region has been significant from military and strategic point of view. It has borne brunt of repeated foreign incursions.

For the above reasons Punjab has been a melting pot of various ideologies, cultures, cross-currents in the socio-political, cultural, and religious thoughts. Advent of politicised Islam in Punjab and its spread over to other parts of India left an indelible impact on the social, cultural, and religious life of the medieval India. It shook the stagnated and degenerated Indian social order to its deep roots. Compulsory conversions and religious persecutions of non-Muslim population were order of the medieval ages. People were petrified and horrified. They were tight lipped due to weak will and state terror.

There are no divisions in human life and culture. It may be made clear that divisions in the historical epochs do not imply that the epochs are compartmentalised and split up into historical periods. The historical epochs are in continuous flux. They merge into one another. It is arbitrary on the part of man to seek for particular points of absolute beginning and ending of historical epochs. Past imperceptivity penetrates into the present and the present passes away unnoticed into the past. Different periods of India's cultural history are arbitrary. Man for his epistemic necessity articulates divisions of epochs. However, for our convenience and pragmatic viewpoint, we can split them up into triad of ancient, medieval, and modern epochs. Thus, beginning and end of medieval period cannot be pinpointed because historical epochs telescope into one another. The medieval period starts with the invasions of the Turks' invasions and ends with the collapse of the Mughal dynasty with death of Bahadur Shah Zafar, the last Mughal Emperor.

Culture progresses and retrogresses through the ages. This is Spengler's viewpoint of the world cultures. Goethe also holds the same view. It is a continuous progress and retrogression through the epochs of history. In the Indian polity transition from the ancient to the medieval period was a gradual departure from the divided princely kingdoms to central rule of the Sultans in Delhi. Delhi remained in the Sultanate period heartland of the Indian polity. Skirmishes and mutual jealousies among alien intruders continued because they did not belong to one racial stock and culture or country.

Then a question comes to our minds: What are the criteria that distinguish the ancient and the medieval ages? Many factors distinguish the two ages. The practice of land grants in the early medieval ages was encouraged. The decline of trade led to decay in towns and centres of trade with the West-Asian countries. The mode of production in villages changed due to supply and demand. This change emerged because of land grants and the decline of town trade. It was apparently a gradual transition from ancient to medieval age. There was a mushroom spurt in agrarian expansion. The medieval period is also marked by the appearance of forced or bounded labour, which was imposed by the invaders and the feudal class on the lower caste villagers. Right to land to the shudras was denied. In social life dowry contributed to the unequal distribution of lands.

Since time immemorial India has been developing her own polity, organisation, socio-religious patterns, languages, dialects, literature, aesthetics and unfolded to the spiritual world and philosophical truth. In ancient times the aliens; like, Greeks, Parthians, Kushans, Sakas, Huns, *et al.*, invaded India and established political supremacy in different regions.

Most of the elements of civilisation came to India from Persia. For philosophy and science, the Arabs look to Greece and the old Alexandrian School of Plato and Aristotle. Reason and faith were being reconciled. Alas! Changez and the Mongols put an end to cultural development. They were warriors and not religious celebrities. They exploited religion to dominate Indian power. They dismantled cultural life of the Indians and created terror in their minds. Nevertheless, they could not successfully establish their supremacy in culture because they came from the uncivilised racial stocks. Nevertheless, we learned many things from the Persian culture. The process of acculturation continued in the medieval ages.

Their supremacy was encapsulated by the Indian culture. However, they had some impact on social, religious, and cultural life of the indigenous rural populace. The core of Indian culture remained in a state of suspended animation immune from the alien cultural influences. During this period Indian culture was a 'silent' culture. Metaphysical foundation of Indian thought continued to dominate because of her quest for the Infinite and restoration of man's dignity and freedom.

The rise of Islam was started in the beginning of the seventh century. In addition, the integrated sovereign state under the rule or power of the Khalifahs (deputies of Prophet Muhammad) provided a tremendous impetus to the expansion of Islam. Their trade began to flourish and their settlements in other countries and on the Indian soil continued to multiply. They were allowed to follow their religion and propagate Islam openly and freely. Till ninth century, they spread Islam over whole of the Western coast of India.

For over a hundred years, the Muslims were established on the Malabar coast. The natives welcomed them on the Indian soil as traders of horses and missionaries. Before ninth century Islam advanced on the Western coast. In India politically unsettled and upheaval conditions prevailed. It mushroomed into new dynasties, which split up the country into splinters. People's mind was polluted. They welcomed Islam. Even mosques were erected and conversion to Islam took place. This trend continued till thirteenth century.

In Madurai (Tamil Nadu) the Muslims made their entrance in CE 1050 under the leadership of Malik-ul-Mulûk, who was accompanied by a great saint, Hazrat Auliya Shah Sahib remained there and was buried near Madurai. In the twelfth century, the Muslims formed a well-established community in these parts. There were other Muslim settlements in Tamil Nadu. Ibn Batuta traveled in these parts after invasion. He states that Ghiyas ud-Din al-Damghana was the ruler of Madurai in his time. It can be inferred from the above facts that the Muslims made their cultural and political advent on the South India in the Western coast as early as the eighth century if not earlier and in the tenth century penetrated into the eastern coast. They had influenced political and societal lifestyles of the Indians. Indian culture was overshadowed by the Islamic culture. The Muslim saints and missionaries built tombs and mosques, which became centres of worship and periodic meeting places for the common folk.

On the contrary, in the North the Arabs, the Turks, and the Mughals adopted the forceful method (sword).[4] The Muslim rulers in the Northern India indulged in forceful conversions for spreading supremacy of the Qur'anic ideology of *tauhid* (unity of Allah). They made many coercive conversions, which smacks of ethnocentricity of Islam. They strived to convert the whole India into *Dar-ul-Allah* (House of Allah).

Syrian Christians in the first century came to South India. Zoroastrianism came from Iran in seventh century. The Muslims came to India in the North-West (sea coast) and the North-West (land). Central and Western-Asian horses had best areas for breeding climate in India—Rajasthan and Kathiawarh. The North remained unsettled due to geographical conditions and the South was comparatively peaceful though it was exposed from the Arabian Sea and Bay of Bengal. Jesuit fathers and missionaries made systematic efforts to understand life, culture, and literature of India. They were active in the Malabar, Tamil Nadu and other Southern areas. After CE 1765, the Mughals granted to the English East India Company the right to collect revenue and administer justice in Bengal. It encouraged the British to gain familiarity with the laws, customs, and history of the Indians.[5]

(ii) Continuity of Indian Culture

What do we mean by the term '*hindu*'? Lexicographical meanings of the term '*hindu*' are given in dictionaries, but no philosophical meaning is made clear. D.N. Jha asserts that: "the use of the term '*hindu*' is equally erroneous. It was first used by the Arabs in the post-Gupta period to describe the inhabitants of Hindu (India). Ancient Indians never thought of themselves as Hindus" (see, *Ancient India*: Manohar, New Delhi, 2004). It is related to the River Sindh of Pakistan which comes down from Tibet and passes through Kashmir, and finally falls near Karachi into the Arabic Ocean (Arabic-Persian-*baharan*). In Persian literature and poetry the Muslims used the word 'Hindu'. It is transferred from the Arabic character '*seen*' into '*hai*'. Thus, the word Sindhu is spoken as 'Hindu' in the Persian literature. Those who live across the River Sindh towards India are called 'Hindus'. Gradually, the term 'Hindu' has been used for those people who are followers of the Vedic tradition. In the contemporary context, the term refers to followers of the Indian religious traditions. In the wider sense of the term, it also covers others religious traditions as well. In this work we shall use the term Indic culture in the complex sense. An endeavour shall be made to argue continuity of the geographical culture of the Indian soil.

The quintessence of Bhakti to Shakti is to realise cultural truth in the practical arena. Indian traditions mostly adopt spiritual discipline for rarefying gradually consciousness that transcends entices from the empirical world. At the same time, consciousness (mind=*mana*) is evolved from gross bodily elements and spirally goes up to identity with the supreme truth or consciousness. It is a process of transforming energy (shakti) into pure consciousness (Shiva). At the apex state, consciousness is simultaneously attuned to the eternal truth and is engaged in the empirical world (samsara). This concept was distorted in the medieval ages. The Bhakti movement came into being to revive original concept of Indian metaphysics. Culture is the necessary by-product of the Indian metaphysics and societal realities are its necessary offshoots. This was the pivotal point from which Sikhism continued from the Indic heritage. It also innovated some philosophical and cultural elements which were cohered with rich ideology of India.

The Bhakti Movement is a precursor to India's cultural revival. Tamil Siddhas represented the Buddhist tradition that is continuation of the Shramanic tradition. It is distinct stream from the Vedic one. Its seat was the Indus Valley Civilisation. In the Vitthala Bhakti tradition of Maharashtra, Shaivism is mixed up with Vaishnavism. The former dominated the latter. In Pandharpur cap on the icon of the deity symbolises Shaivism. This tradition spread in the North. Sikhism continued it and further developed. From this standpoint an endeavour is made to argue that Sikhism is a continuity of Indian culture.

Sikh faith anchors on *nama-simran* for achieving the goal of life *here* and *now* while discharging all worldly responsibilities. Man is not a helpless pawn that can be placed anywhere in the chess game of life. Man has latent freedom that can be aroused. He is, thus, intrinsically free. Every religion postulates his freedom that is to be culled out. For this purpose religion was developed. Religion is a human creation for bringing out the best in man. It transforms the beast in man and makes him a refined cultural person. The founder of every religion often conceives in his mind the ideal image of man. Guru Nanak, the pioneer of the Sikh faith, had in his mind the ideal image of man. His ideal man gurmukh was transformed into the Khalsa of Guru Gobind Singh. This transformation was carried forth in history. It constitutes a unique phenomenon in the history of religions. We do not come across in other religious traditions the process of transforming man in the course of history. It was carried out during the Guru period. Thus, it is the unique characteristic of the Sikh upsurge.

It is believed in the religious traditions that man has the primary "essential" characteristic of *ruh / atman* and a secondary shaping characteristic of the *nafs / jiva*. When both are treated as distinct and independent elements in the human person, it will create diversity in the unity of one. In respect of the former, every person's dynamic ontic identity of the 'I' is the same, but his magnified 'me' is diversified into the multiplicities of the 'me,' which have 'I' latent in them. The 'me' is to be developed into the 'I' with esoteric discipline. Anyone who breathes and wears clothes and interacts with 'others' either subsists or exists! In the true sense of the term, what makes his character distinct from other human beings are the spiritual attributes, feelings, instincts, and the singular personality traits spin around the 'I'. Once a person develops them, he realises his essential "I" in the existential situations as a categorical imperative (*nishkama karma*). He realises in himself the 'I' that mirrors the cosmic Being.

Despite all these, one is to be vigilant about one's self-respect and independent distinct historical identity. In the Kantian sense, he should be treated as a "person", a kingdom of ends and not means. The Sikh scriptures advocate the distinct identities of the gurmukh and the Khalsa. Their freedom and self-respect are to be safeguarded.

The medieval Indian Bhaktas made a radical departure from the prevalent medieval Indian culture and reinterpreted it from the hermeneutical and existential standpoints. They ruled out the hypostatised otherworld and restored social realities and the historical reality of human action. For them everything exists in the nature (Arabic, *qudrat*=energy). There is no acosmic truth in their ecstatic utterances. They have projected man as a concrete social being in nature. Man is real and his historical actions are real. At the time of birth man is a *jiva* ('me'). The eternal self (*atman*) is to be culled from within the *jiva* ('me'). Man creates his 'I' from within and then struggles with it in society to restore peace, harmony, and justice. He is to struggle for bliss (*ananda*) and emancipation of humanity.

Man's life is considered a rare opportunity to realise the ontic reality. The human being is the only species that can transcend the empirical world and enjoy the life of intrinsic freedom. His life in the world is not a gross material life or of pure abstraction from the temporal realm. His life is like that of a moth that lives in the garden and enjoys the fragrance of the flowers without being entangled in them. It is simultaneously in the garden and out of the garden; it has the freedom to move out of the garden as well. Similarly, man is to live in the world, but he should not be over engrossed in it. Man is to go through the tunnel of spiritual discipline before he enjoys this state of ecstasy.

In Sikhism, man is placed in the concrete existential moments created by the historical situations and the societal life. Unlike the Vedantic concept of incarnation, it is held that the incarnate (*avtara*) is dormant within man. It is to be aroused to make man act in history for executing the divine will as a responsible free moral person. The Khalsa should always be ready to discharge his duties for the welfare of all and sundry. Here, the Khalsa means one who is always eager to face any eventuality and risk to life. He is an embodiment of disinterested deeds. In this context, Guru Nanak says, "After washing the vessel and burning incense, go in for milking. Milking is [your] action and absorption in the *Ik* results in disinterested historical action." (GG, p. 728) Man is the miniature representative and executor of the divine will in history. Hence, he is a doer in history. This is the spirit of the Sikh dynamic view of human life.

It may be said that negation of the world and the self were prevalent in the medieval ages. The medieval saints reinterpreted and reaffirmed the existence of the phenomenal world and the self. The Bhaktas ushered in the new trend of voluntarism and the Gurus struck the radical change in the movement. In other words, the Bhaktas dotted the i's and the Gurus crossed the t's. Sikhism propounded the spiritual voluntarist philosophy, which gives precedence to praxis over theory without marginalising the latter. Volition and cognition go hand in hand, but former dominates. Voluntarism reinterpreted action as distanced engagement in the temporal world. All ideals of human life are to be realised in the *sangat* of the householders. It stands for the restoration of social realities and repudiation of the otherworld. It is the singular contribution of the Sikh voluntarist view to the global thought. In the social context, abstract ritualism and formalism of the Vedantic tradition is devoid of spirituality. Sikhism restores human freedom that was epitome of all religions in the past. The Gurus preached and practised their ideals in the course of history. This is how the theoretical and practical teachings have been concretised in praxis. Eternity has been yoked to the chariot of temporality.

However, this blending does not remain the same. Guru Nanak's philosophy of praxis erodes the Greek myth of eternal return or recurrence. It implies that every moment is new. It is revisiting the Heracleitean concept of 'change' and 'universal flux'. Therefore, only man has consciously created the history of humanity. He lives in history and creates history. He is, at once, a creature and a creator. Man, in praxis and history, is the creator of future. He does not live in the dead past and entertain false hopes of the other-world. He is to perform his role in the playground of the 'eternal present'. This concept of praxis symbolises an eternal dynamic life. Man becomes man only if he realises his historical responsibilities for the emancipation of man. Guru Nanak's gurmukh is never alienated from the social and historical realities. He is always active in the welfare of the real human beings.

Man is intrinsically hedonist. All human actions revolve around the pursuit of pleasure. He seeks *moksha* or *nirvana*, which is a rarefied pleasure—bliss (*ananda*). He wants to achieve this ideal by overcoming the existential problems in society. Thus, the concept of pleasure is an innate phenomenon in man. The genesis of religion lies in overcoming the impediments to life caused by the uncanny natural forces; like, floods, earthquakes or droughts. Man is expected to eradicate evil that is embedded within man and society. *Nama-simran* is the means for eradicating evil from within man's self. It is practised both in seclusion and in the *sangat* (holy assembly).

The meaning of bliss is changed from private and empirical pleasure or happiness to the welfare of other fellow beings. This disinterested dynamic involvement in the worldly life is the ideal of the Sikh ethics. Gurus translated this ideal into practice. He is not to fall a prey to the impermanent empirical pleasures that do not represent the lasting bliss. When he transcends his selfishness and ego-centric deeds, he becomes an altruist in practical life. He sheds the sense of possessiveness and involvement in other selves. He becomes the true gurmukh or the khȧlsa when he identifies himself with others and is motivated to be kind to the sentient and the insentient beings. His deeds make him realise the purpose of human life and discover the deeper meaning of life.

Each stage of life strengthens the urge to reintegrate oneself with each transcending stage in order to play its part in history and in the recycling of life in society. In Guru Nanak's "Japuji", the *khandas* (created conceptual spaces) from the *dharma-khanda* to the *sacha-khanda* represent the inward journey of the self towards an enriched and sublimated unity of the 'I' ("*atman*"). It is not withdrawal from the world. It is inward dive into inner recesses of consciousness to merge with the cosmic consciousness and resurrect to life in the world. It is disinterested involvement while discarding worldly desires and the ego-sense. It is a psycho-social development of the self from the 'me' to the 'I' through the inner rigorous self-discipline. The self, thus, becomes an active and voluntarist self.

The meaning of life is valorised and made authentic by man's creativity. Is there any meaning in life at different levels, ranging from an amoeba to human beings or from neurotic humans to superhuman beings and God ? The modern existentialists are preoccupied with this problem. The scientists are engaged in researches to make man happy, but it is the concern of the philosopher and the religious thinkers to work out the solution of human problems. Hence, the problem of meaning and purpose of life is man's articulation for working out the existential problems and their solutions. It is in this context that the exploration of the meaning of life gains ascendance.

Human beings have inherent urge for autonomy, which is present even in lower species. As compared to lower species, man creates the articulated world of his own. Birds and animals construct their nests and dens in accordance with their levels of existence and needs of the specific species to which they belong. They have territorial sense, but they have no higher creativity of linguistic articulation that may help them to have freedom and creativity. Man, on the contrary, knows how to create. He creates his own ideal world to realise autonomy. He knows how to articulate concepts to the appropriate use. He forges tools in accordance with his will and mind. The realised man wills to be in tune with the cosmic law. The whole argument boils down to the point that articulation of the concept of praxis is a universal and self-creative activity. It is to be developed as a free and conscious enterprise. It then evolves in peaceful atmosphere, and it must be preceded by intensity of suffering. The genesis of creativity is put to use in the existential situations. From this concept, the affirmation of historicity of social action follows. If man is a self-creative being, then he constantly creates and changes himself and the world around him. In every altered condition, man recreates a new world in order to mirror the Akala Purakh. The Being is always recycling and reincarnates itself in new myriad forms. The Being remains concealed for the ignorant. The creative genius has the ability to project it in the form of ideology (world-view). It is not the Platonic Being that is pre-existent and beyond time and space. Dynamic Becoming exists in the Heracleitean time of the 'universal flux'.

The well-known Western philosophers Arthur Schopenhauer in *the World as Will and Representation* and Nietzsche in *the*

Birth of Tragedy propound the tragic view of life. Schopenhauer in the second part of his work says the power of transporting the audience or reader is peculiar to tragedy. It arises from our sudden recognition that life fails to provide any true satisfactions and, hence, does not deserve our loyalty. Tragedy guides us to the final goal, which is resignation or self-surrender to the cosmic will.

Man is a prisoner in the cave of *maya*, and his feet are chained to societal relations. His tragic vision of life is symbolic of the blind alley of the existential human conditions in which he is placed. He has been unsuccessfully grappling with the empirical world. Nietzsche, however, tries to wriggle out of the quagmire of the world with the help of the inherent "will to power". Both end their quests with a tragic note. On the other hand, Indian philosophy transcends to the state of the *moksha / nirvana*. Guru Nanak strikes a balance between the two extremes. This is the essence of the medieval Bhaktas and the Gurus.

The tragic view of life needs to be traced from its primordial cause of misery. It is not sufficient to say that the tragic view of life exists only in art, rather it is also found in literature, poetry, and drama. It emanates from the metaphysical underpinnings of life. In the Indian thought, the tragic effects of the *sansara* are overcome by the hero's dynamic and fearless encounter with existential human predicaments. He delivers himself from the overt and avid thirst for earthly desires and transports himself through his artistic and philosophical creativity and esoteric discipline, to a higher existential space of living in the world. Sikhism, thus, views human life from the existential and socialist standpoints. Its 'groundless ground' or self-existent is spiritual, but that is at once secularised and de-secularised through *sangat, ṣeva, Akala Takht,* and so on.

The tragic and pessimistic views of life imply that man is eternally condemned to agony and suffering. In Christianity, it is due to the 'eternal sin' owing to disobedience to the divine command. In Islam, the original suffering is caused by the violation of divine law by Iblis. He is the archetypal cipher of disobedience and defiance in the Qur'an. In the Vedanta and

Buddhism, suffering is caused by intrinsic ignorance (*avidya*) and in Sikhism, *haumai*, as an individuating force from the Being, is at the root of eternal sufferings. The transformation of me-consciousness *(haumai)* into Thou-consciousness is the central lynchpin of the Sikh faith.

The medieval Bhaktas and Guru Nanak boldly face this ticklish existential problem. They leave no stone unturned to create an optimal balance between this-world and the transcendent eternal reality through an overdose of voluntarist optimism and the dynamic life. They try to strike a balance between asceticism and eroticism. According to them, the purpose of life is to attain emancipation from human suffering and misery while living in society.

Guru Nanak's viewpoint advocates the dynamic and existential view of life in the world. He reconciles the Indic and the Semitic religious traditions without suppressing either one. Sikhism assimilates heterogeneous elements of both the cultures. The Gurus strived to eradicate evil and tyranny from India. For this purpose, they exploited the heroic spirit of the multiracial society of the land. Guru Nanak was a different kind of mendicant. He was concerned with the existential social realities and culture of the land. His *sacha-khanda* is an ideal social order, which was concretised in history by the subsequent eight Gurus, and Guru Gobind Singh gave the process final touch by creation of the Khalsa-panth in CE 1699. The Khalsa is a concrete person born in history. Guru Gobind Singh dropped the book and the Prophet as charismatic religious leader. He rules out the concept of incarnation.

The central problem of the book is to highlight the efforts of the Gurus for steeling will of the subaltern marginalised subaltern populace so that they could confront boldly tyranny and rebel against cruelty of the alien invaders. Their approach was existential approach toward societal problems. They successfully unfettered Indians from the alien dominance of the Muslim servility. This was one of the contributions of the Gurus. For this purpose, man is projected as a concrete valiant hero who is ready to stake his life for truth. It is concerned with problematic issues of the medieval ages. It will also enable the readers to have the comprehensive understanding and bird's eye view of the Indian culture.

Bhakti cult was a subaltern revivalist and protestant movement of voluntarism. It was a sharp reaction to the Islamic cultural invasions. In the medieval ages, the socio-religious florescence emerged in the South and spread into the North like a wild fire. It checkmated the malignant influence of Muslim rulers. Its proponents gathered momentum in India. It rejected casteism and despotism, gender discrimination and hegemony of the priestly class and dominance of the feudal lords. The priestly class created the myth of the other-world that resulted in life and world negation. There was a powerful resurgence in cultural revival in India. The medieval Bhaktas emerged as a counterforce. To reverse the prevalent trends the Bhaktas exerted strenuous struggle. The medieval saints (say, Ravidass, Sein, *et al.*) motivated regional Indian rulers of principalities for resisting alien invaders.

The Sikh Gurus made a radical departure from the prevalent rituals and inspired the devotees for self-dignified life. The very birth of Sikhism owes to active resistance to tyranny (*ati*). They owned responsibility to destroy tyranny on the Indian soil. Thus, the Sikh movement emphasises on active resistance to evil and struggle in life. It fortified will of the Indians. It was a voluntarist movement. The purpose of life of Sikh faith culminates in supreme sacrifice. It conquers death and steels will power for executing the goal of human life. It leads to heroic life in the world. It created nation of the Khalsa who defied temporal sovereignty of the Mughal Emperors. This kind of life was missing in the medieval India. It was due to weak will power of the Indians that they wore yoke of servility for centuries. The Gurus strengthened will of the humiliated masses. They developed steadfast faith in their leitmotiv—the supreme Deity. This is a dauntless religious conviction to offer for supreme sacrifice for the sake of higher values. The Gurus evolved cultural concept of martyrdom. Thus, militant element was infused into subaltern people.

In the medieval times, the priestly class separated this world from the concrete social realities. The Gurus concretised the abstract world *here* and *now*. They sharpened edge of revolt against the prevalent morbid social order. The Sikh Gurus made supreme sacrifices and struggled hard to revive essence of ancient Indian spiritual culture. It led to heroic life in the world. The masses successfully realised their coveted goal of self-dignity.

Guru Nanak, also, considers man as concrete unit in historical time and propounds dynamic view of life. In order to strike reconciliation between eternity and temporality, the ten Sikh Gurus from Guru Nanak to Guru Gobind Singh (CE 1469-1708), carried forth their crusade for revivification of the fluxional stark social reality.

Whatever, Guru Nanak preached and practised in his life was carried forth by eight Gurus and Guru Gobind Singh gave to it a finishing touch. Guru Nanak tried to reconcile theory and praxis, which is the central linchpin of almost all developed religions. They wanted to put to 'use' their ideals into practice. Sikhism deals with concrete social life in history from the existential viewpoint. The guru emphasised to reconcile theory and praxis. There was no contradiction in their *saying*, and *doing*. Guru Nanak sums up in one of his hymns in the Guru Granth (p. 62) that truth is higher than all kinds of truth, but truthful living is higher than those are. Guru Arjundeva pronounces attitude toward 'power' as under

> Seek I neither kingship nor liberation,
> Let me repose at Thy feet.
>
> Guru Granth, p. 534.

Notes

1. Vitthala is an epithet of Krishna in Maharashtra.
2. Kosambi, D.D., *The Culture and Civilisation of Ancient India in Historical Outline*. Delhi: Vikas, 1994.
3. It may be relevant to point out that the Sun temple at Konarak was built in *c.* CE 1250. It is near Jagannathapuri in Orissa. It is a Hindu temple. Now it is in a deplorable condition. Recently when I visited it, no guide could give proper information about the history of the temple.
4. See, Tara Chand, *Influence of Islam on Indian Culture*.
5. cf. Jha, D.N., *Ancient India: In Historical Outline*. New Delhi: Manohar 2004, p. 17ff.

2

Rethinking Purposes of Human Life

(i) Introduction

The purpose of this chapter is to present philosophical interpretation of Indian culture which is manifested through plurality of perspectives. It is a creative academic involvement. It is a healthy sign of progression of understanding the text and the cultural phenomenon. One can inhale fragrance of culture only if one's mind is refined.

The nature, meaning and purpose of human life have been perennial questions. Thinkers have been pondering over them since the appearance of the human beings on the earth. It is desirable to analyse the problem of human nature and the purpose of human life. The purpose of human life is evolved from the environment. Philosophers and religious leaders have been pondering over it for making life happy in the society. Sometimes fundamental questions arise: What is this life? Man takes birth, lives in the world, grows up, marries, and dies. Is this the be-all and end-all of human life? In order to unravel this ticklish problem, philosophers and religious luminaries have put forth their respective viewpoints. It is, therefore, pertinent to grapple with the vital problem of human nature and the purpose of life. Discussions are held for making human life happy on the planet. Owing to weak will power and lack of proper development of mind, people *en masse* withdrew from the societal realities and developed an ascetic view of life. It was a dismal historical state of affairs in the medieval India. This negative attitude has led to life and world negation. Indian culture is intrinsically affirmative. For revivifying singularity of Indian culture in the coeval context, the spiritual celebrities made vigorous endeavours. From this standpoint an attempt is made to articulate a philosophical world-view of the medieval Bhaktas and the Gurus.

In the medieval ages societal aspect was relegated to the periphery. The spiritual celebrities in the medieval times continued their strife to strike an optimal balance between the two extremes. In the present work, an attempt is to work out from the perspective of the existential human situation, amidst societal realities. It is steeped in pre-occupied Bhakti in which feeling dominates. This is the cultic character of the Bhaktas. It does not imply that it was devoid of rationality. It finally developed from *bhakti* to *shakti* or spirituality to martial spirit. The movement is steeling of will for living life of dignity and freedom.

Then a fundamental philosophical question arises: What is the purpose of human life in general and in the Western and the Indic cultural and religious traditions? The purposes of human life in the Western (Semitic) and the Indian cultures can be traced from the savage mind. Nevertheless, in the past, the Western culture has been influencing the Eastern culture, but the indigenous character survives in the folk traditions and culture of the land. Briefly, the Indian culture has its roots in the tribal and folklore of the land. It survives in the indigenous traditions. Here our main concern is with the Indian culture.

Language, education, spiritual discipline, and other tools play their respective roles in refining the savage mind from gross consciousness (*shakti*) into self-consciousness (*shiva*). Critical philosophical chiseling cleanses the dross and drags in the mind. Critical analysis arouses creative faculty, curiosity and urge for innovating new ideas which are to be put to use. This process continuously cycles and recycles the whole span of life. Ideologue evolves new ideologies which are need of the existential conditions.

The cultivation or development of the mind, manners, etc., are societal improvements. Refinement of mind, tastes, and manners; artistic and intellectual development are carried out through education and training. Philosophers are divided on this point. Some thinkers hold the view that man has inherent potency of creativity and others are of the view that environment plays a major role in the development of the mind. Inner development of the mind comes within the scope of culture. And particular form, stage, or types of external material tools come under the scope of civilisation.

The practical solutions of the problems of human life remain untouched because the secrets of human life transcend the realm of the phenomenal world, which belongs to the space of values and ideals. Wittgenstein in his book *Tractatus Logico-Philosophicus (TLP)* rightly says, "We feel that even when all possible scientific questions have been answered, the problems of life remain completely untouched. Of course, there are then no questions left, and this itself is the answer" (*TLP*: 6.52). The secret of life is outside the pale of rational comprehension. The problems of life remain completely untouched simply for the reason that these transcend limits of space and time. The meanings of human life have their own realm of values and ideals, which do not belong to the spatio-temporal world.

Again, Wittgenstein asserts, "The solution of the problem of life is seen in the vanishing of the problem" (*TLP*: 6.521). This is possible only if the agent makes out continuous efforts to tide over the ordeals, which come in the way of man in the existential life. Thus, the solution of problems of life lies in dissolving the problems. This is the answer to the ever-present problems of life. The Sikh Gurus' approach towards life implies that one should live active life in society till last breath. So long as an individual lives in the world, he always faces existential problems, and has to shoulder the worldly responsibilities. He is to face them boldly. It will lead him to a heroic view of life.

Life is likened to a dome of multicoloured glass that shines through multifaceted radiance, but the primordial fount of life is in eternal flux. The sunlight is split up into multiplicity of rays. The radiance of genius's utterances or poetry creates eternal human values that reflect deep insight into human life. Tagore's "Geetanjali" is an anthology of eternal values of life. The Vedas, two Indian epics (the Ramayana and the Mahabharata), The Guru Granth, *et al*. are treasure-troves of human values.

A medieval Indian poet of Urdu Ghalib, explains eternal truth of human sorrows with the metaphor of a burning flame (*shama*). He says the flame burns in multi-colours until the bright day dawns (i.e., *shama har rang mein jalti hai sahar jone tak*). Kabir in one of his hymns in the Guru Granth also observes on it in his own unique style. He says that the rays of the sun are split up into multiplicity. These multiplicities of the rays are as real as their primordial source, the sun (*nur*). In the words of the *Gurbani* life is a *joti* (radiance) that manifests through multiplicity of the empirical world. Evil and suffering are also real. Both are human creations. Man is oscillating between the two extremes. He can attain the purpose of human life only if he transcends both and lives at a higher plane. He should not completely negate the ephemeral world because it is manifestation of the holistic truth. It is possible if he creates balance (*sahaj*) within his self while living in the society. This is positive approach towards human life.

The Indic and the Semitic perspectives are taken into consideration for having a holistic view of life. The Sikh tradition and the Guru Granth are the latest interpretation of the Indian culture. Hence, emphasis is given on the Sikh viewpoint that interprets life for eternity through open-ended method. It opens doors for future reinterpretations of purposes of life. Life is an ever-flowing river of suffering and happiness. The postulate of God may or may not exist, but suffering and death are existential eternal twins. Death conceals eternal beauty that is truth. John Keats, the romantic poet of England, in his *Ode on Grecian Urn* says "truth is beauty and beauty is truth". Here beauty and truth are symbolic of the cosmic order. Physical beauty fades away, but physical death is eternal. Physical death can destroy body, but the transcendental consciousness (*atman)* is beyond her clutches. The journey of time is seamlessly dragging towards the threshold of the dungeon of death. Wisdom lies in harmonising life with the fleeting stream of time. Man is to swim across the stream of suffering and happiness, and the flowing time for awakening his mind (*dhyana*) to eternity. Life and death are occurring at once within human person in time and history. One who realises the eternal truth of death realises the secret of life. It is only the privilege of man. No other species has this privilege.

For realising the purpose of life, man initiates into his life for synthesis of theory and practice. In the existential situations, man is always confronting absurdity of 'death'. Ghost of death haunts him day and night. Sometimes death visits him in his dreams. In order to escape from its clutches, he rises above from the horrible dreams. Breath is continuously beating the siren, dragging us towards the dragon of death for extinguishing the fire of life. Nobody knows when the heartbeat comes to standstill, but one fact is certain that death is inevitable. One need not be disgusted and lose heart. The secret of life lies in struggling and tiding over the oddities of life till the last breath.

Man is to develop a distanced attitude towards the world and others (sentient and insentient), but he should continue striving for their welfare. One is not to behave like a fly that falls prey to the cobweb of the spider. Man is, often, caught in the net of entices of the visible world. Once a man becomes aware of the delusory nature of the world, the net will disappear as darkness disappears when day dawns. The life of enlightenment and equanimity is the ideal of life. This state is realised with continuously striving against oddities of life. It follows that the secret of life is beyond the visible world that lies hidden in the ciphers (hidden meanings). The purpose of life is to live in the higher space of values and ideals, and discharge worldly duties for the welfare of others. It presumes autonomy of the self that is to be developed.

Life and death are at once occurring within human person in real time and history. He who realises the eternal truth of death, he realises the secret of life. It is the exclusive privilege of man. No other species has this privilege. For realisation of the purpose of life, man initiates into his life for synthesis of theory and practice.

Every person lives in his own created world. The genius also creates his own ideal world. It is not necessary that the ideal be always translated into actuality, in use. There is always a contradiction between the ideal and the actual. The moment we realise the ideal, it slips away from our fingers. Then we are to reconstruct the ideal. The process of construction and reconstruction goes on endlessly

Without taking up the problem from different standpoints, we look at it from two perspectives—*tragic* and *optimistic* views of life. Here our concern is primarily with the optimistic and the tragic views of human life. The former ends in happiness and the latter in suffering. Indian culture revolves round the vicious eddy of suffering and happiness. The self is to strive to come out of the quagmire of the mundane world and live life of bliss.

It will shed light on the holistic and the dynamic view of the self from within and without in the societal relationships. We can understand man only in the existential situation of being related to other fellow beings. They become part and parcel of my 'me', yet remain also 'not-me' ('other'). When the 'I' remains a distant observer, the identity of the 'I' sees only the manifested behaviour. However, when the 'I' identifies itself with the inner self, it becomes a mirror of the 'Being/ Numinous'. The 'I' identifies itself with its anxiety, greed or the whole 'self'. The 'I' can understand its forlornness, aloneness, alienation or alterity, and hope or love. The 'I' needs to be true to its authentic and unique self that transcends the illusions and self-delusions of the 'me' and the ephemeral world. This is the realisation of the inner most personal identity of man absorbed in the Numinous and his freedom here in this- world. This is the meaning of the dynamic view of life. The 'I' experiences that it is just a drop of water on the crest of the waves. The concern of the 'I' with others is not as an observer, but, rather, as an existential participant in the addities of life. The 'I' identifies itself with others' interests in thought and deed. This is the existential approach of the Medieval Bhaktas and the Sikh Gurus. They identified themselves with humanity for its emancipation.

According to Indian culture, the purpose of human life is to transform physical self for the sake of higher values which man creates for living a life of eternal bliss (*ananda*). So long as man is attached to his bodily self, he cannot have eternal bliss. When man stakes his bodily person and lives life of higher human values (say, spiritual, moral, aesthetic and so on), he is living real human life of freedom. Thus, purposes of human life are divergent in different walks of life. The Vedantic tradition yearns for eternal bliss and the Buddhists strive for eradicating suffering. The medieval devotional dignitaries lived active life for elevation of human dignity and restoration of freedom.

Valorisation creates value out of the given facts. Man has the privilege that he can create values with his creative faculty. It helps man in the process of ratiocination of the purpose of his life. Awareness of selfhood: "I am man" is the singular quality of man that distinguishes him from the lower species. Man potentially belongs to the realm of the Numinous. Man, thus, is the crown of the creation. The lower species are devoid of *curiosity*, *creativity* and *language* of signs and symbols. Man has a sense of a superior being. He becomes aware that he is man and is distinct from animals and other lower species. Man has the potentiality to discern eternity in the world. From this point of view man invents purpose of human mind.

Man, thus, is a creative being. He creates his own world (ideology) and strives to realise it in his lifetime. Then a philosophical question arises: Why is man better than animals? Why is man capable of self-awareness of his identity and others' and morality ? Man has the capacity to understand his own present and past life in this-world or perhaps, in the mythical otherworld. Man learns through language (say, Skit/Punjabi/Marathi). Culture is an escape from beastliness of lower animals, barbarism of the tribal people, pagans, and animals. Man has the potentiality to transcend his limitations with his conscious effort. He can go from empirical self to the eternal self. He can realise his identity with the Numinous that inheres within him.

Purpose of human beings is primarily concerned with cultural life. Creation of culture comes from man's creative mind that stretches temporality (history) into eternity. He lives in the world and creates history for he is not conditioned by history. He determines the course of history and guides destiny of others. For him others are as real as he himself is living as a free 'person'. In the Buddhist thought it is called: "Live and let live others". The genius creates history by his deeds and works of eternal values. He swims with the point-instant ever-flowing stream of eternity that is regulated by the cosmic law (*rita/hukam*). The hero transcends history and creates new history of eternal values. He is at once in time and in eternity. In other words, he is *in* time, but not *of* time.

Then a fundamental philosophical question arises: What is the purpose of human life in Indian culture and in Sikhism in particular? Culture once created continues till eternity. It changes manifestations during the historical epochs. It may be suppressed for some time, but it comes up when congenial conditions recycle. A cultural invasion from alien culture strangulates the native culture. Indian culture experienced such cultural invasions. Indian culture is rooted in prehistoric times. It continued in the medieval times in the Sikh movement. It continues till today as a living societal reality.

In Indian culture man is projected as a concrete 'becoming' unit struggling in the existential life. Every ideology (say, political, religion, social, and so on) is man and social centred and the Deity is the base on which the edifice of the ideology is constructed. The martyrs or heroes create culture and religious traditions. They rejuvenate religious traditions. Gurus sacrificed their lives for the sake of humanity and finally Guru Gobind Singh created a nation of the militant khalsa. Hence, religion is meant for man and not *vice versa*.

The central objective problem of religion is to transform man from creature to creator. In other words: "It is a passage from first person singular perspective to third person singular perspective". He is required to create his distinct identity in society. All ideologies have their own concepts of an ideal man. The Bhaktas had their divergent and distinct regional identities. It is a unique phenomenon that distinct regional cultural identities of India have been represented in Rajab's *Sarvangi* (CE 1596) and the Guru Granth (CE 1604). The former yogis anthology is more or less a compilation in Hindi script (*pandu lipi*) of the holy sayings of the Bhaktas is and the second scripture in *Gurmukhi* script prepared by the Gurus is standardised and edited anthology having verses/hymns of the Gurus and the representative Bhaktas of the Bhakti cult of different parts of India. It does not have hymns of the Dravidian saints. So much so, representatives of Islamic culture are also included in the Sikh Scripture. It symbolises unity-in-diversity of Indian culture. In the context of the global culture, India is called global miniature culture. The editors (the third Guru Amardasa and the fifth Guru Arjundeva) collected and edited the scripture with a view to basing the scripture on unity of Indian culture. The Guru Granth is a symbol of composite culture of India. Since Muslims have been living in India as representative of Islam, their hymns were also harmonised in the scripture. The Bhaktas of Maharashtra possessed distinct identities from those of other denominations. The Kabirpanthi sect is different from other sects. Baba Farid, a Sufi saint, has his distinct identity, but his hymns were adjusted within the metaphysical paradigm of Sikhism. Similarly, the identity of Guru Nanak's ideal man, *Gurmukh*, is different from that of Guru Gobind Singh's Khalsa. In the Sikh tradition, there are different sects (*sampradayas*). Each sect lays emphasis on different aspects. My concern in this chapter is to delineate the generic meaning and purpose of human life in the Indic culture.

The purpose of human life is not a given fact. It is human creation for living a concrete life in the world. It is the outcome of man's creative nature and his passion for social responsibility and for a peaceful life. The Indian sages articulated ideologies for this purpose. Two epics are the foundational pillars of Indian culture. Their ideology has been continuing through the epochs of our cultural history. The Gita is the philosophical foundation of Indian philosophy. It puts forth threefold purposes of human life: eradication of evil, promotion of goodness, protection of saints. Dharma (righteousness) and heroic actions (*karmas*) is the essence of both the epics. In philosophical terms it is called voluntarism. It will be taken up in details in the ensuing [chapt. 8(b)].

The Gurus infused new life into morrows of the subaltern marginalised populace and the feminine folk. Their will power was strengthened. The above goal of human life is revivified in the medieval devotional traditions. Guru Gobind Singh reinterprets the Gita's ideal and gives a finishing touch to this concept. Guru Gobind Singh, in one of the cantos (*chaupis-43*), highlights three objectives of his life: continuing righteousness, elevation of saints, and eradication of evildoers (see,"Bichitra Nataka", in The Dasam Granth).

This forms the essence of the Sikh voluntarism. It aims at trying to restore human autonomy, peace, and justice in society. Thus, *dharma* and voluntarism are inseparable concepts. Both mirror a dynamic view of human life.

The Sikh perspective is continuity and mirror of Indian culture. It sheds light on the holistic view of the self from within and without in the societal relationships. We can understand man only in an existential situation of being related to other fellow beings. They become part and parcel of my 'me', yet remain also 'not-me' ('other'). When the 'I' remains a distant observer, the 'I' sees only the manifest behaviour. However, when the 'I' identifies itself with the inner self, it becomes a mirror of the 'Being'. The 'I' identifies itself with its anxiety, greed or the whole 'self'. The 'I' can understand its forlornness, aloneness, alienation, and hope or love. The 'I' needs to be true to its authentic and unique self that transcends the illusions and self-delusions of the 'me' and the ephemeral world. This is the realisation of the personal identity of man and his freedom here in this-world. This is the meaning of the dynamic view of life. The 'I' that experiences it is just a drop of water on the crest of the waves. The concern of the 'I' with others is not an observer, but, rather, an existential participant. The 'I' identifies itself with others' interests in thought and deed. This is the existential approach of the medieval Bhaktas and the Sikh Gurus. They identified themselves with humanity for its emancipation.

The Western thinkers, with their blinkered perspectives, have projected that *Sikhism: Continuity of Indian Culture* is pessimistic. Arthur Schopenhauer who is called the weeping philosopher tried to seek solace in the Indian philosophical and cultural traditions for over coming pessimism. It is correctly understood as an optimistic philosophy. The Western scholars distorted the Indic perspectives of human life. They have generated the impression that Indian thought is either the Vedantic or the Buddhist. In the medieval ages, this viewpoint dominated the Indic ideology in the East and the West. They did not take cognisance of the Dravidian culture which continues in the medieval ages in the Bhakti cult and Sikhism. Sikh faith came forth with a vigorous optimistic and voluntarist view of life. Many Indian philosophers have been pondering over this philosophical problem since time immemorial. Some thinkers have projected tragic and others optimistic views of human life. Overall, the Indian philosophers are of the unanimous view that one should transcend the seductive clutches of the empirical world *(samsara)* in thought, word, and deed (*mana, vacha* and *karma*). The *tantrics* tried to supplement the theoretical dimension with practical esoteric practices. Despite all such endeavours, the prevalent world-view of the Indian philosophies has been of negation of the empirical world and the life. If it is interpreted from a philosophical standpoint, with purpose of human life is to lead an active righteous life with disinterested attachment with the empirical world and the empirical self.

The Indian philosophy of human life is an attempt to realise eternal bliss. In India, the main exponent of the so-called tragic view of life is considered the Buddha who started his quest for emancipation of human suffering. In the beginning, he was a pragmatist and realist thinker. He is of the view that primary concern of our life is to eradicate suffering. For example, if an arrow pierces into the body, our immediate duty is to take it out. We should not indulge in metaphysical speculations. He, therefore, began with voluntarist view of life for emancipating humanity from the primordial cause of suffering (*dukkha*). Finally, he withdraws from the arena of human struggle and transcends to the otherworld of *nirvana*. He ended his quest in minimising the significance of the empirical world (*samsara*). He zeroed on the transcended state of consciousness.

Largely, the interpreters of the Vedantic and the Buddhist lore declared this-world as illusory. On the contrary, the saints and the Gurus assert that the empirical world is a stark and living reality. For them this-world is concrete and real. *Moksha* and *nirvana* are to be concretised in the society. Earlier the concept of *maya* from the epistemic and ontic standpoints was taken as an illusion or delusion, but the Bhaktas and the Gurus reinterpreted it as the real cosmic energy manifesting through myriad forms in the world. For them the world is both sacred and profane. If one is dominated by one's *haumai* ('me'), it is profane. If one's inmost self ('I') dominates, then it is sacred. For them, the holy congregation is a miniature unity of the society. The *sangat* is an embodiment of the divinity. The Divine is always present in the *sangat*. It cannot be brushed aside as a delusive element because it is a ladder for ascending to the inner space of tranquility that is the sublimated concrete reality of the self. It knits a network of inter-subjectivity of the societal relations. During the process of socialisation in the society, it is projected in praxis. This is the coveted goal of dynamic life while living in society and discharging moral and social responsibilities.

Our ancient sages refined crude and rustic ideas. In this process, religion played a vital role. The purpose of human life is to sacrifice the physical self for the sake of higher values which man creates for living a life of bliss (*ananda*). So long as man is attached to the bodily self, he cannot have eternal bliss. Physical death is immaterial for the hero. He lives in the created world of values and ideals. The hero looks death in the face, real death, and not just the phantom and shadow of it. This attitude of the hero removes his fear of death. Death does not kill the hero rather he kills death. Martyrdom of a hero immortalises and glorifies him as an icon for the future generations. This is what we mean by heroic life in the Indian culture.

(ii) Identity of the Self

In short, it can be said that the essence of the Indian view of life is to bring up cultivated identity of the self within and, then, to struggle in life for the welfare of others. The self is to be committed to social and moral responsibilities towards humanity. It is an endeavour to create an ideal man who can mirror eternity on the earth. Hence, the social philosophy of the Indian thinkers is a ratiocinated world-view that retrieved the existential components of Indian culture in their contemporaneous milieu.

Then a question arises: Why do we articulate the purpose of human life? When we become conscious of what is essential in us, we become conscious of the meaning of life. We are to quest for collective responsibility and welfare for others. The ideologue formulates an ideal social order.

When a 'baby is born' false sense of identity, in the form of ego sense, takes birth. The birth of false identity (ego) incites attachment with the external world and identifies itself with the body and the external world. In order to create an identity of the self from within itself is to make conscious efforts to attain true awareness, which is simultaneously attached in and detached from the external world. In the very beginning, it is the 'first person perspective' in which the 'me' dominates. The 'me' has a sense of possessiveness and egoistic attitude. The baby instinctively identifies itself with the bodily self. It always claims 'this is mine; this is your(s).' The aim of human life is to transcend the over emphasised sense of possessiveness. It is possible only if one develops an attitude of detached involvement from one's bodily self and the material world. Thus, the central issue is to transform the 'first person singular perspective' into the 'third person singular perspective'. This journey is from 'me' to 'Thou'. In the latter state, the 'I-consciousness' of the self completely merges into the Numinous. From this point of view, the inward journey of the ego terminates at the terminus of the Numinous. This directional journey is to be guided by the grace of the *shabda-guru*. This problem has been taken up by Guru Nanak at the end of the *khandas* of "the Japuji". In this section, he wants to lay down the metaphysical basis of the Sikh dynamic philosophy for determining the purpose and meaning of human life.

However, *haumai* (ego) has been used both in negative and positive senses. In the negative sense, it has been castigated. Nevertheless, when one's ego is attuned to the cosmic law, it sheds its separatist existence: it becomes a fount of the autonomous human actions. Indian philosophy tries to convert the tragic view of life into an optimistic one by negating and minimising the empirical human life in the phenomenal world. It suggests inner transcendence or distancing of the self (*sannyasa*) from the empirical world. The term *sannyasa* has been often misinterpreted. It means detachment in thought and not in actuality. In the medieval ages, it tilted towards a static view of life and developed a pessimistic outlook of life. The Semitic traditions came to India with a dynamic and optimistic view of life. In the medieval time those traditions drifted away from the social responsibilities and were swayed by the idea of the other world (*bahisht/* heaven), seeking satisfaction by proxy for all our false longings. The sacred was relegated to the periphery.

Over and above, this was the main tendency in Indian cultural philosophy that negated the empirical world to live in the transcendent visionary other world. That is an abstract view of life that is cut off from the concrete, empirical or societal realities of the empirical world. A concrete life is based on the holistic view of the self, inclusive of reason, feeling, emotions, and instincts. Personal relationships, from the existential standpoint, promote solidarity with other fellows, and sense of belongingness and identification. Man feels the fear of being in seclusion. We aspire for freedom in the society, not the freedom of a recluse who is cut off from the social world. It is the essential purpose of human life and destiny that plays a treacherous part to curb it. This is the gist of Fromm's book, *Fear of Freedom*. The sense of belongingness comes when we identify ourselves with others. This is the existential and concrete view of life that has been emphasised in the Sikh Canon. This is to be rarefied and translated into practice. The medieval Bhaktas and Guru Nanak boldly faced this ticklish existential problem. They triumphantly overcome it. They lived in the world as emancipators of the humans.

The medieval devotional literature is a search for the essence of the dynamic nature of man. Post-experiential articulation of the discoveries of truth is to alter the nature of truth that has been discovered. The tracks of the experience of truth have been discovered by the Sufis, the Bhaktas and the Gurus do appear to have been explored thoroughly. Human nature has nòt been analysed from psychological, neurological, biological, mystical, and other viewpoints. In addition to these, one must have taste of lived mystic insight. All the approaches, put together, give a holistic view of human life. The attempt is to discover a space of the inner holistic, lived experience that is coexistent with the whole spiritual and the material life. The scientific investigation cannot achieve the purpose of life. This is also true that it can never be the case with philosophical investigation. The philosophical analysis of the issues crystallises the issue. It takes one to the threshold of the truth. The mystic or the guru takes a 'leap' to the heart of the Numinous.

In the latter case awareness of the issue gradually deepens, but the achievement of fixing human values results in despair. Human nature is intrinsically creative. Man creates values that are beyond the scopes of sciënces, psychology and positivism. Human purpose transcends the contingent world of facts and is to be visualised as the eternal world that pictures the Being. With a view to realising the purpose and meaning of human life, man is to sharpen his theoretical faculty of articulation and analysis, and evince practical sense. When both are reconciled, the mystery of human beings is unearthed. The cataract of visual opacity is removed. The vision of a realised person sees truth face to face. He identifies himself with all. He becomes a fount of altruism.

The Guru Granth makes abiding social and moral commitments that are derived from its pronounced non-dual dynamic ontology. It logically entails restoration of social realities. It raises ontological, epistemological, semantic, and ethical issues. The central theme of Indian culture and Sikhism is to project the meaning of human life within the societal set-up of life. Man is projected as a concrete historical unit mirroring cosmic reality on the earth. The interpersonal relationships always saddle man with responsibilities towards his fellow beings and humanity at large. He develops a sense of identification with others.

Every person lives in his own world. The genius also creates his own ideal world. It is not necessary that the ideal be always translated into actuality. There is always a contradiction between the ideal and the actual. The moment we realise the ideal, it slips away from our fingers. Then we are to reconstruct the ideal. The process of construction and reconstruction goes on endlessly until one breathes one's last breath.

3

World-view of Sikhism

(i) Introductory

The present study is concerned with philosophical exploration into the hermeneutic articulation of Guru Nanak's world-view in the context of modern philosophical trends based on scientific inventions and discoveries. His ideas came into being in the second half of the 15th century, and culminated in CE 1699 with the creation of the Khalsa by Guru Gobind Singh. He propounds universality of human values and respect for other religious traditions and scriptures. He envisages a global society based on social equality and dynamic world-view. He fathered the Sikh world-view. In the Sikh faith there is a metaphysical necessity of social commitment that logically follows from its dynamic nature. Religious experience is concerned with the Numinous (Akala Purakh) which escapes all linguistic constructs or symbolism. The Numinous transcends all phenomenal categories. Sikhism postulates the supreme truth as a dynamic non-dual unity. And the immanent (this-world) and the transcendent (otherworld or Beyond) are encompassed within the eddy of continuum of the dynamic. The mystic of the Sikh faith is simultaneously concerned with this-world and the otherworld with a disinterested involvement. It is one of the singular contributions of Guru Nanak who tries to reconcile the transcendence and the immanence in theory and praxis. It has been the perennial philosophical problems since the ancient times. We shall, therefore, study this chapter in two parts : the theoretical articulation of Guru Nanak's world-view and philosophy of praxis.

At the very outset, a question arises: What is the connotation of world-view? *The New Shorter Oxford English Dictionary* (Vol. 2) asserts that would-view is a set of fundamental beliefs, attitudes, values, etc., determining or constituting a comprehensive outlook on life, the universe, etc.... (p. 3721). It is self-evident from it that the world-view is a holistic concept, which encompasses all the aspects of the universe and human life. Our concern in the first section is to highlight it. Guru Nanak's outlook or attitude towards the world and human life is positive. An equivalent term of world-view in German philosophy is *Weltanschauung* which also means attitudes towards life and the world. Thus, general conception of the nature of the world is contained or implied in the value-system. From the standpoint of values, total philosophical system may be articulated and practical consequences may be derived from its theoretical formulation. It, then, enjoins upon us to articulate a sound theoretical world-view of Guru Nanak. It will help us to derive his philosophy of praxis, which tries to reconcile theory and practice. The reconciliation depends on the self-creative nature of man. He can adjust to the constantly emerging problematics in the existential conditions of human life.

It will be pertinent to point out the source of Guru Nanak's world-view. Guru Nanak's concept of the world-view is embalmed in the Guru Granth. It is an eternal source of sayings of the Gurus, Bhaktas, Sufis, *et al*. All the contributors gave free and independent interpretations of the world-view, free from the prejudices, traditions, and any scriptural authority and the alike. Their enlightened intuitive insights deserve to be rationally theorised and communicated for their *sui generis* contributions for emancipation of mankind. Their mystical experiences of the Numinous are post experiential utterances articulated through symbolism and signification. If the verses of the contributors belong to divergent cultural and symbolic system, the problem of their intelligibility will crop up. The verses cut across the cultural and regional limitations. As a matter of fact, intelligibility is a matter of ethico-spiritual achievement. It is a continuous process of enrichment through inwardisation and externalisation. It is a process of transcendence of cleavage of 'I-Thou' and outwardly identifying with the 'other' people.

Despite diversities in the verses they reflect identical immediate and absorptive mystical experience of the Ineffable. There has been a gap of time between the utterance of the holy hymns and their recording in black and white. The third and fifth Gurus before incorporating hymns of the saintly contributors in the Sikh Scripture systematically standardised them. Since the text of the Sikh Canon is a standardised and authenticated version, there is no problem of interpretation (hermeneutics) to decipher candid meanings of the hymns.

There is always a conceptual gap of interrelations with the original contextual meaning and the historical consciousness. It implies plurality of understanding of the text's relativity and the praxis of interpretation are to be harmoniously fused into one another. There are degrees of understanding, but we will be objective and rational in this exposition. It needs objective rules of interrelation. For understanding and interpreting Guru Nanak's hymns, it is necessary to have an interpretive conceptual framework of a mind. Guru Nanak's ideal of achieving the highest landscape of spirituality (*sacha-khanda*) and emancipation of mankind (i.e., *sarbat ka bhala*) was a peaceful social and spiritual reform movement. It was an active involvement in the social realities. Initially it was more of spirituality and less of polity but unbearable tyranny of the then despotic emperors coerced the oppressed subaltern masses to turn into a militant or violent movement. It was an inner historical development in the Sikh religion. This development has been derived from the Sikh Canon. There are hymns in the Canon that inspire for revolt against encroachment of human freedom and conscience. Furthermore, it was the dynamic metaphysical basis, which necessitated the movement to develop into an active resistance. It advocates restoration of historical human action and freedom. It sets aside medieval objectivity and absoluteness of truth and authoritarian and tyrant attitude towards underpriviledged human beings. These are creedal polemics against medieval philosophies.

In the modern context there is denial of any fixed meaning, or any correspondence between language and the world, or any fixed reality or truth or fact to be the object of enquiry. In the West this tendency was anticipated by Nietzsche. His *perspectivism* is a philosophical technique for dissolving the presumptions that there can be absolute knowledge. For him objectivity is revealed as a disguise for power or authority. In religious traditions, objectivity leads to religious fundamentalism and bigotry. It culminates in other worldliness and minimises reality of the external world. His interpretation was a turning point in Indian thought. Hence, Guru Nanak's hermeneutics of understanding Indian cultural milieu was a Copernican Revolution in theory of knowledge. He is of the view that understanding of the world and the self is not an activity of consciousness, but a condition of belonging to the world. It was his existential outlook towards this-world. He puts forth analysis of understanding as a mode of disinterested practical involvement or concern with others and with the world. So interpretation of the world and life is always grounded in existential realities. His understanding is in harmony with his contemporaneous scientific outlook.

In this chapter there are certain philosophical issues that need to be analysed. Before taking them up we may like to enunciate them. What is the ontological status of this world? Is there any room for other worldliness? How does Sikhism reconcile spiritualism and materialism or transcendent and immanent? What is the ontic status of time (*kala*)? How is *kala* related to *Akala* (eternity) ? What is man and his existential status of social realities? How does Guru Nanak reconcile theory and praxis? What is Guru Nanak's concept of praxis? These are some questions which will be explored to cull out the underlying hidden meanings in the Sikh Canon and historical consciousness manifested in the Sikh tradition.

At the very outset, some philosophical questions arise: What is world-view? What was Guru Nanak's world-view? Is it viable in the modern conditions with minor outward changes without ignoring the core of the concept? Such questions shall be discussed in this section.

Guru Nanak expounds an idealistic viewpoint of the world-view because he considers spirit is prior to matter. Its metaphysical structure has the characteristics of non-dualism, dynamism and social commitment. At the times of Guru Nanak, Islam was a living state religion of India and other Indian religious traditions of Hinduism, Buddhism, Jainism and the indigenous folk traditions were groaning under the ethnocentric oppression of the Islamic thought represented by the Muslim rulers. Guru Nanak's struggle was to wrench the down trodden masses and humanity at large out of the quagmire of the medieval world-view. Indian and prophetic traditions at that time were dominated by the world-view of other worldliness. This-world was thrown into the periphery. They developed a quietist and pessimistic outlook towards the empirical world in the false hope of perfect happiness in the otherworld. This hope was not present in the antiquity. Perhaps, it was due to the connivance of feudal and priestly classes, the false ideal of the otherworld developed during the middle ages. It resulted in life and world negation. In the medieval sense the advocacy of absolute authority was at the peak in Middle Ages. Despotic power had been exploited for selfish ends by the feudal or upper strata of the society. It is for this reason the absolute despotic personality and authority of the transcendental Being dominated since the time of the first Semitic prophet Adam to the last Prophet Mohammad. And the 'Divine Rights of Kings' is a necessary corollary from it. On the other hand, in India, King has been also considered the representative of God.

The Vedantic and the Buddhist world-views over emphasised the impersonal outlooks towards the supreme Reality. Both developed ascetic trends of self-transcendence that is the central doctrine of Indian philosophy. It was conceived negatively and lopsidedly. Its equivalent term is Indian tradition is *sannyasa*. It has been interpreted in praxis as withdrawal from the world; Guru Nanak's interpretation of the term is positivistic. For him *sannyasa* is renunciation from within from the worldly attachments. It does not mean actual withdrawal from worldly responsibilities. Guru Nanak advocates a dynamic view of life that emanates from his dynamic and realistic world-view. It is true that Buddhism was initially started as a dynamic and realistic world-view but later on its major School of *Shunnyavada* developed an overtone of escapism from this-world. And the Vedantic interpretation of *a Sannyasa* is also overshadowed with *mayavada* or illusoriness or delusory nature of the world. In a nutshell, static world-view was in vogue in the times of Guru Nanak. Though the Qur'an advocates the dynamic world-view of life, yet in the medieval times its followers had also been over whelmed by the dreamy ideals of the otherworld.

Guru Nanak sharply reacted to the life and world negating ideologies of the medieval ages. In the world of a French pioneer philosopher of ideology, Distult de Tracy in his work "Science of Ideas" (1790) would assert that medieval ideologies in praxis represented 'false consciousness' because they were unable to see stark social realities of societal relations and exploitation of the subaltern masses. Its cure lies in progressing consciousness. This duty was performed by the genius of Guru Nanak. He reacted to the existential ills, evils and atrocities in the society. In the worlds of Nietzsche the Indian fourfold hierarchical ideology represents 'holy lie'; a falsehood that cloaks power in supernatural goals of the divine legitimating.

Coming back to Guru Nanak's world-view a philosophical question can be posed. Is this world-view abstract or concrete? If it is abstract, it can be equated with transcendental nothingness or void (*shunnaya*). It will negate the immanent and this-world. If it is to be realised in the pure consciousness of man, then it will be logical construct without phenomenal contents. For him it was a concrete and realistic world-view realizable in history. It is realistic because phenomenal and social aspects are affirmed in it. With dynamic life and world-view he sought to overcome crisis of reconciling the Semntic and the Indian world-views. His concrete world-view encompasses both diametrically opposed world-views without suppressing other one. The eternal and the temporal or the sacred and the profane constitute the two aspects of the non-dual dynamic Being. His all-inclusive world-view also reconciles spiritualism and materialism.

The Sikh world-view was created by the genius of Guru Nanak. Other contributors to the Sikh Canon supplemented it with their hymns. Nanak collected the hymns, the third Guru Amardasa, and the fifth Guru Arjunadeva schematised them. The contents of the Guru Granth are eternal (*amar*), but the Scripture itself is not uncreated (*anadi*). Once it was created, it became eternal because of the eternal values expounded in it.

In Sanskrit the term *sansara* has almost the identical meaning that explains the phenomenal transitory world. The literal connotation of the word *sansara* is that which is evanescent or changing. While accepting the transitory and evanescent nature of the world, the *homo sapiens* are projected as the concrete beings. Their bodies are the real micro-manifestations of the ontic macro-reality. They are destined to live *in* the world, but not *of* the world. They have an affirmative outlook or attitude towards the universe and the human life. This is the essence of the distinct and lived societal world of the Indian concept of *sannyasa* (renunciation). Guru Nanak and other contributors to the Sikh Canon tried to reinterpret it in their own regional dialects and different ways.

The dynamic metaphysics of Guru Nanak does not uphold withdrawal from the worldly duties. His composition "The Siddha Goshti" (GG, pp. 938-46) reinterprets the prevalent static view of the phenomenal world-view. Guru Nanak and the Madhyamikic School of Nagarjuna are in agreement with the philosophy of dynamism. Guru Nanak says that the *sunna* is within and without the self. It is in the three worlds too. He who realises the *sunna* in the transcended fourth state of consciousness is above good and evil. In the words of Nietzsche, the transcendent realm is beyond good and evil. One, who realises this mystery of the dynamic Being, becomes immortal (see, GG / canto 51, p. 943).

In the Vedic period, the concept of the otherworld had not come into being. In the Upanishadic period the esoteric tendencies were developed to find out truth that was hidden. For the common people, it was difficult to visualise its secret. Then the utopian realm of the otherworld was articulated. For the common person it was the dreamy realm of mysticism. It developed into the otherworld. In the Vedic age, the concept of the *moksha* was not developed. It was developed in the Upanishadic period when there was a quest for the truth from within. The development of the otherworld (*baikunth*) and the *moksha* were the post-Upanishadic developments. Consequently, the common people lost faith in the mundane world. It was the period of retrogression in the Indian metaphysics. Similar thoughts dominated the Semitic traditions. The dynamic rational morality and life were built on the metaphysical foundation. It created the knotty philosophical problem of reconciling eternity and history or temporality or the otherworld and the mundane world. This was the fundamental problem that was confronted by Guru Nanak. In the words of Guru Nanak it is to reconcile the visible with the invisible.

Sikhism is critical of corrupt medieval religious practices sanctioned by the above traditions. It bitterly condemns the rulers on the ground that they themselves subsumed or usurped all the temporal powers in their own persons. They became both *de facto* and *de jure* rulers. So much so they concentrated all powers in their own hands. They claimed to be 'God incarnates', and relegated God to the peripheral status. This was the blatant exploitation of their worldly power. The Dasam Granth takes up this problem in the autobiographical poetic composition, "Bachitra Natiká", which is a fictional creative work. The intention of the author is to expose false religious practices prevalent in the society. The anthology does not deal only with his life-events, but also depicts different *avtaras*, both in the Hindu and the Buddhist traditions, who appeared on the canvass of history in the four mythical ages (*yugas*) from the *satyayuga* (pure truth) to the *kaliyuga* (dark age). The Khalsa of Guru Gobind Singh treads on the canvass of history and leaves foot prints for the coming generations.

On the contrary, in the Semitic onto-theology the personal divinity is the key concept. The prophetic revelation is the progressive self-disclosure in the prophetic or historical linear time. The divinity has been revealing in history according to comprehensibility of the people. Prophet Muhammad claims that Allah revealed perfect truth through him. In the Islamic tradition the Qur'an is the consummation of the Semitic revelation (wahy). It is the claim of the Qur'an that the previous revelations were partial that were subsumed in the Qur'anic revelation. It is, therefore, the perfect revelation. The Prophet Muhammad is the last prophet. After him there can be a *murshad* or *pir* and *aulia*, but not a *nabi* or *rasul*. Finality of the Book (the Qur'an) and the lineage of the prophets from Adam culminates in Prophet Muhammad. The Muslims revere Guru Nanak as a *pir*.

The Sikh onto-theology is different in nature and tone. In the Sikh faith, revelation is not the progressive self-disclosure of the Akala Purakh as is found in the Semitic traditions. The Sikh concept of revelation is the outcome of ecstasy (*sahaj*) and absorption in the Akala Purakh (Numinous). Revelation of the Guru Granth is the ideological identity of monism inclusive of all possible possibilities of creation, but it is subject to variations in attributes, which are hermeneutical coeval reactions of the contemporary contributors to the Guru Granth.

In India, the preference for the secular world in favour of the otherworld was displayed in the very early medieval period. Originally even Islam was the religion of this-world, but later it developed tendencies of the otherworld. Before Guru Nanak's asceticism was practised both in India and in the Islamic traditions in pursuit of salvation or autonomous self. The emphasis was laid on giving up one's home causing hardship to one's family. The ideal of the otherworld was adopted in the extreme form of negation of one's own existence. So the concept of the otherworld was common in India and the Islamic countries. Guru Nanak bitterly condemned it in his hymns. The whole of the Guru Granth is a critique of it. The Scripture advocates for wrestling with the oddities of the world for the sake of the subaltern folks.

(ii) World-view of Sikhism

The genius of Guru Nanak created the Sikh world-view. Other contributors to the Sikh Canon supplemented it with their hymns. The third Guru Amardasa and the fifth Guru Arjunadeva schematised it. The contents of the Guru Granth are eternal, but the Scripture itself is not uncreated. It assumed the status of eternity when Guru Gobind Singh raised the Scripture to the status of Divinity. In the Sikh tradition, the scripture becomes eternal because it is true for all the times to come (i.e., *jugo juga atala*). It is not of an age, but of all ages. It presents the view that man has an inherent tendency of self-transcendence because of his creative nature.

Sikhism is critical of the gangrenous and corrupt medieval religious practices sanctioned by the above traditions. It bitterly condemns the rulers.

The Sikh philosophy is different in nature and tone. In the Sikh faith, revelation is not the progressive self-disclosure of the Akala Purakh as is found in the Semitic traditions. The Sikh concept of revelation is the outcome of ecstasy (*sahj*) and absorption in the Akala Purakh. Revelation of the Guru Granth is the ideological identity of monism inclusive of all possible possibilities of creation, but it is subject to variations in attributes, which are hermeneutical coeval reactions of the contemporary contributors to the Guru Granth. We find that all the contributors to the Sikh Canon have identical ideology (monism), but attributes of the Akala Purakh have diversity of expressions in the context of their respective cultural milieus. Baba Farid's hymns outside the Sikh Canon have different tenor and are to be interpreted within the context of the Islamic tradition. When these hymns were incorporated in the Guru Granth, their meanings were transformed within the philosophical context of the Sikh Canon. That is to say that the bigger footprint covers a smaller one. Similarly, the context of the Guru Granth is wider in scope because it covers the Indian and the Semitic cultural contexts. It is not rejecting the other revelations, but to subsume them in the wider circle. Thus, the Guru Granth encompasses the Semitic revelation as well as *shruti* of the Vedic lore.

In the Semitic traditions–book, prophet, and revelation are central. Revelation is horizontal progression and is self-disclosure of reality in historic time. Reality in historic time is accepted because revelation as progression is accepted for approximation and narrowing down gap between the self and Numinous. Complete identity between the self and the personal Deity is not achieved.

Guru Nanak and other Gurus continue as central till Guru Gobind Singh when the Guru Granth was elevated to the supreme Divinity. The Gurus' charismatic personality as central linch-pin is replaced with the *shabda-guru*. The Guru's charismatic personality disappears. The Guru Granth mirrors the Akala Purakh. On the contrary, in the Semitic traditions Prophet's charismatic personality is not done away with. Revelation is progression in the linear time and historical realm. History of Sikhism is interpreted in the Semitic sense. In the Semitic religions personal God is central and in the Indic idelogy tradition of Advaita monism is the ideology and in Buddhism emancipation from suffering is central. The Guru Granth represents restructured Indic ideology (non-dualism/ monism=Advaita is Indic).

When we say that the Guru Granth is an epiphany of the '*guru*' means that the script is an embodiment of Guru's body ('*guru ki deha*). The Guru Granth as an embodiment of '*eternal shabad*' is a living God on the earth.

In Islam, the revelation (*wahy*) is consummation of revelation in the Qur'an. It descends through Gabriel (Zabriel) in intervals to Prophet Muhammad. It is a claim of the Qur'an that earlier revelations were partial that are subsumed in the Qur'anic revelation. It is the perfect revelation. Prophet Muhammad is the last prophet. The Guru Granth is a scripture of different nature and note. In the Guru Grant no hymn of the Qur'an is incorporated while the entire Qur'an is attributed to Prophet Muhammad. In the Guru Granth revelation is not progressive self-disclosure of the Being as is found in the Semitic traditions. The Sikh concept of revelation is the outcome of ecstasy and absorption in the Akala Purakh. The revealed hymns of the contributors to the Sikh Canon cover the period from the sixth to the seventeenth century Christian Era. Revelation of the Guru Granth is the ideological identity of monism inclusive of all possible possibilities of creation but it is subject to variations in attributes, which are hermeneutical coeval reactions of the contemporary contributors to the Guru Granth. Their utterances could not be accepted as such because Guru Nanak was the first Guru who collected hymns of other bhaktas and sufi saints.

On the other hand, in the Indic traditions revelation is not presented in historical time because time in Indian thought is illusory. It is only in the Indian traditions that historical time as reality is accepted which has been reconciled with the cyclic time of the Indian and the Greek traditions. The ideology of the Guru Granth is kernel, but interpretations differ. Revelation is self-disclosure of the Numinous through multiplicity of expressions. The revelation in the Guru Granth has ideological identity of monism but the contributors to the Scripture picture contemporaneous social realities that were in fluid forms. They were critical of the morbid social and political conditions in the society. The medieval Indian culture was in turmoil. The social and religious institutions were static and had lost contact with existential realities. The feudal structure of the Turco-Afghan and Mongol was in conflict with Indian feudal monarchic systems.

It is interesting to note that the Guru tried to create an edifice of the Akala Takht as an embodiment of eternity. The sixth Guru constructed their edifice of ideology on the anchor of real historical time. The Gurus inspired the Indians to imbibe historical sense. It prepared them to rebut atrocities of the alien invaders on India.

(iii) Free Will and Responsibility

The lower species are devoid of creativity and man can develop language of signs and symbols. He can develop his consciousness to eternal freedom and become a spring-well of autonomous categorical imperative (*nishkama karma*) for discharging responsibilities. These are distinct features of man from other lower species. In addition to it, he articulates symbolic language to vent to his views and thoughts. While doing philosophy or creative thinking, past treasure is kept in the unconscious mind and new ideas are articulated to cope with the new situations. Thus, every philosophy is a critique of archaeology of knowledge, which is disintegrated and reintegrated for formulating new coeval world-view. For this purpose, philosophy creates and recreates new values, judgments, and life views in the society. This implies social, political, moral, etc., responsibilities. Philosophy is not philosophy of history, which recapitulates archaeology of knowledge that is preserved in the sacred scriptures, traditions or folklore. It is innovation of new ideas in the contemporaneous existential situations. Thus, genuine philosophy advocates relative truth. It comes forth with new ideologies for ushering in peace and harmony in society for the welfare and emancipation of the fellow beings. Freedom is a precondition for discharging responsibilities towards others. It is basic condition for a good civil society. Hence, man is to be allowed to have freedom. It is symbolic of cultural life. He tries to achieve it in his life-span from birth to coffin. Transcendence from the negative aspects of the person is to be pursued ceaselessly. Continuous striving and struggling in the world constitutes the essence of the dynamic view of life. He should have freedom in every walk of life and should not run away from the moral and the societal responsibilities. The essence of human life is to create balance between the in-born self and the created self. Man's personal resolution determines the criterion of his autonomous voluntary actions. He is creator of the new world-view. He reconciles theory and praxis in resolving moral dilemmas in the existential situations. The personal resolution implies that there should be no clergy, and no imposition of the moral code by the priests. Hence, freedom is personal autonomy of the self without any constrains.

Voluntary action presupposes that the 'other' and the world are real. The 'other' is to be treated as a real 'person', an embodiment of freedom. The other persons and the holy assembly of persons (*sangat*) are real. The *sangat* is miniature unit on which the super structure of society is built. Evil is inherent in man and real at the same time. It is to be weeded out from within the self. It is also a motivating force pursuing moral struggle in the world. Hence, evil is necessary for taming beast in man and making him an ideal person.

Voluntary service (*seva*) without conceit is real. It makes man oblivious of worldly seditions. These are products of the societal life. The *sangat* can be useful in checkmating the egoity and the enticements of the world. Man is to be a cultivator and not a parasite or only consumerist and hoarder. He can be a mendicant, but not a recluse. Every person is to be a householder and not a priest. It means that the collective responsibility and the will prevail over individual will.

In Indian culture an endeavour is to triumph over death and attain eternal freedom where vicious cycle of birth and death does not recur. Man continues living detached life in time without having the fear of death. Man can dissolve this contradiction by overcoming the fear of death. Though there is no commonality of doctrinal identity among Indian thinkers, the core of Indian culture anchors on its dynamic view of life. When the self transcends the limits of the empirical consciousness and merges in the cosmic consciousness, all linguistic constructs disappear. The self, then, realises absolute freedom.

The dynamic view of life necessarily entails the empirical world, social realities, and societal relations, family, etc. Indian culture reconciles eternity and temporality (historicity). Thus, Indian philosophy and culture largely reel round four-fold values (*Purasharthas* : *moksha, kama, artha* and *dharma*). The highest goal of Indian philosophy centres round the concept of *moksha* (eternal freedom). It is self-evident and self-sufficient principle upon which all other principles depend. They are derivatives from it. The trio scheme is a means to realise *moksha*. They perform the role of responsibility to *moksha*. Therefore, freedom and responsibility are inseparable from each other. Freedom and responsibilities should go hand in hand. Realisation of freedom is man's authentic existence.

Authentic existence of man is at once culmination of the temporal existence in eternity. Man has the potentiality to stretch his temporal self and merges into eternity. It brings in the issue of immortality of the self. It is impossible to conquer or stop physical death. It is an inevitable absolute certainty. It can be postponed but it cannot be put to an end. It has been a wild goose chase for achieving victory over the physical death. Even Ravana who tied *kala* (death) to one leg of his bed could not defy it. Thus, human existence has been a ceaseless striving to overcome the spectre of death. Indian religious traditions do not declare that human existence is a total failure. They target at achieving eternal freedom (*moksha*) from vicious circle of birth and death.

In Sikhism, human action in history is restored. It is the form of realism because the reality of the external world is accepted. Consciousness is 'intentional' because it is directed towards others, apart from the subject. When it transcends the 'me,' then it cuts across all the phenomenal categories (i.e., space, time, causality, etc.) and the self realises its oneness or mystic identity. It realises its intrinsic autonomy. The self is attuned to the cosmic law (*rita/hukam*).

The sages of antiquity in India and Greece had a real sense of the time (*kairos*). In the early ancient history of India they had a historical sense. We might have not recorded the chronology of the historical facts and the events, but we had the notion of logic of the ideas. The notion of the otherworld was not developed in ancient India. It was developed in the medieval ages. The concepts of life and world negations became current in the medieval ages. The cardinal emphasis of the cyclic view of time is to transcend from the historical time. On the other hand, the prophetic or linear view of time emphasises advancement towards the goal where time ends at a particular point. This is the basic difference between the Indian or the Greek, and the Semitic views of time. When both are blended into one whole, self-transcendence and advancement can be possible. Guru Nanak tried to reconcile both in theory and praxis. This viewpoint advocates the dynamic view of life and world. Hence, the ideology to represent such a view is to be dynamic. The ideology is to be structured and restructured from time to time in conformity with the changed social conditions. Thus, Sikh onto-theology is a blending of the cyclic and the prophetic perspectives of time.

Guru Nanak's concept of time is existential and phenomenological. The foundation of the Gita is the mythical or articulated linguistic construct of time that motivates the person to *nishkama karma*. The central message of the Gita is the epitome of the Vedic lore. With the passage of epochs, we find in practical life a wide gap between theory and practice in the existential situations. In the medieval times, the gap was at its peak. This was the main concern of Guru Nanak to restore lived time in the practical life. This concept has close affinity with the Semitic concept of time. Prophet Zoroaster has the similar viewpoint of time. The Semitic and the Zoroastrian traditions have no significance of the other and the mythical worlds. Guru Nanak had a coeval existential problem to reconcile the Semitic and the Indic views.

In the medieval ages people lacked genuine awareness of the historical time. The mythical time shadowed the historical time and, consequently, the phenomenal world was conceived as *maya* and a magic show. The medieval world-view, on the whole, was cut off from the stark social realities. It resulted in negation of the empirical life and the world. The medieval Bhaktas and Sikhism reinterpreted the prevalent negative Puranic and the Qur'anic world-views of the middle ages and revived the ancient Vedic affirmative historical world-view, which is primarily concerned with this-world.

Guru Gobind Singh highlights the role of the invincible will in the existential situation as the social and moral responsibility. The khalsa, attuned to eternal Self (Akala Purakh) and dominated by divine will, defied the temporal state or rule. According to Guru Gobind Singh the khalsa is not purely created by history. It is a natural creation by the divine will for the realisation of the eternal freedom of the self. The Dasam Granth reiterates the voluntarist thoughts *passim*.

An individual is granted free will though he has inherent devilish elemental traits in him. Spiritual discipline assists man to subjugate the evil in him. The fundamental dictum of morality is that: "as you sow, so shall you reap". The ideal of the human life, based on the new model of morality, is not to be realised through ecstasy and meditation in the solitary jungles, but it is to be attained in the societal world while living the life of a householder. Regeneration and transformation in the society is to be consciously ushered in. Every person is to contribute his might to the cause of amelioration and transformation of the existing abnormal conditions in the society. Everyone is bound to carry on incessantly the duty of redeeming pangs of the human beings in accordance with the divine will. The individual will is the executor of the divine purposes. Thus, the cosmic law functions through the individual will. He is capable of carrying out the mission.

The best service to God is to be rendered through active service to His creatures. The creation is the manifestation of God. Hence service to creatures is service of God. One is to identify oneself with others in mind utterances and deeds. The trio should constitute unity of will to do action. Real good life is to be lived disinterestedly amidst the worldly joys and sorrows. Thoughts in the conscious mind and utterances are to be translated into practice. It is the essence of the practical and dynamic view of human life. The voluntarist lives unto this ideal triangle of thought, utterance and deed.

Bhakti movement is onto-theological ethics. It is emancipator of the self. Self-reflection is freedom from self-imposed immaturity. It is dependent on giving a rational reconstruction of the autonomous self. Will transcends causal necessity and spontaneously action on categorical imperative. Only free man can act categorically. Transcontinental freedom and moral law are interchangeable Hence, in the ultimate analysis it needs no mentor and tutelage or authority. Pure will is identified with freedom. Culture and freedom are synonyms. Kant has placed freedom and perfection (holy will) at the centre of his moral thought. Principles of practical reason are universal and ends in themselves, 'kingdom of ends', freedom, etc. These are bases of human rights. These are bases of state, culture, and religious identity. State is to respect man's freedom.

The devotees assemble in the Hindu temples to listen to religious discourses and exegetical expositions of the texts. It is not true religious activity. The congregational activity is lacking freedom in the Hindu temples, mosques, and gurdwaras or churches. In India it was developed in some medieval sects, such as those of Chaitanya and Vallabhacharya. On the other hand *nama-simran* through *shabda-yoga* is basic cardinal religious activity. The *ardas* traces Sikh faith from myth of creation to different stages of the Sikh history. With a view to invoking spirit of self-sacrifice, names of the Sikh Gurus and the Sikh martyrs are repeated. It ends in glory of the '*waheguru*' and welfare of all. The supplication is surrendering one's will to Akala Purakh for inspiration to do action.

The chapter can be concluded with the remark that freedom for discharging moral action for the welfare of others is the ultimate goal of human life. This leads us to the concept of *Sikhism : Continuity of Indian Culture*.

4

Sikhism: Continuity of Indian Culture

(i) Introductory

Before launching an analysis on the philosophical issues involved in the above title, it enjoins upon us to explain the vital philosophical questions which can unlock the vexed problems of culture. (i) What is culture? (ii) What is uniqueness of Indian culture? (iii) How can diversity of regional cultures be harmonised within the Indian culture? Can we rationally justify that Sikhism is continuity of Indian culture in the medieval and modern epochs. We shall take up identity of Sikhism vis-a-vis Indian identity. (iv) What is globalisation? (v) How can we retain India's cultural identity in the context of globalisation in the coeval scenario?

Our understanding of Indian culture is that of rope dancers. We are unconsciously interpreting Indian culture from the Western perspective. It is unfortunate that Indian religious discourses continue limping alongwith Hindu Ashramas, Siddha or Yogi Mathas, Sikh Gurdwaras, Muslim mosques, Shaiva Shivadwalas, Jaina Mandirs, and Buddhist Pagodas/Stupas.

Precondition of interpreting others' culture is sound grasp of their culture with critical and creative mind. They are to abide by objective rules of hermeneutics and logic. Liberal quoting from the texts does not show creativity. The lenses of Eurocentric methodology colour the interpretation of Indian culture. We are to interpret *Sikhism: Continuity of Indian*

Culture from the Indian standpoint. This will, perhaps, be a singular contribution to the Indian philosophy.

In the present scenario, technology has revolutionised the global scene. The means of communication, media information and internet have squeezed the world into a global village. It has placed humanity on the volcanic mouth. Modern science might have contributed to the development of civilisation, but it has checkmated our spiritual culture and values. It has bulldosed minor cultures. No culture in the modern world can be isolated from others. Man is always in flux and engaged in internal conflicts and external tyranny. He is to confront twofold fronts at a time. Then, what can be the net outcome of fluxional nature of the world and man? In the modern technological age, the academic philosophical community has come closer because of means of communication, internet and television. These are the main information sources of today. Nevertheless, visual sources are mostly superficial. They don't take us to the heart of 'others' minds and cultures of the insider and the outsider. Culture is a lived experience. It is a symbol of human freedom.

Indians lived under alien servility since the Turks came to India and later the British ruled over us for more than three hundred years. Mere looking at a bhakta meditating in *samadhi* does not leave deep impact on the onlooker. The onlooker himself must undergo this experience. We need an integration of others' minds and their world-views into one unity. Sheer mental colonisation of other world-views will not be sufficient. We need to develop an integrative world-view that is to be put to use. This experiment can be done on the soil of India because Indian culture, being a composite culture, is a world within the world. India is a miniature global world-view. India is a world within the global world. It has developed a composite culture which encompasses elements of the Semitic, the Greek and the Indian philosophical traditions. Therefore, it is easy for the Indian philosophers to develop an integrative *Sikhism: Continuity of Indian Culture* that can be a guideline for both India and the global world. It enjoins upon the philosophers to formulate the integrative world-view that subsumes the past and the contemporary issues. Hence, the problem of rethinking crops up. Such philosophical explanation analyzes the current issues and carries forth the past traditions, and blends them into one coherent whole. Both horizons are blended into one unity. It is to be translated into praxis. Indian culture is a micro-culture that mirrors global cultures.

Sikhism is a re-interpretative exposition of India's integrative culture without making departure from its essential unity. It is continuity through the epochs of ups and downs of history. It incorporates Western, Semitic, Greek and other cultures within its fold without deviating from the essential unity of Indian culture. It mirrors a holistic picture of our culture.

(ii) What is Culture?

In Sanskrit it is called '*sanskriti*' and in Arabic language it is called is '*tahjib*'. It is often used as synonyms of *dharma* or religion. The root of Sanskrit is to cleanse or polish. It deals with knowledge (*vidya* or *ilam*). With the help of practical wisdom, we formulate some laws. These are man-made laws. These rules are made for living a peaceful life where justice prevails. These are concerned with values which are eternal. Culture is primarily concerned with spiritual values and ideals. Modern science has eroded moral and spiritual values.

The values are ideals which are expressed through customs, traditions, and conventions. These laws should be based on natural principles. The captive should not be deprived of food to the extent that he can't survive. Mahatma Gandhi's hunger strike is justified because it was undertaken for higher moral principles. Man thrown before a lion loses hope to live. Secondly though laws of nature are empirical and contingent, these should not be violated beyond limit. Lastly, laws of logic and cosmic laws are foundational and fundamental. They cannot be violated. These laws cannot be set aside. Natural laws and human laws have to abide by the laws of logic. Cosmic law regulates the process of the cosmos. All laws abide by the laws of the cosmos and logic. Wittgenstein remarks, "It used to be said that God could create anything except what would be contrary to the laws of logic. —The reason being that we could not *say* what an 'illogical' world would look like." (*TLP*: 3, 031). It means that it is impossible to explain logically what is contrary to the laws of logic. The above-mentioned laws are applicable to culture as well. Man makes cultural laws that are to be applied on man in the society and the nature.

Thus, there would be a *diachronic* relationship between the two. Hence, relativity of interpretation is the essence of modern philosophical hermeneutics. Interpretation is a process of objective understanding and absolute objectivity of meaning is a hermeneutic mirage. It is reproductive and creative articulation and not merely a repetitive and productive epistemic endeavour. There is no fixed meaning in itself. With what you speak and write earlier about words (*shabdas*) intelligibility of the meaning is deepened when the interpreter goes deeper and deeper into significance of the text and the facts.

In the modern era there is a denial of any fixed or absolute meaning, or any correspondence between language and the external world, or any fixed reality or truth or fact to be the object of hermeneutic inquiry. The meanings are relative and contextual. This dynamic nature of the conceptual articulation enjoins upon the hermeneut to develop new hermeneutical articulation of the meanings of the text of the Sikh Canon. In this context, it will be pertinent to mention Gadamer. He is of the view that understanding is comprehension of two horizons of the original meanings and historically stationed text for understanding. Gadamerian hermeneutics brings back to life the text by blending historical consciousness with the present textual context of the scripture. In this sense, it is a productive and creative process of interpretive context. Therefore, every text is to be reinterpreted in the modern context (see, *Truth and Method*, pp. 264-80). Hence, the meaning of the text is always diachronic.

The transcendental identity of consciousness is acosmic and beyond history and time. Its reflections are manifested in history. It is eternal that can't be reduced to the empirical world. It implies that consciousness as such can't be reduced to the empirical self because it is the transcendental precondition of all representations (knowledge/judgment) and pluralities. This is the central concept of Indian culture's dynamic vision. However, it can be harnessed to time (history) for carrying out real historical actions as categorical imperatives. It will be voluntarism where cosmic will (*hukam*) is active in history through realised dignitaries.

Consciousness (*shiva*) is at once transcendent and immanent in the *shakti*. It is to be emancipated from it. In other words, it is to be freed from the cocoon of the phenomenal effects. The self is not a finished soul-substance. It is an activity and unifying principle of consciousness. It is because of its dynamic nature that creativity comes in man. Creativity depends on development of human mind. A person who is more developed, he is more original and cultural. Mind of the man is more developed as compared to ordinary persons. Hence, it plays significant role in the creation of values and culture.

(iii) Culture and Creativity

The rock does not know that it is a rock. It is only man who is aware that it is a rock. It is said: where the sun cannot go, a poet can penetrate into it. The creative imagination of the poet can cut across all the hurdles and reach out to the coveted target. At the same time it is difficult to understand the creative mind of the poet. To understand a poet is to be a poet. A mystic can understand a mystic. Thus, to understand a mystic one has to be a mystic.

In addition, a creative thinker is always ahead of his time. His contemporaries, often, fail to appreciate him. In this context, Iqbal in his inimitable style says that a flower resembling an eye (*nargis*) sheds tears for thousand years to find a person who could appreciate its beauty. At last an appreciative eye is born. Similarly, only another appreciates the work of a creative poet or thinker. In this hope, he brings forth a piece of creative work. He hopes that another great person will appear to appreciate it and will make improvements upon it. Only another poet and mystic can appreciate a great poet and a mystic. Both masterminds are attuned to the echoes of the cosmos and eternity. So long as consciousness inheres in man, it is possible for a creative mind to create something new. It is in this hope that the creative persons live in the world and continue producing creative pieces of literature.

The creative genius garners ideas from the utterances or writings of wise persons and reinterprets them in the light of his contemporary conditions. He, often, interacts with other wise persons. In this way our mind cultivates new ideas which strike him in moments of solitude. Then he formulates new ideology for putting in for use in the practical life.

More the suffering richer is the creative maturity. Creative thinking must precede suffering and sorrows. It is also a general view that suffering precedes creativity. There are exceptions to this general principle. For instance, Lord Buddha was a prince. He had all the luxuries of life at his disposal. It is not known as to what was the cause of his sensitivity for the sufferings of the living beings. Perhaps, sensitivity was in-built in him. He identified himself with sufferings of the sentient beings. Similar is the case with the Gurus who identified themselves with the marginalised people. The Buddha renounced his palace in search of causes of suffering and death in the world. He found that root-cause of all suffering in the world is ignorance about our own selves and the world. He found the solution in *nirvana*. It was negation of the *sansara*.

Some achieve maturity in the early age and others in the later life. The general theory of creativity is that it should be persistently continued. There are degrees of creativity among human beings. The great creative thinkers go on keeping company of great masterminds that sharpen their creative faculty only if he is willing to develop it. For example, a knife becomes sharper, when it is used more and more. Similar is the case with the creative faculty of the talented person. Once the creative process is initiated, it continues recycling and rebounding till death.

The creative sensitivity of the artist transcends natural or object language (words) and enters the realm of meta-language of ciphers. Twilight language (*sandhya bhasha*) also encompasses the phenomenon and the beyond. The words of natural language exist in the minds of the etymologists, philologists, linguists, *et al*. The words divorced from the spoken language are dead leaves that don't yield gnawing secrets of life. The holistic vision of truth is represented by the ciphers that yield secrets of life. The ciphers are found in the utterances of the mystics and in the esoteric scripts All scientific questions can be answered, but the question of life remains unanswered. Wittgenstein correctly remarks, "The solution of the problem of life is seen in the vanishing of the problem...." (*TLP*: 6.521). He continues to say that logic can't find the sense or meaning of life. It is only mystic who grasps the sense of life, but he can't express it. It means that the whole truth of life escapes from rational apprehension. Being a logical philosopher he is not concerned with mysticism of silence. The meaning of life is intuited and then values are articulated to picture it. It means that meaning or value of life lies outside the empirical and contingent world. The mystic can intuitively realise it that can't be explained or 'said'. It can only be 'shown'. For example, the dumb can't say, he can show sweetness with facial expressions.

History of the traditions is the treasure of the past culture that continues as an evergreen treasure of ideals and values. It never withers away or dies. Its reminiscences remain which are revivified when new congenial situations arise. Man values his past and holds on in great esteem than his corporeal life. He is not willing to give up his consciousness of the past at death even. It gives birth to continuity of life after death. The oral traditions are revered. The creative thinker changes them with new values.

The Indians have been slaves of old customs and traditions. The Gurus tried to wash them off and Guru Gobind Singh finally baptised or replaced them with new ones. The majority of Indians are still cherishing old outdated ethos, beliefs, custom, conventions, etc. They are living in the past at traditional level. In order to live in eternity these are to be restructured in accordance with new changed conditions.

Self has the dual role of creation and creator. Transcendental consciousness in the self is the cause of creation of the cosmos. Its creativity is the cause of all forms in time and space. It is only creativity of the creative mind that bridges eternity and historicity. Individual self is a micro-cosmos. Therefore, cosmic law controls functioning of the self. The

Divine executes its Will through the individual will. It is to be attuned to cosmic law to make him ideal man. A person whose will is attuned to the divine will, is a realised perfect person. Human consciousness travels from first person to third person perspective. It is journey from 'me' to 'Thou'.

In other words, life and will are coeval terms. Thus, reality or truth is 'becoming' and not the thing 'having-become'. The world and life have definite meanings that are closely allied to the concept of 'becoming'. Past is being actualised and future is created with values. Thus, it is the 'present', which epitomises eternity. Sikhism lays emphasis on it.

(iv) What are distancing and *sannyasa*?

It will be pertinent to point out that distancing and *sannyasa* are synonyms. It is simultaneous involvement and detachment. It involves goal oriented action Hermeneutics of distancing is necessary for arriving at truth. What is theoretical detachment or distancing? What is the significance of distancing in the cultural discourse? It is very important in the case of interpretation of the cultural tradition. In order to be candid and objective in the interpretation of distancing is necessary. So long as the river of time flows, people will continue stumbling over the repetitive nature of the philosophical problems unless one realises that nothing is repeated in the next moment. It is a fact that nature is not repeating and history is progressing in a unique and chequered way. The Greek myth of the eternal return states that the identical event repeats endlessly. The dynamic onto-theology does not accept 'return of the eternal'. How are things changing? In the modern times, the myth of the eternal return has been eroded.

Understanding dispassionately is distancing from prejudices and bias. Seed and lower species are not capable of detachment. Only man is capable of detachment because of his developed mind. He can reflect upon others' problems without being involved in them. For example, mother can't detach herself from the ailing child. She is generally dominated by feelings, sentiments, and emotions. The doctor, for instance, dispassionately diagnoses the patient and comes to the right conclusion of the treatment. He is concerned with *how* and *why* of the problem. Thus, the argument is that all practical problems can be dispassionately solved only if we have a sound theory. Feeling and reason should go hand in hand. It is called 'paralysis by analysis'. No action should be done in haste. Hence, both have close family resemblances. It means that one is to be involved without attachment.

(v) Meaning, Creativity and Communication

Then some philosophical questions arise. Does the meaning exist in the text or we insert in it? For an ordinary reader, the meaning is in the text but for the creative thinker or interpreter it is at higher level of understanding. His effort is to weed out interpolation in the text. He tries to articulate universal principles from these meanings.

This creative process proceeds without any pre-given suppositions. It is not primarily due to radical departure from pluralities of the cases/facts, but is due to transcendence from the empirical world with his creativity. The discourse doesn't remain within the limits of purely linguistic constructs or signs. It, rather, goes beyond them and reaches out the core of truth that transcends linguistic tools. This is how the meaning of the text and understanding of the reader are fused together. The fusion results in communicating the meaning in the text to the reader. The statements in the texts represent sense (meaning) or signification. It means that form of a proposition doesn't contain its sense, but the sense lies in the content that is to be interpreted by the creative mind. It implies that the proposition has the possibility to communicate its meaning which requires interpretation. The meaning of the text/tradition is to be creatively interpreted that is not in the text/tradition itself. Hence, creativity plays a vital role in interpreting the meaning.

Real epistemic service to truth and humanity is to enter continuously into restructuring and reinterpreting the scriptures and the traditions to avoid irrational religiosity of the rabid fundamentalists and dogmatists. Under the normal tools of linguistics and analytical epistemology, it is an arduous job to justify the crusted prejudices and fossilised religious dogmas and beliefs. The meanings of the scriptures should be taken as treasure-troves of innovative concrete religious consciousness in human history. They carry forward spiritual legacy of the hoary past in the contemporary context. The significance of the sacred scriptures will be a dead log if they are not continuously reinterpreted. It will be smothered under the dust of time.

(vi) Culture and Values

What is culture? Wittgenstein states that "culture is a big organisation which assigns each of its members a place where he can work in the spirit of the whole" (*Culture and Values,* p. 6). In this definition, emphasis is on the interlocked relationships in a whole in which individuals are assigned their duties. In the light of this definition, Sikhism doesn't make any discrimination among the members. All are treated equal. Wittgenstein further asserts that no culture dies. The great culture never dies. It is like the sun that sinks at night and rises again in the morning. It goes on rotating ceaselessly. Likewise, the values are eternal and are for the ages to come.

No one will be there to observe the progress as that of a "culture as an epic". Epic is a written prophecy. One can foresee one's death (ideology) in the future as an inevitable phenomenon, but no one is definite about its exact form and moment. When death comes, we can't experience it. Wittgenstein rightly said: "Death is not an event in life. We don't live to express death..." (*TLP:* 6.4311). The essence of life is activity and death is cessation of activity. Eternity is not infinite temporal duration that encapsulates past, present, and future. Eternal life is to live in the present without the burden of the past and anxiety for the future. Likewise, epic is an eternal lesson for the present generations and no one can predict the exact happenings in the future. Culture is to be lived in the 'eternal present'. The very fact that we become aware of it makes us existentially responsible to the historical responsibilities.

Culture is the way of life of the people including their attitude towards other people and the world. This positive attitude towards the world enjoins upon man the commitment to the moral, social and political responsibilities for the welfare of humanity and justice. Attitude implies values, beliefs, arts, aesthetic sense of sensibility, vision of social ideals, or values, habits and various customs, ethos, conventions, and other societal activities. Cultural patterns of life are acquired and cultivated in society. These patterns mirror through values, beliefs, and religious ways of living. Formation of culture through religion plays a very significant role.

Values are articulated for institutionalisation of societal life in society. It is an attitude and mode of dealing with objective reality and subjective personality. Three points are noteworthy in understanding perspectives on culture. First, culture is a human creation. Second, it provides 'objective reality' and 'subjective interpretation of inner self' is churning of ideals, values, ideology, and so forth. Third, it represents interpersonal relationships for harmony and justice. It endeavours for adjustment that emanates from spontaneity and freedom of action. One can formulate ideology for bettering the existent social order. Here revival of Indian culture means restoration of freedom and self-dignity of man. This determines cultural identity of India.

Then the question arises: What is value? Why does man create value? What is the existential significance of values in life? What is the relevance of values in social life? How are the values to be reconciled in theory and praxis? The values are human creations and are not the God given gifts. The creation of values necessarily follows from the dynamic nature of the onto-theology. Values are created ideals for seeking justice and peace for the welfare of the people. Man creates values because he is intrinsically free and creative. He wants to better his existential conditions and aspires to live life of peace and harmony. He, therefore, creates values. Take, for instance, there is a hungry dragon waiting for the prey in the ditch and the rope is going into the well. The rat (time) is cutting the rope of life. Baba Farid, a Sufi saint, symbolises time with crow that is a symbol of death. Every born man is facing this absurd predicament. Time is continuously dragging us towards death. The significance of values in existential and social life is that they make us transcend the empirical world and land us on the higher landscape to live life of equanimity. He lives in the world with a strong will power.

The poet, for example, is going down the ditch. He sees a flower coming out of the wall. He changes the track at the sight of the flower and starts appreciating its beauty and fragrance, and forgets the fear of death. It is the attitude of the poet, artist or philosopher that makes him to change his attitude towards life and death. It is more applicable to the creative sensitive thinkers and not to the dullards and insensitive persons or lower animals. Forgetfulness of the cutting of the rope [death] creates new values. The values try to reconcile life and death in a higher state of consciousness. Guru Nanak in one of his hymns says if anyone wants to love truth, he should forget death (i.e., *jau tau prema khelan ka chau / siru dhari tali gali meri au...* (20) / GG, p. 1412).

The evil is also a human creation. The moral and cultural values emanate from one's attitude towards others and good and evil. At human level these are ratiocinated, but finally transcendence from these is intuited in the labyrinth of solitude. The value is not a factual phenomenon, but it is an attitude that creates values. It transcends the realm of the factual world.

Epic is a human creation as a cosmic picture of human life with conflicts and sufferings of the human beings. In the Indian culture Valmikah created the Ramayana. The Mahabharata was the cosmic vision of rishi Veda Vyasa who created the epic for humanity for the past, present, and future. It is pole star for man for finding ways to come out of the quagmire of human suffering and problematics of human life. These are the treasure-troves of human values and ideals presenting perennial guidelines for the coming generations. Thus, artist, poet, scientist, philosopher, and other creative thinkers create new configurations of values for humanity.

It will be pertinent to point out that it is only man who can create values and configuration of culture. It comes out of man's autonomous nature. Hence, man is pivotal in the process of creation of all possible values. Values are not *anadi* (eternal). These *are* created in time. Once they are created, they can't be destroyed. They become eternal. Man dies but the value of truth survives forever. The values live forever in the memories of the people from generation to generation. From this standpoint history is significant. The values are context bound. They are not part of the world. These are acosmic in the sense that rules of nature don't work at volitional level. They transcend the factual world. The sense of the world is outside the world. Whatever exists in the world is contingent and accidental. The values are outside the world because they are eternal (see also, *TLP*: 6.41). Here Wittgenstein is not explicit about the use of values. He takes up the use of values in his later works (see, *Philosophical Investigations and Culture and Value*). The values are *attitudes or interests* towards given fact(s).

So man is not only a creature (say, rock or log of wood or any other object presented to the eye), but also creator of values. Man creates values in time but they become eternal. The values (good/evil) are not uncreated (*anadi*), but are eternal (*amar/ ananta*). Since the values are created in time or history, they are to be put to use (tested) in history. Hence, values need history. Though the values are outside the world, yet they are to be descended to the world to test their viability. God is an absolute value-construct. He is uncreated, yet is to descend on the earth to emancipate humanity from suffering. The mind creates a conceptual space, which is independent of the ephemeral world. This conceptual space is the realm of the values.

Communication and solidarity of mankind are interconnected. The former creates interpersonal relationships. It is a stepping-stone for solidarity. If anything of value is good, it must be of use for all and for all times (altruism). Solidarity is the ideal of the epic for which we are to strive. The values create unity in the social structure and remove dissipating forces. This process of creation and destruction continues endlessly in history because social and historical conditions are in constant flux. New social structure needs new values of equality, liberty, fraternity, *et al.,* for the welfare of all and sundry. Hatred for injustice should be developed. There should be an active resistance to injustice. Solidarity is to be ushered in by deeds and not by sheer words.

(vii) Uniqueness of Indian Culture

Here, I want to focus attention of the readers on culture and person from the Indian perspective. In the age of science and technology, search for global peace and justice seems to be a wild goose chase. Shadow of death is hovering over our heads. Humanity is burning in the cauldron of the fire of terrorism, violence and religious fanaticism and bigotry. The frenzied politicians are doggedly knocking at the door of death by falsely banking upon science and technology. The volcanic eruption of atomic bomb may usher in dooms day at any point-instant. Human beings may perish and God will have to restart the process of creation *de novo*. Oswald Spengler in his classical work, *The Decline of the West,* has warned and blown the siren of annihilation of humanity. He gives the idea that science and technology cannot yield any spiritual healing to the moral and spiritual needs of humanity. It is only and only genuine religions can save humanity from cruel clutches.

The age of science and technology is the beginning of the end of humanity. Science and industry have caused immense misery to humanity. It cannot yield peace in the world. The idea of great progress is a delusion, alongwith the hope that truth will be known. It is just a mirage (*mriga trishna*); a deer tries to find water in the summer season in the rising and ebbing away waves in the deserts. From the point of view of culture, there is nothing good or desirable about scientific knowledge. It is unfortunate that people are doggedly falling prey into the trap of the scientists. No doubt, science is good to a limited extent for satiating man's bodily comforts. Beyond certain limits, it is injurious for humanity. It has taught us how to fly in the skies, dive deep into the oceanic waters, but it has not taught us how to live peacefully on the earth along with other human beings. It strengulates human freedom. Thus, moral and spiritual values are in crisis.

Uniqueness of Indian culture lies in that it does not advocate possessiveness of property and power. It advocates progressive detachment from the world. The Western culture is antipodes to it. It is science and technology oriented. Wealth or money is a part of power. It corrupts human mind. The phenomenon of global terrorism is the natural outcome of it.

The Western culture, science and technology are opposed to Indian culture. Wealth or money is a part of power. It corrupts human mind. The phenomenon of global terrorism is the inevitable outcome of it. Use of power for selfish purposes is to be shunned. Indian culture advocates sense of disinterested attitude towards both wealth, power, and pleads for distanced involvement in the societal relations. This is the meaning of *nishkama karma* of the Gita and *subha karma* (good voluntary deed) of Guru Gobind Singh. Meaning is hidden as amber is in the ashes.

The dominance of material values, in the age of science and technology, is the beginning of the annihilation of humanity. Matter has the potent quality of attraction whereas the spiritual values lay emphasis on ascent of the mind from the clutches and seductions of the mundane world. Material values relegate spiritual values to the periphery. Hence, the present crisis, of cultures and civilisations of the East and the West, has come to the fore. Science and industry have caused havoc and immense misery to humanity. It cannot yield peace and harmony in the world. Sufferings of human beings are increasing day and night.

In the light of the above given global gloomy and dismal picture of the world, it will be pertinent to discourse Indian culture and values (*dharma*) which survived through the ages. It is a historical fact that Egyptian, Samarian, Greek, Persian and other fountainheads of civilisations perished from the map of the world history, but Indian civilisation survived through the epochs of history. This credit goes to the spiritual values of Indian history and cultures which are treasured in the traditions, ethos, the Vedas, Puranas, Upanishads, the Gita, Buddhist literature, the epics (the Ramayana, the Mahabharata, etc.), and in the medieval Bhakti literature).

Then a question arises: What is the essence of the culture? It is not concerned with the progression of civilisation. It surrounds the civilisation. The spirit of civilisation lies in its unity and continuity. Culture is an ideational pole star that guides and determines progression of civilisation.

It is true that wisdom of India is found in the scriptures and oral traditions, but we have wasted time in garnering chaff instead of grain. The scriptures are the Vedas, but we have wasted time binding the manuscripts. The central linchpin of the sacred scriptures is "life" which the scriptures, the epics and the traditions emphasise, but we have glossed over the hidden ciphers in them with exegetical expositions and explanations, which remain at superficial level.

Indian culture mirrors India's unity-in-diversity or identity and otherness. This undercurrent runs in Indian philosophy. There is no commonality of doctrinal identity amongst all Indian thinkers; like, Buddhists, Vedantists, Naiyyaikas, Sikhs, Gandhi and purveyors of the Western thoughts; like, Marx's and Wittgenstein's. The core of Indian philosophy anchors on its dynamic monism. The philosophy of India largely centres round the basic notions of *karma, rebirth, moksha, chit* and four *purashârthas*. The religious celebrities and philosophers have been trying to continue these in the past. The identity of Indian culture is dismantled in the contemporary scenario. Need of the present time is to reformulate cultural identity that should not digress from its essence. It should be mix of tradition and modernity

What is Indic (Buddhist, Hindu, Jaina, and Sikh) culture? What is the unique characteristic of Indian culture? What was the scenario of medieval India? How did the medieval religious celebrities contribute to the revival of the Indian culture?

The essence of 'Indian culture' is the basic question before us. Distinctness of cultural identity ensues from scriptures and traditions. Since the advent of the Arabs and other alien invaders, we were not free to express ourselves due to Muslim rulers' atrocities. Indian culture has undergone through dark channel of servility of the barbarian alien Muslim cruelties and the sophisticated British rulers. During these periods, Indian culture was pushed to the periphery. It subsisted, but it did not perish. The Muslims and the European scholars interpreted Indian culture in their Semitic cauldron of scriptures and the traditions. The Muslim scholars had biased and superficial understanding of Indian culture and scriptures. They could not cast off cataract of their bias.

For the last three hundred years, we have been aping the Westerners. It is unfortunate that we have not come out of the cocoon of the Western expositions of Indian culture, religion and philosophy. The Westerners being 'outsiders' could not do justice to our culture, religions and philosophy. We can overcome their entrenched bias and subjectivity if we objectively follow rules of language and logic. Bias is natural for an outsider because of his sentimental affiliation and attachment to his faith. He sees 'other' religion through the lenses of his faith. Error stealthily creeps in due to non-lived experience of others' culture or religious traditions. Books without coeval interpretations are sheer dry leaves. Interpretation waters the texts and new leaves (meanings) come up and blossom. It infuses life in the text in the coeval context. Creative interpretation sprouts new meanings in the contemporaneous idioms and resurrects life in them.

The uniqueness of Indian spirituality is that it gives scientific spiritual discipline of yoga (yoking to the Numinous), which is the basis of different schools of Indian philosophy. The Gita is the key of the Vedic Indian philosophy, which is its practical dimension and Sankhya School is its theoretical base. The non-Vedic traditions (Shramanic) also emphasise on practical aspect. Both put together constitute perfect voluntarist philosophy of life. Spiritual discipline (*sadhna*) concentrates on rarefaction of consciousness through different states of yoga. It is transformation of the self from the empirical self to the eternal self without dissolving man's 'personal identity'. It is transformation from jiva to *atman* —'self-consciousness' (*viveka budhi*). In other words, the *jiva* is transmuted into *atman* or the empirical gross self is transformed into the subtle self. Thus, our concept of spirituality does not negate the world. This lands us into the realm of all pervasive spirit.

Culture is manifested in religion, art, literature, spiritual values and the like. This concept can be extended to different cultures and civilisations as well. Man does not live by bread alone. No human being can afford to live without bread or at least some form of food because it is necessary for his survival or subsistence. In addition to it, man lives in higher space of values and ideals that constitute his real culture. It manifests in man's behaviour and societal relationships. It can be extended to society for fashioning its character.

Both culture and civilisation are different and closely related to each other. For the progression of civilisation, we require external tools (brush, colour, oil, water, etc.) for painting. We need chisel, hammer, stone for hewing stone for bringing out image from the stone. Some material tools are required for progression of civilisation. The material culture flowers out of civilisation. Culture is the fruit and flower of creativity of mind, and intellect transcends the nature. Man with the help of civilisation changes nature (e.g., course of rivers, dams, electricity, means of communication, transportation, etc.). Man improves upon food, gender, cow, dog, and tools. In short, man adapts himself to the environment. Man improves upon morality, painting, and magic by controlling natural environment, water, fire, air, natural gasses, etc. He develops better relationship with the nature. Culture surrounds the civilisation. The spirit of civilisation lies in its unity and continuity. Culture is what we have self-cultivated being and civilisation is what we use as tools in day-to-day life.

Progress of culture and civilisation has different paces. Civilisation is improvement of material tools that advances rapidly and culture is inner advancement of ideals/values that moves slowly. There is, thus, always-a-cultural lag between the two. I have used revival and progress two terms, which express at once both. The former restores ancient cultural heritage, which was suppressed by the Islamic and the Christian cultures. It came up and advanced in the new congenial conditions. Cultural progress is goal/value directed.

Culture is a human creation that is concerned with style of life of the individuals and society. Human creation deals with ideals and values. It never dies. Once it is created, it becomes eternal. Our ancient sages were engaged in both civilisation and culture. The former was revealed through different disciplines of science. The subject matters of these disciplines are medicine, medicinal plants, surgery, agriculture, astronomy, astrology, and such allied subject matters. These disciplines studied different aspects of the universe. For them the world is manifestation of the Brahman. Their views are recorded in ancient Sanskrit and Prakrita manuscripts and oral traditions, which are preserved by scientists and the spiritual celebrities. Culture digs out truth from within the human person. Thus, civilisation and culture are complementary to each other. Both are closely interlaced.

In the modern times, science is legitimately credited. The present material progress and the advancement of civilisation is the net outcome of it. No doubt, science has given us knowledge, but it has failed to give wisdom. It has not taught us how to make a beast a human being, and godly person. This is possible with wisdom, which we find in our ancient spiritual culture, which has come down to us mostly from the sages through oral traditions. The technique of transformation of the self from within comes to us with wisdom. Our ancient sages (*rishis*) taught us the secret of the art of living a non-involved way in the world that helps in having eternal bliss. The values do not come within the domain of science. This is the essence of spirituality and the Indian spirituality in particular. Hence, relativity and contingency is the essence of modern concept of truth, which manifests through sciences and spirituality.

Culture, on the other hand, is the inner motivating force of values and higher human aspirations, which determine the course of development of human history and civilisation. The values emanate from man's creativity and his inherent freedom of will. He can create better world and demolish tyranny and injustice in society. He has the inherent capacity to historicise new values in praxis. For this purpose, Sikhism emphasises to cut down *manmukh* (egocentric self) and tries to transform him into a cosmic conscious being (*gurmukh*). To be a *gurmukh* is a dire necessity for execution of the divine purposes. In addition, realisation of purposes of human life is carried out in this world *here* and *now*. It is through the individual consciousness the cosmic echo (*anahadanada*) is realised through the reed of individual life in the cosmos. In the cosmic consciousness there are no extraneous constraints and compulsions. And individual consciousness gets freed from these. He wants to be free in the practical life as well. The materialists project man from the viewpoint of a naturalist and positivist. The Gurus are non-behaviourist functionalists in the socio-cultural world of values and ideals. They are spiritualists and realists. Their lives were governed by spiritual values. They were realists and pragmatists in the empirical world.

In the existential human conditions, man is pitted against oddities of human conditions in the concrete world of societal situations within the cosmos. The dynamic ontology of the cosmos implies that man can create his own self. Wittgenstein's 'Tractarian' view correctly asserts that man's creative mind is operative in all-comprehensive reflections on all possible perspectives on the problematic issues. In the course of this work, I am trying to argue *passim* that man transforms his empirical self (ego) into self-reflective identity of the self. He simultaneously carries out his existential historical responsibilities.

Many cultural invasions on India had significant impacts on our lifestyles. Many good elements of culture came to India from Persia. Despite all these variant factors, the core of Indian spiritual culture assimilated the alien cultures into its deep-rooted fold of antiquity. It will be pertinent to point out that India did retain her distinct cultural identity. Our spiritual culture is an admixture of spiritual and material values, but the former dominates it. It is full of vitality and energy. Our Indian culture is the culture of struggle in life. It is dynamic culture. Our sages refined spiritual culture through the ages.

Culture is an escape from beasthood of lower animals, sheep, animals, and barbarism of tribal people. In religious language, it is to kill Satan or devil in us. Division of labour is the outcome of civilisation. Man has the potentiality to transcend his limitations. He has the potentiality to realise his identity. In every religion, the central objective is to create distinct identity of man. In the Bhakti cult, there had been divergent identities of the bhaktas of different regions. The Bhaktas of Maharashtra have distinct identity from other denominations. Kabirpanthis are different from others. Similarly, identity of the Sikh is different from the khalsa. In the Sikh tradition, there are different sects (*sampardayas*). Each sect lays emphasis on different aspects.

Culture or civilisation may be spiritual or material. Civilisation is a progress in the material tools (e.g., structure of buildings, architecture, and material tools, etc.). On the other hand, culture is inner refinement of consciousness. Culture is also cultivation of the mind. Both are continuous processes going on forever. Both require reason and insightful comprehension for having picture of continuity of both.

Civilisation is characterised by the term 'progress.' Progress is its outer form rather than its spirit. It is concerned with means to construct a new structure and civilisation concerns with material means and models. Civilisation emphasises on means to an end and not on an end in itself. Civilisation itself is not independent of end culture. The creation of the mind develops from the syntax or configuration. The clarity of the whole configuration would mirror meaning of a culture. This is the epic view of culture. The epic description of a culture is seen through great figures and characters. In addition, a culture is foreseen when a work is composed. When the two epics, the Ramayana and the Mahabharata, were composed, it was envisaged by their authors that there would be nobody to describe them, but the message will remain till eternity. Every age and generation need new interpretations of the spirit of the epic culture, but the very spirit of the message continues till posterity. Everybody knows that death will occur one day, but it cannot be pinpointedly forecast. Hence, one is to live in the present.

This is the spirit of medieval Indian culture and the world-view. The morphological study of ideology proceeds from lower forms to higher forms and recycles. It mirrors recycling progress of culture and civilisation. Culture is a guiding principle for life. Culture being an ideational phenomenon it is always ahead of civilisation. This is development of consciousness to higher forms of consciousness. Knowledge advances with the advancement of culture and civilisation.

Spengler describes this approach as the morphology of the mechanical and the extended science, which discovers and orders nature-laws and causal laws. It is called systematic paradigm. The morphology of the organic, of history and life and all that bears the sign of direction and destiny is called physiognomic.[1] It is not a mechanical progress. It is teleological or goal directed process. This is a morphological concept of culture, which is applicable to the medieval Indian culture as well.

What is the morphological concept of culture? It refers to 'forms' of culture in progressive and ascending pathway toward apex of the goal of life–*moksha*. Indian culture is an excellent example of morphological concept of culture. Indian culture was almost gasping for survival under the Muslim servilities. In the medieval times, it resurrects as a phoenix comes out of the ashes. In this chapter my endeavour is to portray revival of Indian culture though it waded through vicissitudes of chequered history.

John Dewey, an experimentalist and instrumentalist thinker, rightly said in his book *Inquiry* that man creates and modifies new material tools to adjust with the environment. This is progress of civilisation through history. In addition to it, culture is the progress of inmost 'soul' non-material tools, values, ideals, norms and so on. Tribal people cultivate land and grow grains. Army had old skill but it has changed into new ones—artillery, navigation, and aircraft. The *idea* of a culture is the sum-total of its inner possibilities from its sensible phenomenon or appearance on the canvas of history as a fulfilled actuality. It is the relation of the souls to the living body, to its expression in the light world perceptible to our eyes. The history of a culture is the progressive actualising of its possible forms. Cultural is the end and civilisation is a means. Means as tools are modified and improved. For example, cart is replaced with motor-cars, aircrafts and so on. The end cannot be realised. The end is like a fish that cannot be caught. When we try to catch hold of it, it slips away from our fingers. Culture is a continuous process of realising ideals in actuality.

There would be a diachronic relationship between the two. Hence, relativity of interpretation is the essence of modern philosophical hermeneutics. Interpretation is a process of objective understanding and absolute objectivity of meaning is a hermeneutic mirage. It is reproductive and creative articulation and not merely a repetitive and productive epistemic endeavour. There is no fixed meaning in itself. With what you speak and write earlier about words (*shabdas*) intelligibility of the meaning is deepened when the interpreter goes deeper and deeper into the significance of the text and the facts. The ciphers are treasured in the sacred scriptures, which need to be digged out and explained. These can't be explained with exegesis. Exegesis is a branch of theology that is concerned with explanatory and expository interpretations of the scriptures. It is not concerned with understanding the ciphers.

In the Sikh tradition, exegesis remained limited to explanation or exposition (*kathakari*). It remained at superficial level of literal explanations, philological explanations, etymological derivation of roots (*dhatus*) of the words and the history of word (semantics) derived from different languages. There has been multiplicity of meanings. It lacked fixed meanings and one-to-one relationship with the meanings. It lacked logical syntactic study of language. In the words of Wittgenstein, it has been "an abuse of language".

Then, we are confronted with a philosophical problem: How to make first person experience public? Then how can we talk out the religious or mystic experience? In this process there are some elements involved in it. These are: (i) Numinous, (ii) prophet, (iii) experience of the Numinous, (iv) oral utterance and written word (scripture), (v) meaning, and (vi) real identity of the self (*atman*). Language is considered the foundational universal medium. Thinkable is *said* and unthinkable is *shown*. Hence follows ineffability of mystic experience (*akath/abola*).

Consciousness is transcendent and immanent in the *shakti*. Because of Indians' search for the infinite spiritual truth, they have been bred on mythology, tradition, religious beliefs, and so on. They transcended rationality and lived in the realm of the 'Beyond' where reason commits happy suicide and one enjoys eternal bliss (*mukti*). On the other hand, the Westerns built their philosophical and religious beliefs on rational sound grounds could not bridge the chasm between this-world and the 'Other'. The Indian spiritual celebrities stretched the finite into infinity. The Indic thought and spirituality have travelled far and wide and left deeper footprints that Eurocentric perspectives have so far acknowledged. It is unfortunate that the Europeans over shadowed Indian thought with power and better rational methodology. Indians largely live on traditions and religious faith. Truth being in flux they could not pace with the point-instant changing events of the dynamic time (*waqt / kala*). The Westerns are ahead of us in this respect. We need philosophical understanding of the texts and the traditions. Thus, philosophical understanding or (hermentics dives deep into the text and the traditions. It brings out hidden meanings and formulates new pattern of the scattered elements. New pattern mirrors understanding of the text.

Culture is concerned with inward states of consciousness or mind in its blossomed forms. It may diminish or shine with historical epochs, but the essence of a culture continues for ever. Culture is a lived experience and traditions are likened to dry leafs which shed them with the changing conditions. Outmoded traditions are dropped which are cut off from the societal realities and new traditions come up. Thus, this dynamic cultural process ceaselessly cycles and recycles for times to come.

(viii) Dharma and Culture (Values)

Dharma and culture are lived experiences. It is only confession, self-discipline, and values with strong will power that can emancipate humanity from the perennial sufferings and sorrows. These will determine the healthy future of society. Of course, past culture and religion are to be carried forward as motivating forces. The fossilised and dead theological beliefs hamper human beings and the societal progress. When the mystics replace these spurious beliefs with new genuine beliefs, they dismantle pride and cleanse scum of worldly seductions they cleanse opacity of spurious beliefs. The pioneers of religious traditions come forth with noble and prophetic beliefs. The prophetic beliefs are the holy utterances of the realised selves or mystics. These swerved humanity on righteous path (dharma). If the reader is to enjoy the scriptures, he is to see into it as an insider of culture. He is to identify himself with experience of the author because the texts are the lived experiences of the authors.

Philosophical interpretation helps in understanding meanings of the text. The ciphers of the sacred scriptures are comprehended with intuitive insight (*diva drishti*). Barriers of religious language are to be taken into cognizance while interpreting the sacred scriptures. We cannot enter the palace of truth unless veil of language is torn. The scriptures can take the reader to the threshold, but he is to take a leap of his own to the heart of the truth. Truth is realised in a state of ecstasy, which is an ineffable experience. It can be expressed in dusk language (*sandhya bhasha*). It at once represents eternity and temporality.

Writings on the Indic scriptures have laid more emphasis on the exegetical expositions and anatomy of linguistic analysis. The common reader does not make a distinction between the historical heroes (say, Rama and Krishna) and in the texts. Both the heroes of the epics are elevated creations of the visions of Valmikah and Veda Vyasa. Their leitmotivs anchor on dharma that is hub of societal relations and justice. Originality does not lie in the facts, but in the mind of the author and the interpreter. With new similes originality steps in. Thus, subjectivity of interpretation cannot be ruled out while culling meanings. It is the outcome of man's creativity. Hence meanings are contextual and relative.

The meaning or value of the book is not on the surface. It is hidden at the bottom. By gazing at the facts, the creative thinker gives value to them. Meaning or value is in the mind of the creative thinker (say, Valmikah, Vyasa, *et al.*). When we try to dig it out, the pristine meaning is at the bottom, "all in flux". It is in the syntax of the facts that is in the mind of the author and the interpreter who deciphers it.

Culture mirrors inner self of the person and the nation. Therefore, culture is the way of life of the people including their attitude towards other people and the world. Attitude gives value to the facts. It implies values, beliefs, arts, aesthetic sense of sensibility, vision of social ideals, or values, habits and various customs, ethos, conventions, and other societal activities. Through the epochs of history, cultural patterns of life are acquired and cultivated in society. These patterns mirror culture through values, beliefs, and religious ways of living. Formation of culture through philosophy, religion and aesthetics plays a very significant role. Religion is often mistaken for a fashionable institutionalised substitute of beliefs. Such a religion cannot emancipate humanity from suffering. Sheer doctrines or dogmas cannot emancipate humanity from suffering. The prophetic religion has been saviour when truth is eclipsed by falsehood.

The scriptures and the ethos or the folklore is chosen from the history of the nation. Their leitmotiv is integrative life as a whole. They mirror ethos or culture of the land. They are treasure-troves of the past culture of the nation; characteristic spirit of a community and people. They have universal signification for eternity. They are not of the age but of the ages. The *atman* (inner self) is the culture has close affinity with '*sankriti*' because both focus on inner dimension of the self. If we go deeper into the meaning of the term 'culture', consciousness is 'culture'.

If we go into the etymologies of the term 'culture', in Latin ('*cultura*') and German ('*kultur*'), both emphasise on cultivation of the mind. It is cultivation of the self from within and taming of nature with material tools is civilisation. It is manifested in religion, art, literature, spiritual values and the alike. Culture is refining beast in man and churning out divinity in him. This concept can be extended to different cultures and civilisations. Man does not live by bread alone. No human being who can live without bread or at least some form of food is needed because it is necessary for his survival. In addition to it, man lives in higher space of values and ideals that constitute his real culture. It manifests in man's behavour and societal relationships. It can be extended to the society to fashion its character.

Culture emphasises on a way of life, social structure, etc. Civilisation is development of material tools and artistic artifacts, buildings, mosques, etc. Culture is distinct from creating petty human things. In simple words, civilisation is concerned with external side and culture with inner aspect of human personality, i.e., beliefs, attitude, moral ideals, relationships of man and man, man and group, group and group. Morality comes within the scope of culture. Development of civilisation is faster than that of the culture. Culture is a guiding force and civilisation follows the direction of culture. This process goes on continuously. It proceeds from lower to higher forms of culture. There is sometimes progression or decline.

Culture is inner cultivation of the mind. It means that real culture reflects innermost self of the person and society. It emphasises a way of life, social structure, civilisation (material and non-material). The epic focuses its prism on it. It is distinct from creating, creativity, and petty human needs. It deals with higher values and beliefs. Civilisation is concerned with external side and culture with inner aspect of human personality, i.e., beliefs, attitude, moral ideals, relationships of man and man, individual and group, group and group. These are subject-matters of ethics.

Then a question arises: What is the Indian culture? Indian culture is spiritual in essence. In the ancient ages, the material or physical culture was relegated to the background by priestly class. The roles of the sages and the saint/gurus were to create harmony between the two. Both spiritual and material cultures go hand in hand, but the former should dominate.

The balanced viewpoint is the essence of India's dynamic life and voluntarism.

Disappearance of culture does not mean annihilation of values, but the disappearance of certain means of expressing values. Norms and their expressions may change, but the values once created become eternal. Once value is created, it becomes public. The hero is a public property. He is no more of his parents. Evil also becomes public (e.g., Ravana and Duryodhan). The created characters become independent of you. They become icons for the suffering human beings.

The values of the Vedic times did not wither away. The earlier culture becomes a heap of rubble and finally a heap of ashes, but its spirit continues hovering over the debris. History of cultures of the world reveals that cultures recycle in the progressive process of history. Spengler has elaborated this point by giving 'family resemblances' from the epochs of the world cultures. Spengler's observation of the world cultures is from the holistic standpoint of development of forms of cultures. The Indian epics may trace development of Indian culture and civilisation from Spengler's viewpoint.

New cultures are rebuilt on the debris of old culture. In the course of history the ethos, traditions, convention add new horizons to the culture. For instance, when the snowball falls from top of the hill, it gathers more snow around it till it reaches the ground. Similarly, culture of the land is enriched through the vicissitudes of history.

In this sense, culture deals with values, which are eternal, and its spirit hovers over heads of the people. For example, for welfare of the people, various means may be used. Non-violence and violence are means for restoring peace and harmony in society. For realising values and ideals, material tools are improved, but the spirit of values is eternal. Earlier we used sword for peace and justice. Now sophisticated weapons are used for the sake of same ideals.

In the existential human conditions, man is thrown in the concrete world of societal situations within the cosmos. The dynamic ontology of the cosmos implies that man can create his own self. Wittgenstein's 'Tractarian' view correctly asserts that man's creative mind is operative in all-comprehensive reflections on all possible perspectives on the problematic issues. This holistic view is reflected in Indian culture that was carried forth by Sikhism.

Valmikah portrays Rama not as a supernatural being or incarnate of Vishnu, but as an embodiment of dharma and virtues. He is hero of this world struggling for restoring peace and justice in society. Some lapses and shortcomings are found in his character when he confronts existential dilemmas. He encounters moral dilemmas and overcomes them by simply adhering to the *dharma*—the righteous way. There are several instances narrated in Valmikah's Ramayana, which cast shadows on the pristine character of the hero and reinforce the theme of Rama struggling with mortal flaws and prejudices whilst striving to follow the path of *dharma*. He never swerves from the path of dharma.

The central theme of the epics is the multifaceted dimensions of dharma. Dharma operates within the gamut of monistic philosophy of the Indian culture. The ideal of human life is moulded according to the principle that determines 'form' within the 'cosmic form'. The process of progressive ascension of the self culminates in the highest form of *moksha* that subsumes other three purposes (*pursharthas; kama, artha* and *dharma*) as derivative integrative goals of monistic view of life. The way to solve the problem you see in life is to live in a way that will make the problematic to disappear. Dharma in the epics of the Mahabharata has been hermeneutically reinterpreted in the contemporary context and has been reformulated in the The Dasam Granth. Guru Gobind Singh in the "Bachitra Nataka" reinterprets it in the medieval context. Defensive violence for eradicating evil from the earth is reinterpretation of *ahimsa* (non-violence) of the epics and the Buddha and Jainism.

Ahimsa is not an absolute term. It is open-ended and relative to the coeval social ethos. It is always in a flux. Means and end are ensconced within the ethico-metaphysical structure.

India's resistance to terrorism mirrors Indian culture of ahimsa. On the contrary, the Western and Islamic coercive ideologies and metaphysics are poles apart from the Indic culture.

Dharma as a moral principle is linked up with metaphysical cosmic principle (*rita*) that is self-sufficient and *sui causa*. It was transformed into moral principle for preparing Arjuna for *dharma-yudha* to discharge moral and social responsibilities as 'duty for the sake of duty'. The process of progressive ascension of the self culminates in the highest form of *moksha* that subsumes other three values of life. Then the religious celebrities within the contours of the Indian culture evolved purpose of human life. In the Indian epics, voluntarist view of life has been derived from the prevalent ethos. Man creates culture, which is the prime phenomenon of all past and future world-history.

It may be pertinent to point out that it is difficult to interpret alien culture from outside because it is *subjective* and *singular*. It can be viewed from inside because it is inner experience of the people of the land. The Westerners have presented a distorted perspective of Indian culture. They have visualised our culture through the glasses of Christianity. We have been aping the Westerners for the last three hundred years. It is unfortunate that we have not come out of their domination though they have trivialised our culture and the sacred classics. The prevailing knowledge of the English knowing Indian elites is the post-colonised impact.

Thus, the false concept of tragedy leads to misconception of destiny and fate. Destiny is the living idea of 'becoming or flux', which unfolds itself immediately to the intuitive vision. The Mahabharata forecasts destiny of the Pandvas and the Kauravas. Destiny transcends causality and reveals trans-empirical realm. The idea of destiny and the principle of causality are different. Causality is limited to the Nature. Destiny goes beyond the Nature and is not controlled by causal necessity. Destiny is to be derived only through religion and art. The idea of destiny demands life-experience, hope, happiness, despair, devotion that is salient element of love.

Inward certainty is the meaning of life, which is found in self-determinism.

Fate is related to our attitude towards future and past. In religious terms, our life is determined by God's will. Then a philosophical question arises: What is the status of man's autonomy of will? Religious faith is commitment to a system of reference (others). At the initial stage, man's actions are determined. Nevertheless, he has the potentiality to come out of the cocoon of determinism. The realised person transcends with grace and spiritual discipline. The *jiva* is transformed into *atman*. It can be compared to climbing a ridge where one faces risk of slipping on his left and right. Once he reaches the apogee of the ridge, he is free to move. It is inner transformation from the first person perspective to the third person singular perspective. There are three stages of self-transcendence. The first stage is of self-surrender that is sacrifice of one's ego, conceit and pride. The second stage is that of identification with humanity and the Numinous. The last is complete surrender to *rita* (divine decree). We constantly struggle against our will to attune to the eternal principle. When one realises truth, one overcomes the fear of death.

Members are to be drilled into society for internalising cultural action. Savage mind is to be refined, tamed and trained to cultivate cultural mind. Synchronic existing interpersonal relationships are to be transformed into *diachronic* harmonious mutual relations. This recycling creative process is to be carried out in history. History is always in chronic tension or conflict between tradition and social change. Philosophers can suggest remedy beyond conflicts and tensions and implement their suggestion in practice. In the post-independence epoch the imperialists left legacy of education that drove a wedge between the middle and the countryside illiterate people. The elite middle classes are exploiting the poor illiterate, ethnic linguistic groups that are ruled by the privileged middle classes.

The creative thinker lives out his life spans and survives for eternity. He is not prisoner of tradition and his culture. Ordinary man is the prisoner of his culture and tradition. The hero or martyr is not the slave. He transcends the hackneyed traditions and creates new ones. While living in his culture, he creates new culture, which will suit new social conditions. Culture is not a matter of choice in which man is thrown by birth. However, he is condemned to be free. He has the freedom to create culture and, then, strive to realise it in praxis.

Indian culture discards compartmentalisation of human life and discrimination in society. It is inner self-cultivation or inward journey from ego to *atman*. Process of self-transformation or self-transcendence ends its inward journey in full actualisation of humanity through spiritual discipline. The small mind inwardly heads towards the cosmic vision. We are to recognise sovereignty of the individual person as a person of self-dignity, which is only within human beings and interpersonal and social relations.

Notes

1. Spengler, O., *The Decline of the West*, Vol. I, p. 100.
2. See, Dharmendra Goel, "Culture and Reality" in Rekha Jhanji (edit.), *Essays in Honour of Dharmndra Goel: Knowledge, Culture, Action.*, pp. xxvi-xxxi.

5

Language Mirror of Culture

(i) Language and Creativity

Time and the world open doors of creativity. It is possible only if the self gets emancipation from the chains of constraints and stresses, and seductions of the world. The inner and subjective sense pulls our thoughts out of the personal and private experience, and brings out a kind of reality of the past and envisions for the future life and the world-view to be yearned for. By coming out of the prison of suffering and dark chamber of emotions, sentiments and other allurements, one can have a flight to the future destiny on the wings of imagination and the ascending ladders of historical time. It may be kept in the mind that human freedom is different from taming the coercive laws of the nature and logic. The laws of nature cannot be violated absolutely. If a man is to survive, he can't remain hungry for a long time. On the other hand, the laws of logic can't be set aside at all. These are absolute laws. Creativity is developed with continuous efforts from within while abiding by logical consistency.

Man projects ideas of his inner self and realizes them through material tools, say, marble, brush, canvas, paints and so on. For an artist or thinker human life is an improvised material out of which he articulates form and expresses it through different genres: poetry, fiction, drama, short story, and so on. Aspirations of man transcend the confined world of traditions, conventions, texts, scriptures, etc.

Art is a stimulus and means to deliverance from the physical world. It sharpens sense of sensitivity. Education of art heightens our sense of the world. Genuine education, through art, philosophy, and literature, widens consciousness beyond the contours of the 'present' context. Artworks or art-forms are concretised ideas. Looking at them (idols) transforms our consciousness. For the artist the idol is a living human figure. He experiences feel of higher sensitivity of life. Inventive churning of mental activity sparks off new ideas. In education, the art of thinking is to be taught. It crystallises ideas and removes logical contradictions.

Liberal education is an education for freedom of thought and action. Aesthetic appreciation is not possible without freedom of thought. Every creative thinker is philosopher and artist in his own way, giving concrete form to his ideas in his own unique way. Man's intrinsic nature manifests in creative activities of philosophy, aesthetics, sculpture, and other creative fields. The artist brings out form from the rough stone by hewing it. Creative thinker visualises the ideal form from individuals and configures network of their interpersonal relations. He formulates new societal relations in accordance with envisaged ideology. Then he creates a syntax out of which he finds new ideas. This should be the goal of liberal education.

Language, besides a vehicle of communication, is an instrument of power. Reins of power are controlled through education. Education is, often, used as a tool for lording over others. Strings of power are pulled through language. It can be said that language and education are not neutral. Both are either for domination or domestication or for free cultural action. The ruling elite class of the Muslim rulers indoctrinated their Islamic ideology through Arabic and Persian languages with a view to casting out Indic thought. Their ideology was not the true Qur'anic one. It was a politicised ideology. For this reason, Guru Nanak castigates Arabic or Persian as *malech bhasha* (dirty language). Their language lacked glow of spirituality. In order to cast off alien ideas, wrapped in Arabic or Persian language, Guru Nanak advises us that we should empty our minds from morbid and alien ideas and replace them with new healthy thoughts of our native culture. This idea can be substantiated from the verse of Guru Nanak. The verse is rendered into English as under:

> After washing the 'churn', sit down in poise, burn incense,
> And thereafter, pour into it milk,
> Our action is the milk, our absorption [in the Numinous] the yeast; Thus, make curd with desires cast out (1).[1]

Guru Nanak in this verse has taken the metaphor of butter-making churn (*bhanda*). The language of the Canon is twilight. Its mystical referent is the Numinous, but it is simultaneously applicable to the phenomenal realm. We can apply it to linguistic and educational perspectives. In this context, "*bhanda*" is posed as human mind, which is to be emptied, and new ideas are to be poured into it.

Instilling of revolutionary ideology is carried out through language and education. From this standpoint, the medieval Bhaktas' revolutionary ideas instilled new ideas, cast off old dead thoughts and forcibly indoctrinated Islamic thought or ideology. Theoretical thoughts or ideals are reconciled with praxis. All these are communicated through language. Education simultaneously de-schools the mind and pours in new ideas (reschooling). In this sense, we can say that 'language is the house' of culture.

Education of man lies in demonstrating his capacity for transcending what is merely given. At the initial stage, his lower self naturally determines him. He has an inherent desire to be autonomous. Language and education play a vital role and man regains pristine freedom. Beginning on the path of freeing the self from *jiva* to *atman* is inner progression from inauthentic action to cultural freedom. It augments revolutionary education. Revolutionary education brings in changes by ushering in new ideology.

Man is superior to other species because of his creative consciousness. He is the only living being who articulates language for communicating his ideas to other human beings. Social life is a necessary condition for living in the dynamic world. He articulates ideology for living peaceful and harmonious life. Man is always caught in the eddy of human sufferings. In order to come out of human suffering, man envisages ideal form of life. In all the religious traditions we come across ideologies which mirror purpose of human life. In this chapter I am dealing with Indian standpoint from the comparative perspective.

Among the *homo sapiens* in the kingdom of lower species man is man because of invention of language. Language is the most significant tool that distinguishes between man and lower species. Apart from vehicle of ideas, it is creator of culture. It also wedges societal relations, which yield social unity. Man is the only species that has the potency to develop language. He develops language that facilitates him to make him autonomous. Language facilitates in developing his autonomous 'cultural action'.

Man transmits knowledge through language to next generations whereas animal instinctively passes to next generation. Man with his creative faculty evolves new material, mental, and intellectual tools to communicate to the coming generations. In this context, language is very necessary for adaptation to new tools and techniques of culture and civilisation. Furthermore, man has the monopoly of symbolic language through which he evolves civilisation and culture.

Language is very important dimension of culture. Revelation, *shruti* and *wahy* in the Vedic and the Semitic (Islamic) traditions played significant role in the development of civilisation and culture. The sacred ideas of the scriptures are treasured in languages of the respective countries and regions. Language is a vehicle of ideas. It is a means of communication of ideas and sharing feelings and thoughts with others. Language is a cementing force of individuals into a unity. Oral language (memory) has been a means of communication from generation to generation till paper was first made in China. Oral language mainly depends on memory. There are dangers of lapses of memory. In order to overcome this difficulty man discovered paper, which replaced inscriptions on the *bhojapatras*, stones, camel's hide, goat leather, trees, etc. It was better way of preserving and recording culture.

Scripts were developed. Characters of scripts have different faces.

In the Indic traditions, revelation is not presented in historical and real time because time in Indian thought is illusory and mythical. It is only in the Indian traditions that the Bhaktas and the Gurus accepted in praxis historical time as dimension of reality. For them language is a social phenomenon. The Gurus reconciled historical sense of time in practice. The historical linear time has been reconciled with the cyclic time of Indian and the Greek traditions. It is interesting to note that revelation in the Guru Granth is not linear self-disclosing progression as we find in the Semitic traditions.

Cultural language is symbolic which man creates and refines. In the primitive culture-form, abstract thinking was not possible. Imagination of the child could not visualise image or form. Unless the form is projected, abstract thinking is not possible. In the primitive stage, man had not developed symbolic language as a tool to communicate subtle ideas. Gradually culture advanced and, correspondingly, language is chiseled from gesture language to symbolic language of higher sciences and logic or philosophy. The language of the mystics is of ciphers. Meanings are hidden in the text. Expert and critical mind is required to interpret them.

The language of poetry is emotive one. The language of the mystic is higher than that of the poetic diction. The mystic evolves twilight or dusk language (*sadhya bhasha*) of ciphers, which at once comprehends eternity and temporality. Thus, the twilight language of the mystic communicates two meanings. The first is concerned with the phenomenal world and the second one refers to the ciphers The ciphers (*para bani*) are beyond natural language. These can be deciphered by symbolic language. Their symbolic import can only be understood by the developed mind. It was refined and advanced from concrete to abstract thinking. It is refined to express subtle ideas. It carries the higher symbolic functions of the ensuing cultural development. Sanskrit and Pali are highly symbolic languages in which Vedic and Buddhist thoughts are expressed respectively.

Devotional literature of the medieval Bhaktas and the Gurus is symbolic and communicates hidden ideas.

The traditional distinction between "being" and "becoming" misses the essential point that shows distinction between the two. Spengler expresses the contrast through "becoming" and "the become". It necessarily follows that "the become" is founded on "becoming".[2] It implies that the phenomenal manifestation is in point-instant (*kashan*) and universal flux. Thus, culture is an ever-flowing stream that is always in constant flux. The culture that is 'becoming' creates higher 'form' that gradually transcends limits of the temporal world. Higher the form corresponds to the higher culture. In this sense, Goethe's "Faust" is the protestant representation of the whole culture. Thus, the Guru Granth is the highest 'form' of Indian culture. Creation of the Khalsa-panth is concretisation of the cultural form envisaged by Guru Nanak.

When the Turks came to India, the Persio-Arabic script and their phonemes were gradually adapted to vernacular languages and dialects. Indian Muslims and non-Muslims neither adopted the Arabic script and sounds for their purposes. They evolved an altogether new script and developed new vernacular phonemes and characters. Ultimately, the Urdu literary tradition, as mirror of the Indo-Islamic culture and civilisation, came into being in both Deccan and North India. Amir Khusrau called it 'Hindvi'. The use of the new Persio-Arabic script greatly facilitated the direct transmission of the Islamic terms and the ideas. It carried into Indian vernacular traditions; the Arabic and Persian culture. Original Arabic culture penetrated into Indian stream of thought. The Turks brought civilisation in tradition, art and architectural culture from Persia. It necessarily involved a good deal of creative engagement with Indic literary genre.

Creative writers of the greater Punjab in the medieval times popularised Punjabi language though they used Persian characters or scripts and embraced local sounds. Punjabi was language of the creative narratives (*kissas*) and poetry. Narratives of Warrish Shah, Pilu and Hashama. Baba Farid used pure Punjabi, but his hymns were recorded in Arabic. His hymns in the Guru Granth are in newly developed Gurmukhi characters.

It will be pertinent to point out that the ruler determines court language. It is interesting to note that Persian continued as court language during Maharaj Ranjit Singh's regime in Punjab. Ranjit Singh had a short span of time to rule over Punjab. He had threats from all sides. The British and other Sikh rulers posed perpetual danger to him. Intrigues in the palace did not allow him to materialise his plans. Thus, during Ranjit Singh's reign from CE 1801 to1839 in the greater Punjab, Persian was the official language. He could not introduce Punjabi in his state. He did not induct Punjabi in Gurmukhi script as the court language. Arabic or Persian was the court language since the Turks settled down on the Indian soil. Persian was used by common people though their pronunciations were changed according to native dialects. Mostly Persian characters were in vogue. On the other hand, common people preferred Persian because it was easier for them as compared to Sanskrit which was language of the elite Pandits and classical Hindu scholars.

Ranjit Singh's practical wisdom did not permit him to replace Persian characters with Gurmukhi script. He, perhaps, realised that script is secondary and the language is primary. It is true that garment of a beautiful girl is important, but what it conceals is more important. Likewise, language is more important than the script. Therefore, the meaning wrapped in the script is of great significance. Hence meanings in Persian language were understandable for the ordinary scholars.

Shivaji, on the other hand, introduced Marathi in Maharashtra as the court language. He was a rebel. He could afford because he was openly confronting Aurangzeb. The Gurus replaced Devanagari script with Gurmukhi script in the Guru Granth. They also replaced Devanagari script of the Bhaktas and the Persio-Arabic script of the Sufi saints into Gurmukhi characters. Indian Constitution has accepted Hindi as the *lingua franca* because it can be the common language for having national integration of the country. The regional languages are not to be overpowered. If both Hindi and regional languages go hand in hand, the ideal of national integration can be realised. The linguistic problem of the minor cultures remains unsolved till date.

The process of creativity of a new culture has three elements: retention (memory), impression, and recall. New configurations suddenly strike new ideas and thoughts. Alertness of mind and deep involvement in the problem is a precondition. The creative mind concentrates on a problem and, then, new ideas suddenly hit upon my mind. These ideas may be recorded on the paper. Such new ideas never occurred earlier. It must come before in time with intensity of feeling. It presupposes deep involvement of consciousness. The Gurus were seized of the existential social problems. They might have often struck upon new ideas in intense states of ecstasy. Guru Nanak was existentially aware of societal problems. In intense states of mind new ideas emerged. He, then, envisaged *sacha-khanda*. When proper or congenial conditions occur, then suddenly new ideas spontaneously come to my imagination. Similarly, new ideas come when one is experiencing suffering and pangs of life. It implies recall and expression (creativity), reconfiguration of elements, enjoyment, self–satisfaction to a person (poetry, music), and communication (sharable with others). That gives expression through revelation or *alham*, *shruti* / *wahy*. New ideas (patterns) come, which are expressed through language. Man, is a peculiar type of animal that has the potentiality to create new ideas. These are expressions of ideas. It is a process of creativity.

The last stage of creativity is seclusion. Indian mystics attained *moksha* in seclusion of mountains. The Buddha got enlightenment under a Bodha tree in Gaya. *Wahy* descended from Allah to Prophet Muhammad in a cave of Hira. Guru Nanak had his first revelation at Sultanpur on the bank of the River Bein in CE 1490. He spontaneously uttered : "There is neither Hindu nor Muslim". His first prophetic revelation means that essence of man is humanity and all racial distinctions are man-made divisions. Temporary retreat is found in other religions as well. The realised person comes back in society for sharing his realisation of truth with others. Sharing with others is most important aspect of communication. It is enjoyment of creativity that is shared with others (say, poetry, music, *ghazals* of Ghalib, and singing of Begham Akhtar). Creativity is not repetitive. It is always a new configuration of words, sentences, and ideas. Creative genius, poet and thinker do not tread the beaten track. It is said that a lion, a poet, and a genius create new paths. Their creativity is responsible for progression of culture and civilisation. The world-history can be seen through continuous advancement and decadence of civilisation and culture from chaos to order. This process continuously cycles and recycles.

It is a creation of new norms and values. It follows that gradual creation/evolution of norms and values follows after its genesis. It is not a mechanical drill. Rotation of buckets of a Persian wheel is a mechanical process. It is not true in the cases of civilisations and cultures. There is always gradual improvement or decadence in both the cases.

In addition, culture is inner transformation of the self that advances towards realisation of possibilities of the potential ideals, which are created from time to time. Culture is creative process of developing new beliefs, moral ideas, and norms of conduct. These are functional ways of life. The institutions are gradual creations and evolutions of norms. It is a creative process of developing new beliefs ideas, and norms of moral conduct. These are ingrained in creative ways of human life. Martial spirit (*vira-rasa*) was ingrained in our tribal culture and ways of life. With the advancement of civilisation needs are multiplied and their degrees are increased. Culture refines and modifies needs and desires, which improves quality of life. Beast in man is refined into a tamed cultural unit of society. It implies man's creativity. He takes help of language and galaxy of values. Creative thinker creates and evolves values and new norms to fit in the changed conditions. Culture also means to harvest so far achieved by man and create new values for the future.

Paulo Freire observes that 'culture of silence' is alienation, oppression, dehumanisation, and deprives of liberation, freedom, autonomy, and self-dignity. Education theory is introduced in the womb of the culture of revolt. In practice, it becomes the voice of the culture. Education instills new revolutionary ideas to plant a seed of revolt only to achieve the right to speak its word fearlessly for assuming direction of its own destiny.

Validity of thought-language is known through praxis by which man transforms reality. Humanisation is transformation of social relations. Animals have no historical sense and value dimension. Since the animals do not have value sense, they are incapable to demythologise the old myths. They are also not capable to transform the myths into historical realities. To put them to use requires creative energy. Consciousness is to be emptied and it must be filled with new ideas. When Guru Gobind Singh created the Khalsa, he first emptied minds of his baptised naiveté. Then he injected martial spirit in their minds. This is process of transforming 'culture of silence' into 'culture of revolt'. Resonance of cultural cycling and recycling continues to echo in society.

In the medieval ages, the shudras were kept illiterate. They were divested of awareness of social phenomena. It manifested by depriving them of education of historical, social, cultural and economic realities. They lacked philosophical perspective of all these cultural phenomena. They were relegated to the periphery of society. The illiterate lives on the fringe of society. He is not treated as free person, but a thing (without freedom). Thus, inauthentic or dehumanised self lacks freedom and the authentic self is autonomous.

Brahmanical indoctrination reinforces the mystification of reality by keeping it opaque and by filling the empty consciousness of the learner with innumerable alienating words and phrases. The literary process through education is a cultural action for freedom, and an act of knowing in which the learner assumes the role of knowing the subject through dialogue (*samvada / goshti*) with the educator. For this reason, "it is a courageous endeavour to demythologise reality" held by the tradition for centuries together.[3] The Bhakti insurgence is a clarion call of revolt against the prevalent conventions and traditions. Age-old oppressive knowledge was object of critical awareness. Illumination sheds light on the path to free action.

Apathy of 'culture of silence' is eroded with critical self-assertion of consciousness. Theoretical contextual analysis and concretisation in praxis sets the ball rolling for autonomous action. In the 'culture of silence', to exist is only to subsist or live. The peasant carries out orders from above. Free thinking is difficult and speaking the word is prohibited. The under privileged shudras and women folk lack language of the texts of the sacred and revealed scriptures. They are deprived of sharing power and social equality.

Abstract theoretical context of dialogue determines meaning. Dialogue is concrete and real if it is tested and referred to social realities. Analysis is abstraction of concrete reality (society) and construction of abstract picture (configuration) that creates new syntax that is to be tested on social phenomena. This existential experience is holistic. In illuminative vision, the pragmatic view transforms abstract reality into concrete reality. Synthesis of both is the ideal of the present work.

Learning is creative process of acquiring knowledge. Reflecting critically is not stuffing mind with rotten and outmoded ideas. Creative thinking is churning of ideas and creating new configurations and syntaxes. This is one of the most profound significance of language. This is the central function of doing philosophy with critical analysis of the current philosophical problems of language.

Language, thought, and world are closely interlaced with one another. Mythical, logical, historical (temporal), and real worlds are creations of language. Man creates historical and mythical cultures for the free action in society. Language is related to thought. Paulo Freire asserts that language is impossible without thought and language and thought are impossible without world to which they refer.[4] Without language, ideas/thought cannot come into existence. Wittgenstein presents this problem differently. He holds that 'Language did not emerge from reason" (*On Certainty,* 475). This remark from *On Certainty* differs with Paulo Freire. If, for example, a dog rushes at the child, it recoils and cries and the dog runs away. This reaction is not outcome of thought or reasoning, but an instinctive behaviour. This is an immediate expression of pain, fear, surprise and so on. Wittgenstein's examples cannot be true in creative thinking. In creative thinking, first idea (thought) strikes and, thereafter, words are chosen to express it. Hence, thought precedes language. Mythical world and otherworld are created by language with the help of creative faculty of man. Word as an utterance implies reflection and action. It is word-and-action. Human act is not act if it is not at the same time associated with self-expression and word expression of creating and recreating in deciding and choosing and ultimately participating in society's historical process.

Consciousness without world is impossible. A phenomenologist and existential philosopher Husserl asserts that consciousness presupposes external world for bracketing subject and object schism. If the world is not an object of critical reflection, then that object does not exist. It will be solipsism and subjective idealism that negates the objective world.

Level of consciousness is known in cultural historical reality. The culture of silence was created by the alien culture of the Islamic world from seventh to eighteenth centuries and later by the British rulers who created clime of cultural dependency. The dependent people by definition mirror silent culture. Their voice is not of the authentic voice, but an echo of the dominant culture.

Cultural action and concretisation refer to the process in which men are mere recipients, but as knowing subjects; achieve deepening awareness both of socio-cultural reality, which shapes their lives, and of their capacity to transform that reality.[5]

He at once transforms the world by his action and grasps and expresses the world existing reality in his creative language—hymns and oral messages. On the contrary, lower species (animals, birds, and others) are incapable of abstraction and objectification because they do not have symbolic language. Animals cannot reflect and analyse the abstract issues. For them consciousness *of* and action *upon* reality are incapable for them. Reconciliation of theory and praxis is impossible for them. Animals cannot reflect and analyse. Man has the capacity to transcend his present existence in the world through symbolic language and potential creativity.

(ii) Language 'House of Culture'

Language as the "house of culture" means that ideals and values are found in the language through which the ideas are expressed. We are primarily concerned with Indian and the Islamic cultures, which were prevalent in the medieval Muslim rule. One most serious flaw in the writings of Indian scholars is that they gloss over the Islamic impact on Indian culture during the medieval ages. In the medieval times, religion and language were the most significant elements, which influenced Indian culture. Persian was the state language till the fall of Mughal dynasty. Arabic as the original language of the Qur'an and the Islamic sciences continued fascinating attention of the Indian Muslims and the non-Muslims. It was imposed on the Indians. The Muslim travelers who came to India carried with them their culture through Arabic and Persian cultures.

Language carries forth heritage of repertoire of culture, civilisation, and religion and other treasures of knowledge. It is the most important artifact of culture as it preserves philosophy and culture of the land. It is reflected in a particular language or dialect. India's ancient languages were Sanskrit, Pali, Prakrita and Apabhransha. These were the languages of the elite learned scholars. The Vedic and the Buddhist, and the Jaina sacred scriptures are recorded in Sanskrit, Pali, and Prakrita respectively. Regional tribal dialects were relegated to the periphery of the illiterate tribal people. Their tribal culture survived in oral tradition and folklore.

Arabic and Persian languages came from Arabia and West-Asian countries. Christian missionaries inducted English, but preferred Indian language and dialects for preaching their Christian ideology. De Noble came to Madurai, which is in Tamil Nadu in the South of India. He first learnt Sanskrit and the Hindu customs, religious rituals, dresses of Hindu priests and so forth. He communicated the message of Christianity wrapped up in Sanskrit. Thus, language is a powerful weapon to fire at other culture and convert into their fold followers of other faiths and cultures. Nevertheless, objectivity in meaning can be possible only if we strictly follow linguistic and logical rules and put them into use.

Language requires value system that is found in the scriptures, edicts and in traditions. Value system implies internationality for the future without making the future a prisoner of the present. Present is subordinated to tomorrow. Hence, progress is a continuous transformation of servility into freedom of conscience. Thus, authenticity of identity anchors on freedom and sense of belongingness with 'others'.

The common points between antiquity and medievalism were the *varnas, jatis*, and the patriarchal family of male dominance. There were some differences as well. The beginning of Turkish rule is considered the end of the ancient period. In the process of transition of culture languages play a significant role because all traditions, conventions, customs, and other social institutions are treasured in oral traditions and written literature. When the Turks came to India, they carried with them their culture through their language of Arabic. The Persian culture infiltrated through Persian.

Migration of primitive cultures through incursions of alien hordes ushered in decline of Sanskrit and emergence of Arabic and Persian as well as vernacular dialects of different regions. It initiated a process of mutual adjustment and acculturation. Indian culture being of the vanquished was overshadowed by the Islamic ideology. This process continued till collapse of the Mughal Empire. Then reverse process of revival of Indic culture stepped in.

It is wrong to assert that any language is divine. It was claimed by Indian Brahmin scholars that Sanskrit is gods' language (*deva bhasha*). Once we accept it as gods' language, we treat it eternal, which is not subject to change. Language being a social phenomenon, it changes with time, space, and region. After change of time and region, it changes. With the passage of time, old or classical and canonical languages become archaic and out of date. Sanskrit, which was a spoken and scriptural language in the Vedic times, became archaic with the passage of time. The Buddha was the Indian thinker who recognised that language is a social phenomenon. He preached his message in spoken dialect, Pali.

Our ancient Indian culture is treasured in Sanskrit, Pali, Prakrita, and Apabhransha. All these languages became archaic and stagnant during medieval periods. In this period, Arabic and Indo-Aryan Persian languages came to India when the Mongols, the Turks, the Afghans, and other invaders came to India. These languages carried along with them their cultures. India became an arena of multi-cultures, multi-religions, multi-dialects and so on. These languages immensely influenced the indigenous and regional dialects. These alien languages impacted the language of the mendicants and their pronunciations adjusted to the folk sounds. During this period *sadha-bhasha* was developed as a common regional language, excepting south Indian languages of India. Language of the *Sarvangi* and the Guru Granth is *sadha bhasha*.

The regional dialects were developed in the Middle Ages: Tamil, Oriya, Malyalam, Kannad, Marathi, Rajasthani, Awadhi, Braj, etc. These dialects revived Indian culture. The ancient scriptures (e.g., the Gita, the Mahabharata, the Ramayana, the Puranas, *et al.*) were translated into regional languages. Among Rajab's *Sarvangi* a disciple of Dadudyala in CE 1597, compiled. It contains sacred hymns of different Bhaktas in Devanâgri script. Earlier the hymns of the contributors (say, Dadudyala, Kabir, Ravidasa, Gorakh, Sein Surdasa and many others) were recorded in regional dialects which were current in the oral traditions. These were transcribed in Devanagri.

Similarly, Guru Nanak, the pioneer of the Sikh Faith started the process of collecting the sacred sayings of the medieval saints of India and the West-Asian countries. The third Guru Amardasa and the fifth Guru Arjunadeva also got collected hymns of the Gurus, the Bhaktas, the Sufi saints and others from Devanagari and Arabic scripts. Both edited and compiled them under their personal supervisions. The main scribers of the breviaries (*Goindwal Walian Pothian* or *Mohanji*

Dian Pothian)[6] were Sahnsar Rama and Bhai Gurdasa. The former was grandson of Guru Amardasa and the latter was maternal uncle of Guru Arjunadeva. The Guru Granth was prepared in old Gurmukhi script. The language of the script is *sadha-bhasha.* It is also called *sadukhadi-bhasa* because it symbolises a box, which contains valuable hymns of the contributors. The hymns are likened to precious gems, jewels and other costly stones. The Guru Granth has hymns of the Sikh Gurus, the sufi saints, the Hindu Bhaktas, the bards of the Gurus, and so on. The Sikh Gurus evolved the Gurmukhi script. The language of the Guru Granth was the spoken language of India except the South Indian languages of Tamil Nadu, Orissa, Kerala, Karnatik, and Andhra Pradesh. It shows Catholic attitude of the Sikh Scripture.

It will be pertinent to point out that cultural attack on India was made through language. Language preserves culture of the people. When the Turks, Afghans and Mughals came to India, they came with their languages of Arabic, Persian, and other West-Asian dialects. The Arabian and Persian 'outsiders' imposed their Islamic culture by imposing Arabic and Persian languages. They channeled religious communications from their perspectives. This tidal shift of culture generated eddies and undercurrents in India. This was not a linear advancement. As the tide rises, the ocean bares its bosom to the moon (ideology/ religious celebrity). This example illustrates India's medieval scenario when clouds of Arabian invader's fleets started hovering over coasts of Indian Ocean near the southern coasts near Gujrat and Maharashtra. The alien invasions in the North created ripples in the Indian culture, which spread like wild fire in India. The Islamic culture was a ground swell. The common masses embraced it under duress.

Sanskrit language of the elite upper class was in dismal condition. There was a rapid rise of vernacular dialects. The drastic changes in social life ushered in new epoch. Islamic influence started in the seventh century onwards when the Persian and the Arab traders were allowed to settle in large numbers at different ports on the western coast (Malabar) of India and married Indian Hindu girls. King of Malabar in

Gujarat embraced Islam and mosques were built on the Malabar coast. These traders openly observed their religious practices and rituals. Before the ninth century, they spread over the whole of the western coast of India and created a stir among the Hindu populace. They were encouraged to settle down in India.

Arabic and Persian languages carried along with them Islamic culture. Indians adopted the languages of the aliens. The priestly Brahmin class was dancing to the tunes of the ruling class. The priestly class considered the *shudras* filthy and the women defile and incompetent to read Sanskrit language. It was the view of the Brahmins that they could not correctly pronounce Sanskrit words. They ignored real grain and thrashed chaff. They committed a grave fallacy. The mystic ciphers are winnowed from the sacred scriptures with critical analysis and 'intuitive insight' (*diva dhrishti*). It removes the husk of language that conceals the meanings, the core of language.

For the Bhaktas and the Gurus the dry husk of Sanskrit was no more relevant because it was an archaic language. It has lost its contact with common folk. Without communication of ideas, language is sterile. On the other hand, the regional dialects continuously rejuvenated with fresh husk. They were blindly following the Pannian criterion of correct pronunciation of the Vedic hymns. They ignored hidden meanings in the Vedic hymns.

Unnecessary emphasis on grammar and rhetoric does not help reaching out the hidden meanings of the sacred scriptures, literature, and poetry. Its precondition requires developing insight of aesthetic sensibility. The Indian scholars developed literary aptitude for Arabic literature to be capable of writing any original work of outstanding merit. Persian language immensely influenced Indian psyche of the littérateurs through official language. The attention, therefore, of the scholars was focused on the Qur'an and its exegesis (*tafsir*) and commentaries, the tradition (Hadith)/ *Sunnah* and so on and so forth.

Persian lost its impact at the fag end of the Mughal period. It was due to transfer of the border area of Kabul and Kandhar from the Mughal Empire. Fresh waves of speaking Persian immigrants had ceased to flow into the country; partly due to development of Urdu as a common language, *lingua franca,* for social intercourse and literary compositions. Persian had been the official language till CE 1634. It aroused interest mainly in literary and cultural activities—Dara Shikho's *Majma-ul-Brahrain (The Mingling of the Two Oceans)*, Mosan Fani's *The Dabistân (School of Manners)*, reflect mastery over language, and deep interest in classical literature of 'Attar, Sinai, Rumi, *et al.,* gradually faded away. Urdu over shadowed the oriental learning centres Dar-ul-Islam of Deoband and the Nadwat-ul-'ulama of Lucknow. Amir Khusrau, Syed Husan, Faiz (poets), Barani, Farishta, Badauni and Abu-'ul Fazl and many other prose writers were well-known Lucknow and Rampur became centres of Urdu.

In the medieval ages, no single language was either spoken or written. In the fluid situation, new language was the need. The people, therefore, developed Urdu as a market parlance medium for communicating ideas among themselves. It derives its roots from Arabic and Persian. It flourished during the Muslim rule in India. Delhi was the centre of it. It was also called the *khadi boli,* the market dialect, used for the convenience of the Indians, the Arabian and the Persian masses. The, Turks, Afghans and the Arabs were good at Persian and Arabic and the Indians were well versed in Sanskrit, Prakrita, and other regional dialects.

Culture needs sufficient leisure time. Creativity comes in peaceful time. Best creative work is done in peaceful times. Its opposite thesis is also true. When man is in crisis or critical predicament, he tries to come out of it. Intensity of feeling and concentration of mind dissolves the problem and hits upon the solution. Creativity is carried through language. Thus, culture can advance only with language. All literature is miracle of language. Above all these, it is the attitude and development of mind of the person that plays significant role.

The role of the Bhakti literature was twofold. It is refinement of intellectual understanding by education, development of manners, tastes, artistic and intellectual development. The culture of a social group is characterised by its distinct customs, outlook towards life and the world. It is inner development of mind and intellect. Its manifest side is civilisation, which is visible in society. In the medieval times, Islamic and Indic cultures came into conflict. The medieval Bhaktas tried to revive Indian culture in their contemporaneous cultural conditions.

An Indian thinker considers culture as inner consciousness and cultivation is an expression of the mind. Civilisation is concerned with external side and culture with inner aspect of human personality, i.e., beliefs, attitude, moral ideals, relationships of man and man, man and group, group and group. These are subject matters of ethics. It means that real culture reflects innermost self of the person and the society. It emphasises a way of life, social structure, and civilisation. It is distinct from creating, creativity, and petty human needs. It deals with higher values and beliefs.

It is evident from the above statement that every culture passes through chequered phases of history. Indian culture in the medieval times was degenerated and defeated at the hands of the Muslims. It was overshadowed by the Islamic culture. The Bhakti cult rejuvenated it and developed it to new heights of actualisation of possibilities in history. It carried forth the rich heritage of the past Indian culture and subsumed the alien elements of other cultures. Its consummation was realised in the creation of the Khalsa-panth on the earth. It decayed in the confederation period. Culture recycles like wheel but every point-instant it traverses new track. It may go in any direction: up or down, left or right. It is continuing process of ballooning higher and higher stages of cultural progression.

Spengler gives importance to language for articulating abstract ordered thought. Language is a powerful tool for refinement of culture. Higher forms of history or progression of world-view is realised through language. New ideas are carried forth through language. It is container and preserver of culture. It also generates language to communicate new ideas and thoughts, which are the outcome of creativity. Nevertheless, at the beginning of every culture, an inner change takes place in the language that makes it adequate for carrying the highest symbolic tasks of the ensuing cultural development. It may be pointed out that language is not mere human utterance, but a culture-language as such is non-existent among primitive men and inaccessible to children. Language is a powerful tool to create culture and preserve it. Heidegger rightly says that 'language is the house of culture'. All ideas, values, ideals and other constituents of culture are contained in language.

Higher history is related to life of freedom that is closer to actualising the possibilities of freedom. Culture and civilisation progress from chaos to order. The higher forms of life are first actualised within body (*deha*) and, then, these are put to use in society. Here I want to point out that the medieval Indian culture was chaotic and disordered. It was given new higher forms by the Bhaktas and the Gurus. They collected improvised material from the society and provided new egalitarian ideology. During medieval ages, stagnation of Indian culture was natural. When Indian religious celebrities made efforts, our culture developed by leaps and bounds.

What is our place in the universe? Lion, dog, cat, and hen and so on have territorial sense. Even birds have similar sense (nest). Oral tradition, collective beliefs, ethos have territorial sense. Ethnic gods have mutual habitats. The gods live on common mountains *Kailash Parvat*. Beliefs, systems and ideals have common aspirations. Greek gods live on Olympic Mountains. Culture is a process of constantly refining or reformulating collective memory and past heritage. It needs sufficient leisure time. Creativity comes in peaceful time. Best creative work is done in peaceful times. Culture is refinement and outcome of history. Uncivilised stage to civilised one is normative adaptation. Culture is a continuous process of reinterpretation and creation. It is manifestation of recycling of dynamic view of life and the supreme reality.

What is the place of man in the universe? The lower species do not have the potency of creating values. They do not have language for articulating values. Lower species do not have language of signs and symbols. It is through language that man creates cosmos, world, values, customs, and culture. No civilisation/culture is possible without language. Man becomes civilised and cultural through language. Language is the most powerful means for making man civilised and cultural. Thus, culture is an outcome of refinement of human behaviour and interpersonal relations. It manifests in history from uncivilised to civilised stages. Development in civilisation is a normative adaptation to the Nature and development of material and linguistic tools. Culture is a continuous inner developmental process of reinterpretation and creation, recycling dynamic view of life.

Existential human situation of the medieval society was inter-faith and multi-cultures. Brief synopsis of the salient features of medieval India is multi-religious and cultural milieu. Indic culture is acculturation of Semitic and other religious traditions, and Sikhism is further synthesis of Semitic and Indian traditions. It's religion, *sangat, pangat, langar, golak,* etc., are its ingredients in social context. Spirit behind all these is to keep religion immune from commercialisation and politicisation. In the present scenario, politics has muzzled spirituality.

(iii) Culture and Reality

Doing philosophy is rigorous analysis of the current philosophical issues while keeping in mind the past treasure-trove of knowledge. New world-view is built on the foundation of old traditions with new articulations. New ideologies are formulated that are put to use for their viability. This creative process continues incessantly.

Is Indian culture or thought archaeology of knowledge? It is not all archaeology of knowledge. The very ontic matrix on which Indian culture anchors is dynamic onto-theology. Knowledge is an ever-flowing stream of consciousness. It changes continuously. It requires continuous reconstruction. Therefore, reinterpretation is a hermeneutical epistemic necessity. If it is not accepted, it will lead to deviation from the truth. Interpretation should be coeval and contextual. To understand culture requires historical and social contextual sense in the situation.

As compared to philosophy, culture is a wider concept. It covers whole gamut of human life and society. In the present interknitted global scenario, no culture of the world can remain isolated from others. Thus, man is always engaged in internal conflicts and external tyranny. He is to confront at once two fronts from within and without. He is to transcend his ego-self and identify himself with the cosmic Self. This is the spirit of Indian concept of renunciation, which is to live with others with disinterested involvement.

The benefit of philosophical perspective on culture is that it deepens the level of cultural discourse, crystallises issues objectively. Dispassionate conceptual logical dialogue deepens philosophical issues. In Indian tradition, religious discourses were common feature of Indian culture. These were used as tools of communication for persuading others. In India it has become disadvantageous to declare one's background with philosophically surcharged environment. People despise over intellectualising or philosophising. By and large, they are not trained in abstract thinking.

Philosopher's practical wisdom is the recapitulation of the dispassionate experiences of talented persons. They have their own innovative ideas for having an ideal social order. They want to foster norms of society for sharing in the civilised society. Without norms the social order is fragile. Some geniuses do not have formal education. The Buddha, Kabir, Guru Nanak, *et al.*, did not have advantage of formal education in higher centres of learning. However, with their personal efforts they realised truth.

What do external realities denote in cultural context? They denote existential constitution of descriptive, prescriptive statements, events, attitude, etc. Domain of culture consists of several dissimilar elements in certain properties of individuals' society. It initiates the process of creating values, ideals, etc. Refusion of one or more dissimilar elements of a culture among themselves may result in emergence of more compound elements of culture. It can be exemplified with the instance of language. Language itself is a complex configuration of objects, concepts and rules. It gives birth to literature through fusion with like ideas and values. It preserves them in the depositories, which is called tradition. Literature shapes the subsequent culture-behaviour of the individual and society if it is translated into praxis, modified or reconstructed.

Culture is related to systems of norms. Norms are created or formulated to improve upon the existing conditions. These cannot be absolute for being a social phenomenon. Time and space determine their relative validity. The word as reality we accept in connection with culture. It takes different modes of elements of culture that are equally valid for self-disclosing criteria of truth. The criteria are not imposed from without. These are imposed by man. These are man's created constructs.

Rules, laws, and norms play a vital role in forming culture. They determine hierarchy of values According to the context, they offer a workable criterion for preferences for our social 'perceptions'. Values and laws provide preference in new social conditions. Values and laws act only as dispositional norms. These have no Platonic ontic Being either. A dispositional norm is understood only through its applicability to the relevant scenario.

The term culture is not used in the metaphysical sense of having its ontic status. It refers to a space of values, believes, ideals that are between the 'Beyond' and the concrete empirical world of objects. These are guiding principles preserved in oral tradition or in the written documents. These are in the collective consciousness (tradition) of the masses. Fossilised or outdated ideas are changed or discarded. Therefore, culture and reality should continue as living ideational realities for guiding the detracted souls.

Classification of cultural hierarchy enables to make judgement about what is good or poor. The criterion of hierarchy is norm or value, which determine cultural actions. Since the lower or subcultures live at lower values, they are lower cultures. This may give sense of superiority to the members of the higher cultures. It is the cause of ethnocentricity, which means that while evaluating others' culture, our culture should be the criterion for determining their validity. This we found in Christianity and Islam. On the contrary, the male supremacy focuses on men. The latter is closer to truth. Indian culture based on relativity of truth and dialogue is male dominated.

Cultural form of activity is a sign using activity (language). Animals do not have articulated language and creative faculty of resuscitation, interpersonal communication, refinement of emotions and taming of beast in them. Culture is applicable to human level. It is reinventing creative process of new ideology. Traditional model and modern models are the outcome of geniuses' creative feats.

Thus, I have pointed out earlier that meaning given to the value or norm is not in the text, but in the mind of the creative genius's eye (vision). My aim is to draw focus on the spiritual voluntarist culture that steels human will for confronting alien incursions on our culture. The historical heroic facts need to be infused with spiraled development of consciousness. The teachings of the spiritual celebrities are to be interpreted at oneness of temporality and eternity. For articulating new world-view (ideology), the creative social thinker or the mystic (guru) at nodal point stretches historical time to eternity with his cosmic vision. His vision at once encompasses temporality and eternity. From this perspective, the concept of culture is resuscitated in the present work.

It may be kept in mind that difference between facts and values always remains. Culture is an ideational category. If studying or thinking is inspired to think originally, it is doing philosophy. New culture, thus, is created with new values. Ought is inbuilt in the facts. For example, if I warn a person that he should not cut his hair and beard, then ought is implied in it. The Akal Takht at Amritsar (Punjab) is a monumental architectural fact. It inherits norms of moral conduct for every member of the Sikh community. The argument can be extended to philosophy of culture. Every philosophy is a critique of various types of cultural identities, religious traditions, disintegration and reintegration. For this purpose philosopher creates values, judgment, culture and moral philosophy.

Culture is not a sheer concept or postulate, but a lived experience of innermost forms that are potential and actualised.

The former are hidden forms, which come to the surface. The world history oscillates between the two. Progress of human history is from potential to actualisation of culture-forms through world-history. In the words of Spengler, "...the *idea* of a culture, which is the sum total of its inner possibilities, from its sensible phenomenon or appearance upon the canvas of history as a fulfilled actuality."[7] The primitive culture-form underlies all the individual cultures of the human history. Culture is, thus, the *prime phenomenon* of all past and future world-history.

Optimism of man proclaims that one day we shall be successful in knowing it. It is continuous progression from chaos to unity, and ignorance to knowledge. We are trying to transcend our finitude for becoming one with the Truth/ Numinous. Our quest for truth is to cut across limitations of our finitude. From this standpoint, the present study is rejection of essentialist conception of abstract culture. The temporal and the eternal are being clubbed together. It is exposition of the medieval world-view from the existential standpoint.

Culture is a system of the pattern and modes of aspirations and expressions of values, institutionalisation of life in society. It is an attitude and mode of dealing with objective reality and subjective personality. Three points are noteworthy in understanding perspectives on culture. First, culture is human creation. Second, it provides 'objective reality' and 'subjective interpretation' churning of ideals, values, ideology, and so forth. Third, it represents interpersonal relationships for harmony and justice. It endeavours for adjustment that emanates from spontaneity and freedom of action. One can formulate ideology for bettering the existent social order. Here revival of Indian culture means restoration of freedom and self-dignity of man. This determines cultural identity of India.

Then a question arises: What is spirit of the culture? The present study revolves round these vital issues. If we go deep into the meaning of the term 'culture,' we will find that it is concerned with mind or consciousness. Culture is a principle of interlacing society into a coherent unity. It brings connectivity between hearts and minds of the people in multi-cultured society. It is not concerned with the progression of civilisation. It is concerned with progression of the inner self (*atman*).

Now the philosophical questions arise: What is the concept of spirituality? Is Indian culture spiritual or non-spiritual? What is uniqueness of spiritual Indian culture? Can it be motivated and learned? It means that *atma*' (consciousness) is representative of 'culture'. If we go into etymologies of the term 'culture' in Latin ('*cultura*') and German ('*kultûr*'), (Arabic—*tahjib*), we find that both emphasise on cultivation of mind. Culture in Sanskrit language is '*sanskriti*', which means cultivation of mind. It is said that "*atma che sanskrite*". The term '*atma* stands for consciousness. Consciousness guides all human activities. At the initial stage, it is dominated by the sensuous and beastly desires. These are refined by *shabda* and spiritual discipline. It lacks deep 'insight', which mirrors truth. When it is cultivated, the truth is realised.

Culture (*sanskriti*) is cultivation of mind for fashioning its beastly, barbarian, and uncivilised nature. It can be extended to society. Therefore, culture is a way of refined life of the people including their attitude towards others and the world. Attitude implies values, beliefs, arts, aesthetic sense of sensibility, vision of social ideals, or values, habits and various customs, ethos, conventions and other societal activities. Cultural patterns of life are acquired in the society. These are revealed from values, beliefs, and religious ways of living. In lower and higher culture-forms, religion plays a very significant role.

Culture is a lived experience. Mere looking at a Buddhist monk meditating or a yogi in *Samadhi* does not leave deep impact on the onlooker. We need an integration of others' minds and their world-views (weltanschauung) into one unity. Sheer mental colonisation of other world-views will not be sufficient. We need to develop an integrative lived experience of culture that is to be put to use. This experiment can be done on the soil of India because Indian culture, being a world culture within a culture is a composite culture that is a world within the world. India is a miniature global culture. India is a world within the global world. It consists of world within the world. It has developed composite culture, which encompasses elements of the Semitic, Greek and the Indian philosophical traditions. Therefore, it is easy for the Indian philosophers to develop an integrative Indian culture that can be a guideline for both India and the other global world. It enjoins upon the philosophers to formulate the integrative world-view that subsumes the past and the contemporary issues. Hence, the problem of rethinking cultural identity crops up. Such philosophical explanation analyses current issues, carries forth the past traditions, and blends them into one coherent world-view. Both horizons are blended into one unity. It is to be translated into praxis. Indian culture is a micro-culture that mirrors the global cultures.

Then what is culture (*sanskriti*)? Culture spirals round human life. It is self-cultivation of the inner self and undercurrent of inner life of collective psyche of the people. Its nature and purpose mirror inner life. It is a living and dynamic phenomenon that accompanies man from womb to tomb. It is a principle of interlacing society into a unity. It brings connectivity between hearts and minds of the people in multi-cultured society of India. It is concerned with progression of the inner self (*âtman*) and live active life.

Hence, inner self is culture. Visual sources are outwardly superficial. They do not take us to the core of others' minds and cultures of the insiders and the outsiders. It has been pointed out above that mere looking at a meditating Buddhist monk does not leave deep impact on the onlooker. We need to dive deep and develop an integrative world-view that is to be put to use. This experiment can be done on the Indian soil because Indian culture, which is a world within the world.

Man creates culture, which is always in a flux. It, thus, is self-cultivation of mind and society for taming its beastly, barbarian, and uncivilised nature. Therefore, culture is a way of life of the people including their attitude towards other people and the world. Attitude implies values, beliefs, arts, aesthetic sense of sensibility, vision of social ideals, values, etc. Cultural patterns of life acquired in the society mirror through values, beliefs, and religious ways of living.

Cultivation of mind is inward ascension of consciousness, which is incessantly engaged in ever narrowing down circle within a circle of rarefied consciousness culminating in transcending forms and merging in the formless Being (*nirankara*). Then, the external world is not an object for the inward pilgrimation. The self realises its autonomy (*moksha*) and identity. The mystic brackets the subject (self) and the object into the transcended state of ecstasy where identity of the self is realised as an epiphany of the Being. At the nodal point, duration of time is stilled and it is stretched into eternity. It portrays all-inclusive concrete self-luminous identity. It is also all-inclusive because past, present and future are encompassed in it. It transforms them into 'eternal present'.

Consciousness (*chit*) is an anchor on which metaphysical structure is raised. Transcendence of consciousness from gross to subtle state of ecstasy is called spiritual ascension. The external world is no longer an object apart from the subject. The self regains its autonomous status (*moksha*). Buddhism does not favour personal identity of the self, but advocates for fluxional transcendental state of rarified consciousness (*nirvâna*). The mystic brackets object and self into higher state of ecstasy where identity of the self is realised as an epiphany of the Being. This is the quintessence of identity of the Indian philosophy that has been overshadowed by the Western materialistic and the Semitic ideologies.

Indian identity of the self (I) is a miniature cosmos. It is culled out of the micro-*jîva* (me) with meditative spiritual discipline, which stills mind and quiets thoughts. Identity of my 'I' (*âtman*), the continuer of my transformed and rarefied 'me' (*jîva*) attuned to the cosmic law, realises 'personal identity' and autonomy of the self. Thus, the authentic self is an embodiment of freedom that is the essence of man. The personal identity is not a given fact. It is cultivated at once with meditative continuous striving both from within and without. From within he advances towards autonomy of the self and from without he identifies himself with others and socialises in society. The inward journey of the self culminates when the

'I' merges in the cosmic consciousness A person who attains cosmic vision (*vishavrupa*), he acclaims that the external world is the epiphany of the Numinous. He is no more in the world of *maya*. He is spring fount of *nishkama karma*.

The Divine executes the cosmic law through the realised self *(sthitaprajña /sant-spahi)*. He is representative of the eternal Being for restoring justice in society. The medieval Bhaktas and the Gurus abolished charismatic personality of the incarnate (*avatâra*). Consequently, all responsibilities of restoring justice and rule of the divine law in society fall on man's shoulders.

Suppression of culture does not mean annihilation of values, but the disappearance of certain means of expressing values. Expressions may change, but the values once created become eternal. Values have origination in time and space, but they transcend both once they are created. In this sense, culture, which deals with values, is eternal and its spirit in the form of ideas and ideals hovers over heads of the people. For example, for the welfare of the people, various means may be used. Non-violence and defensive violence are means for restoring peace and harmony in society. For realising values and ideals, material tools are improved, but the spirit of values is eternal. Earlier we used sword for peace and justice. Now sophisticated weapons are used for the sake of same ideals. Here civilisation and culture supplement each other.

The above discussion leads us to a vital point that culture is concerned with ideals, values, religious beliefs, customs and conventions, ceremonies and rituals. The mystics and religious celebrities or the visionary ideologues for the sake of restoring peace and justice in society relate these purposes to human life, which are created by man.

We can say that culture is a big configuration of divergent elements, which are coherently interlaced and are contributing to progression from the standpoint of the whole. In this sense, emphasis is on the interlocked relationships in a whole in which individuals are assigned their duties. In the light of this definition, Sikhism does not make any discrimination among the members. All are treated equal persons and founts of autonomous deeds. We may, further, assert that no culture dies. It is like the sun that sinks at night and rises again in the morning. It goes on rotating ceaselessly. Likewise, the values are eternal and continue for the ages to come.

No one will be there to observe the progress of a "culture as an epic". Epic is a written prophecy. One can foresee one's death in the future as an inevitable phenomenon, but no one is definite about its exact form and moment. The essence of life is activity and death is cessation of activity. Eternity is infinite temporal duration that encapsulates past, present, and future. Mystics and religious celebrities assert that at death a timeless state begins. The philosopher will argue that they are not aware that the words "after it and begins" are built in temporality in the grammar/language. In fact, the mystic stretches temporality to eternity. Our thoughts about the world are locked up in the natural language. Truth lies at the bottom where all forms disappear. Guru Nanak's verse can be cited to substantiate this point as under:

> He who absorbs all the visible forms into the 'Formless Form', With 'artless art', he stills truth in the Truth.[8]

Eternal life is to live in the present without the burden of the past and anxiety for the future. Likewise, epic is an eternal lesson for the present generations and no one can predict the exact happenings in the future. Epic is a cosmic mirror of human life. Culture is to be lived in the 'eternal present'. The very fact that we become aware of it makes us existentially responsible to the worldly responsibilities.

The epics of India have created and preserved culture of the land. They represent cosmic vision of life. Both are long poems narrating the deeds of the heroes or legendary figures that are chosen from the history of the nation. Their leitmotiv is integrative life as a whole. They mirror ethos or culture of India. They are a treasure-trove of the past culture of the nation; characteristic spirit of a community and people. The idea of the whole life is prophesised along with clarity of means and end. Their authors of the epics envisaged that ultimate victory would be of good. They had perfect vision of the epics.

Thus, man creates culture, which is the prime phenomenon of all past and future world-history. Goethe's morphological perspective, explained from the seed to the plant and the sapling, is the idea of 'becoming'. Every culture passes through the ages; phases of the individual man. Each culture has its childhood, youth, manhood, and old age. The Bhakti period is the blossoming period of the Indian culture. It came into being in the 6th century on the Tamil Nadu soil and consummated in the end of the seventeenth century. We find the ripened creative power that actualised all the possibilities accomplished prior to fall of the Mughal Empire. It was a collective endeavour of the saints who left no stone unturned for revivifying the Indian culture, which was nearly crushed by evil eyes of alien invaders. Wittgenstein rightly observed that, "The earlier culture will become a heap of rubble and finally a heap of ashes, but spirits will hover over the ashes".[9]

History of cultures of the world reveals that cultures recycle in the progressive process of history. New cultures are rebuilt on the debris of old culture. Sir Mohammad Iqbal, a modern Muslim poet philosopher has expressed this idea in his own inimitable style. He says, "There is some secret that the spirit of our culture does not perish though the enemy has been continuously invading us (i.e., *kucha bât hai ke hastî mitatî nahî hamârî, daurai jamâ raha hai dusman hamârâ.*)"

Spengler explains progress of the world's higher cultures. He is of the view that every culture passes through different stages of retrogression and progression. He says, "Every culture, every adolescence and maturing and decay of a Culture, every one of its intrinsically necessary stages and periods, has a definite duration, always the same, always recurring with the emphasis of a symbol."[10] Manifestations of all cultures pass through adolescence and maturing and decay, but the spirit of old cultures recycle in the present. It never perishes.

The idea of destiny and the principle of causality are different. Causality is limited to nature whereas destiny goes beyond nature and not controlled by causal necessity. Destiny is derived only through religion and art. The idea of destiny demands life-experience, hope, happiness, despair, and devotion, which are salient ingredients of love. Inward certainty as the meaning of life is found in space of self-determinism. Logic is causality based on rational arguments. Thus, destiny is the living idea of becoming or flux', which unfolds itself immediately to the intuitive vision. For example, Valmikah's epic vision of the Ramayana determines destinies of Râma and Ravan. The epic Mahabharata envisages destiny of the Pandavas and the Kaurvas. Guru Gobind Singh divined destiny of the fall of the Mughal Empire with his creative eye, which transcends causality and reveals trans-empirical realm.

The concept of progress may be linear or cyclic. It is primarily based on the cyclic view of time and the concept of time is 'all is in flux'. Disappearance of a culture does not imply annihilation of values, but temporary cessation of expression of means of expressing the values. The values are eternal but their expressions go on changing. It is difficult for an ordinary person to comprehend the cyclic continuity in history. The world's cultural history oscillates between progress and decay, but continues forever. It is a lived existential experience, which needs cultivation of mind. It is evinced spiritual discipline. Reason and insight both put together can discern continuity between eternity and temporality. It is only the mystic or the genius that lives in the 'eternal present' and discerns its continuity. The genius brings out spirit of culture-forms in new forms and puts them to use in history. This is how the human history retrogresses and progresses in different epochs. This is not a straight and linear prophetic path, but a zigzagged circuitous journey.

(iv) Solidarity with Sacred Tradition[11]

What is tradition? It can be seen from three perspectives. First, it is glorification of one's ego or personal identity that one is Sikh and belongs to a high caste of the Gurus, Jâta, Kshatriya, Brahmin, etc. Second, when we try to interpret we have narrow contours of ethnocentricity superioerity of our religion, tradition, and caste. Third stage is that of a creative thinker or mystic who transcends the tradition to which he belongs by birth and identifies himself with humanity. Guru Nanak's first prophetic utterance in CE 1493 was: there is neither a Hindu nor a Muslim (nâ *ko hindu, nâ musliman*). He refers to core of human identity. Thereafter he starts resuscitating new ideology (*sacha-khanda*) of ideal social structure. He made radical departure from the old traditions and set the process of creating new culture. He wanted to develop concrete and viable social order, which could be feasible in the existential conditions in history. He was not an escapist thinker from historical responsibilities. He had full sense of historical time, which he evinced during his odysseys to the Islamic West-Asian countries.

Then a question arises: Why should we reconstruct our cultural tradition? It is to be reconstructed because tradition is dynamic phenomenon. Knowledge of the sacred scriptures and the tradition developed thereof is to be reformulated in the changed contemporaneous context. It is wrong to assert that any truth can be absolute. All truth is partial and relative because contexts are always in flux. New issues crop up in new contexts.

Symbiotic of different religions and cultures implies influences on each other. In addition, confluence of Islamic and Indic cultures has submerged without destroying either one. Being culture of the conquerors, Islamic culture continued dominating Indian culture from the sixth century to the collapse of the Mughal Empire with demise of Aurangzeb. He tried to destroy Indian culture, but failed. No culture dies but it goes to the periphery and subsists. Its debris remains. When congenial conditions emerge, the buried culture comes to the fore.

The idea of tradition can be split up into three units. First, inner struggle of man is for rediscovering his personal identity. Second, is interpreting and understanding art, artifacts, literary texts, as well as cultural norms, archetypal themes, that display the gradual enfoldment of cultural sensibility. Third, is modernisation or articulation of an objective system of society that rediscovers its identity beyond outer clusters of ritual and conventions. It is inner churning of new ideology.

Tradition is further divided into great and minor traditions. The former traditions of Indian society stretch on the top of smaller regional traditions. They overshadow minor traditions. The great traditions themselves are fraught with contradictions and conflicts. For example, the Vedantic and the Buddhist traditions are constantly at loggerheads with each other. Both are alienated from the smaller traditions. It is difficult to say that regional traditions are manifestations of the great traditions. In this context we can say that Croce has given us his theory of simultaneity of the non-contemporaneous tradition. For him all history is contemporary history. Outer forms may change but the under current of fluxional ideology continues forever.

Ideology is a normative structure of values, ideals, beliefs, etc. Creative faculty carries out our selves. We create words of sense, symbols and signs, having meaning, laws. This is how a society gets continued in history. Society in brief carries three-fold dimensions;

(i) Private individuals,

(ii) Public, cultural values, ideals, beliefs, etc.

(iii) Structure of political ideology, economic or religious structure.

Members are to be drilled into society for internalising cultural action. Savage mind is to be refined, tamed and trained to cultivate cultural mind. Synchronic existing interpersonal relationships are to be transformed into *diachronic* harmonious mutual relations. This recycling creative process is to be carried out in history. History is always in chronic tension or conflict between tradition and social change. Philosophers can suggest remedy beyond conflicts and tensions and implement their suggestion in practice. In the post-independence epoch the imperialists left legacy of education that drove a wedge between the middle and the countryside illiterate people. The elite middle classes are exploiting the poor illiterate, ethnic linguistic groups that are ruled by the privileged middle classes.

The creative thinker lives out his life spans and survives for eternity. He is not prisoner of tradition and his culture. Ordinary man is the prisoner of his culture and tradition. The hero or martyr is not the slave of both. He transcends the hackneyed traditions and creates new ones. While living in his culture, he creates new culture, which will suit new social conditions. Culture is not a matter of choice in which man is thrown by birth. However, he is condemned to be free. He has the freedom to create culture and, then, strive to realise it in praxis. He is simultaneously in history and creator of history and culture.

Indian culture discards compartmentalisation of human life and discrimination in society. It is inner self-cultivation or inward journey from ego to *atman*. Process of self-transformation or self-transcendence ends its inward journey in full actualisation of humanity through spiritual discipline. The small mind inwardly heads towards the cosmic vision. We are to recognise sovereignty of the individual person as a person of self-dignity, which is only within human beings and interpersonal and social relations.

Notes

1. Guru Granth (Guru Nanak), p. 728.
2. Spengler, *The Decline of the West*, p. 53.
3. Freire, Paulo, *Cultural Action for Freedom*, p. 29.
4. id.
5. id., 29 (51fn).
6. The breviaries (*pothian*) are called "Goindwaa Walian Pothian" because these were prepared at Goindwal village. Baba Mohanji, elder son of Guru Amardasa got them compiled.
7. Spengler, O., op.cit, p. 104.
8. *nirankar mahi akaru samavai* /
   akala kala sachu sachi mikava /

   Guru Granth, p. 414.
9. Wittgenstein, L., Culture and Values, p. 3e.
10. Spengler, O., op. cit., Vol. 1, pp. 109-110.
11. See, Dharmendra Goel, "Culture and Reality" in Rekha Jhanji (edit.), *Essays in Honour of Dharmndra Goel: Knowledge, Culture, Action.*, pp. xxvi-xxxi.

6

Restoration of Historical Time

(i) Introductory

We find that the hermeneutical understanding of Sikhism from Guru Nanak to Guru Hargobind is a diachronic logical and historical development of the original faith. Sikhism itself was a diachronic interpretation of previous religious and philosophical traditions of India and other traditions. It is a logical development from spirituality to synthesis of the temporal and the spiritual. It is, perhaps, a singular contribution of Sikh culture to the world thought. I, therefore, propose to discuss logical development in the Sikh social philosophy from Guru Nanak's *sacha-khanda* (ideal articulated space of social structure) to the Khalsa-panth (militant social structure created as an ideal space of ideology). Though it started as a peaceful religious upsurge, yet it culminated in the militant civil society of the Khalsa-panth.

The philosophical question arises: Why did martyrdom (*shahadat*) not occur before the 5th guru? The Sikh movement had not developed into a mass movement and the Mughal rule in India did have a strong hold over the land of India. Jahangir was a fanatic and bigoted Emperor. He wanted to create pan-Islamic states.

Prior to the advent of the Sikh movement the Indians did not have practical sense of history. They lacked sense of historical time. It was only after the coming of the Turks, the sense of historical time was developed by the Gurus and the same was applied on the Indian social structure. We were living in the world of mythical and speculative philosophies. We were preoccupied with the quest to find out meaning of human life in the other world. Historicity of human action was negated. We have been trying to find out meaning of human life from the hagiographic literature (genre) of Jatak stories of the Buddha and the Puranas or the epics of the Ramayana and the Mahabharata.

Guru Nanak also demolishes naïve realism as well as a purely speculated idealism and the myths. For him Brahman as a metaphysical assumption is a pure speculative make-belief. It is to be translated into 'usefulness' in practice. If Brahman is all-inclusive reality, it should reflect in practical life as well. Killing of sentient beings is discouraged. For example, killing of a hen is negation of life. Thus, negation of existential beliefs would automatically demolish the practical workability of truth-judgments as real and false. This is the highest good of every religion and Sikhism in particular.

Before launching my analysis on the philosophical issues involved in the above title, it enjoins upon us to explain some philosophical questions: What is social philosophy? What is doing philosophy? Distinguish it from history of philosophy. Philosophy of history is recapitulating archeology of knowledge that is treasured in the sacred texts and traditions. In addition, doing philosophy of culture is rigorous analysis of the current philosophical issues while keeping in mind the past treasure-trove of knowledge.

Historical sense of history warrants that every event or fact occurs in historical time and space that is real. Significant event occurs in history and creates history for the coming generations. The Gurus were concentrating on the essence of man than on a particular man. They had total vision of mankind in their minds. No doubt our forefathers did have idea of social and moral commitment because they created gods and goddesses for the welfare of the people. It may be pointed out female deities were not created in the Semitic (say, Islam) tradition. It is priviledge of the Indian minds.The deites existed in theoretical speculations. In the Medieval Ages people withdrew from historical responsibilities. Wisdom lies in putting deals and values to use in historical time and practice.

The fundamental philosophical question was how to translate the ideals into practice. Earlier the Bhaktas had historical sense of time. The Gurus picked up the thread and further knitted the structure of historical sense. In the hands of the Gurus the historical sense of time became explicit. They had voluntarist approach towards time and history. But the Gurus created new value-system of reconciliation of the ideals of moral and social commitments with praxis. From this standpoint martyrdom of Guru Arjundeva was the most significant event in the global history. It was a turning point in the Sikh history and religion.

(ii) Eternity and Time

Unlike Vedic traditions, Buddhism doesn't accept divine origin of the world and the society. *Dharma* is the structure of reality, as indicated by the teachings of the Buddha including *nirvana* that is to be realised in the transcendental experience in this very life. The teachings of the Buddha were designed for the *saga* including the lay disciples. Brahmins and Muslims or covenant tried to break up the saga. Social order is a sort of contract. *Sansara* is a timed reality and *nirvana* is timeless state of consciousness. There seems to be a dichotomy between the two realms. It is a perennial problem in the philosophical and religious traditions since beginning of the world. The Indian and the Western thinkers confronted it. The Being has been conceived beyond time. In the medieval ages the Being was practically alienated from the phenomenal world and haven of eternity was posited in the visionary otherworld (heaven/ *swarga/bahisht*). There has been a chasm between the immanence and the transcendental. In the dynamic Sikh onto-theology both realms of the immanence and the transcendence are in time. Man can transcend this-world with his creativity which is the necessary outcome of the dynamic nature of the Being. In the modern times Martin Heidegger tries to resolve this problem. His Being is in the world. The beings of small character "b" are encompassed wiuthin the capital character "B". He restored reality of human action and historicity of the world. On this point Sikhism and Heidegger are in agreement with each other. It lands us into the existential human situation. Human action in history is considered real.

The existential human situation poses a question whether freedom or voluntarism is possible in this life or thereafter. Sikhism came with a rigorous philosophy of freedom or voluntarism that is to be realised *here* and *now* in this-world. The human will is to be strengthened with the grace of *shabda-guru*. It is possible only if historicity of time and the world are accepted as existential realities. The historical reality of time implies that action is to be real because time is an inseparable aspect of eternity. Eternity is stretched into temporality and vice versa. This would reaffirm the empirical world and life in it. It will enjoin upon man historical responsibilities. It will lead to social involvement and moral commitments. Freedom of will is precondition for all such activities.

Now I will take up the eternity and time which are interconnected philosophical issues. Time has multi-dimensions that includes mystical, mathematical, historical, psychological, seasonal and other aspects around which human consciousness lives and develops. Human creativity coils around time and reaches out to eternity. Man tries to make experience timeless. Here timeless means that Akala is inclusive of time. The rarefied experience of the mystic is stilled in eternity. The Zen Buddhism calls it '*satori*'. The essence of mystic experience is that it comes out of the cocoon of time and is at once also in time. Man's creativity is capable of it. As a result of it man's creativity is capable of achieving this coveted ideal in the world. As a result of it, it creates desire in man for immortality. Man's experience doesn't transcend time rather it absorbs in it. As, for instance, a piece of salt is absorbed in water. A man can remember the past because his memory is free from the control of time, and the past events active in his 'me' that are functioning in time. In the 'I' the realised self conquers time. His 'I' is in 'eternal present' inclusive of past, present, and future. Memory is in time and will remain in time. It gradually fades away in time or it transcends time through spiritual discipline.

If man is wholly left to the experience of the present moments and is oblivious of memory, then he would easily change with time and be a floating bubble in the stream of events. He could never be conscious of time for consciousness implies duality. Attuned consciousness to eternity doesn't transcend time. Mind is simultaneously in time and also transcends it. The mind transcends time to grasp it in rebound; it must have stood outside it in order to be able to reflect upon it. This doesn't apply merely to the specially transcended moments of time (ecstasy). As, for instance, we can't be conscious of sorrow until sorrow is over, but it is a part of time. If we could not free ourselves from time, we could have no knowledge of time. One is simultaneously *in* time and *beyond* time. This is dual triumph over time in this-world. The mystic's ecstasy is attuned to the transcendental consciousness and is living in the empirical (psychological) time as well.

In order to understand the condition of timelessness (*akala*), let us reflect on what memory rescues from time. What transcends time is only what is of interest to the individual, what has meaning for him; in fact, all that he assigns value to it. Uninterested things and events are often forgotten. It is the value that creates the timelessness. We forget everything that has no value for us even if we are unconscious of that absence of value. We remember only the things or events that have value for us even if we are unconscious of that value. Hence, values are trans-empirical and eternal at once.

What has value, then, is timeless; or, to put it the other way round, a thing that has more or lesser value. It is affected by time. The norms are affected by time but values are eternal. In the world norms are in proportion to dependence of time; only norm that is more durable has a positive significance. This is what I take to be the subtle difference between norms and values. The values are eternal and the norms are in time. Both constitute the comprehensive concept of values and norms. On the basis of this distinction the Sikh moral norms of conduct (*rahat maryada*) have been evolved from the scripture and the tradition. These norms are to be changed with the changing conditions of social life. It may be moral conduct is to be dynamic and for the good of "others". Rigidity in moral conduct erodes its usefullness.

A brief survey of above facts will suffice to make clear the relation between value and duration of time. We are always inclined to pay little attention to the views of those whom we have known only a short time, and, as a rule, we think little of the hasty judgements of those who easily change their ideas. On the other hand, uncompromising fixedness gains respect, even if it assumes the form of vindictiveness or obstinacy. A man dislikes to be told that he is always changing; but let it be put that he is simply showing new sides of his character and he will be proud of the permanence through the changes. The dynamic character is the sign of the creative thinker. He always comes with new ideas. Man fed up with life will resist to be up and doing. He will see the empty buckets of the rotating Persian wheel. In simple words, he develops cynic attitude towards the world and "others". The voluntarist breaks up the cocoon of passivity and jumps into new problematic situations. He is active and optimist in all walks of life.

This law of values is the chief reason why men are interested in their death and future. The desire for value shows itself in the efforts to free us from time, and this pressure is exerted even in the case of the problematic situations, which sooner or later must change. For instance, riches and position and everything that we call the goods of this-world are bound to vanish. Here lies the psychological motive for making of the wills and the bestowal of property. The motive is not care for relatives, because a man without relatives is very often more anxious to settle his goods and not feeling. Perhaps, like the head of a family wills that some kind of permanence and traces of him will be left after his own death. The values he creates live after his death. He is remembered as an innovator of new values. These, thus, make him eternal.

Form and timelessness, or individuation and duration, are two factors, which compose value. The first general conclusion to be made is that the desire for timelessness, a craving for value, pervades in all spheres of human activity. And this desire for real value is deeply bound up with the desire for power, property, and wealth (including ornaments, woman, and immovable property: *jar, joru,* and *jamin*). The desire for immortality itself is merely a specific case of the attitude towards life and death that only things have a positive value. This is connected with memory. The permanence of experiences of man is proportional to the significance of norms and values for him. Putting it in a paradoxical form, it may be said that past creates values. Only that which has a positive value is retained and protected in memory from the jaws of time and so it may be with the individual's psychical life as a whole. If it is of real positive value, it must encompass time.

This draws us incomparably nearer to the innermost motive of the desire for immortality. The complete loss of significance of life will follow if life ends without contributing anything to humanity. The contributions to the world make man immortal; otherwise life will be purposeless and meaningless.

Goethe said to Eckermann that it leads to the demand for immortality. Goethe agrees with common-sense of Schubart and confirms it that, "...To me, the eternal existence of souls is proved from my idea of activity; if I work on incessantly till my death, nature will give another form of existence when the present one can no longer sustain my spirit." *(Conversations With Goethe...,* February 4, 1829). The strongest craving for immortality is possessed by the genius, and this is explained by all the other facts, which have been discussed above. He craves for immortality through his works that transcend time. In the above quotation, the term "activity" is a dynamic process that is very significant. It lays more emphasis on activity than on any static entity that is a 'soul-substance'. I have also argued in favour of it in the present book. Goethe made a radical departure from the traditional Biblical interpretation that in the beginning was the 'word'. He said it was 'deed'. Memory only fully vanquishes time when it appears in a universal form, as in universal men. The genius is, thus, the only timeless man that he has passionate and urgent desire for immortality. He has the strongest passion for eternity as the greatest value. Man is made to transcend the fear of death that checkmates activity. The value of continuous process of transcendence from the fear of death occurs in the Guru Granth *passim.* It is very significant for dynamic view of life.

Pure logical thought can't occur in the case of men; it would be an attribute of the deity. A human being must always think partly psychologically because he possesses reason but also senses, feelings, emotions, and his thought can't free it from the temporal experiences, but must remain bound by them. Logic, however, is the supreme standard by which the individual can test his own psychological ideas and those of others. When two men are discussing anything, it is the conception and not the varying individual presentations of it that matter. The conception, then, is the standard of value for the individual presentations. The mode in which the psychological generalisations come into being is quite independent of the conceptions and has no significance in respect to it. The logical character, which invests the conception with dignity and power, is not derived from experience for experience can give only vague and wavering generalisations. Absolute constancy and coherence which can't come from sheer experience is the essence of the conception of that power concealed in the depths of the human mind whose handiwork we try hard but in vain to see in nature. The conceptions are the only true mirroring realities. The conceptions and values transcend nature.

The secret of Erich Fromm's *The Fear of Freedom* is that man alone in the world is in tremendous eternal isolation. He is of the view that freedom is the cause of his isolation and insecurity. He is in a dilemma of solitude and insecurity. Man stands above social ethics that he is all alone. Like Defoe's Robinson Crusoe he doesn't have the moral sense that there can be no moral obligations and duties towards others. The only remedial viewpoint is to be committed to one's historical responsibilities. From Fromm's standpoint it can be inferred that without social relationships between an individual and others there is certainly no essential self ('I'), and that would mean there is no historical personal identity of the self. My personal identity is because of others. Others reflect in 'me' and *vice versa*. Both are complimentary and indispensable for each other. To accept reality of 'others', in the existential situations, is to posit dynamic view of the external world. Then dynamic view of life will necessarily follow from it.

When man is in the company of others, he gains consciousness of himself. This is Kantian argument that being conscious of others, one's existence is established. This is why a man is prouder in the presence of other men than when he is alone. In his hours of solitude his self-confidence is not damped down. Rather his self is elevated to the realised self-identity. He who himself destroys destroys at the same time the whole universe of others as well. One who murders another commits the greatest crime because he murders himself in his victim. Absolute selfishness, in practice, is a horror that should rather be called nihilism; if there is no "thou," there is certainly no "I" and that would mean there is nothing. I am because of others. Others reflect in me and *vice versa*. Without others man is sheer abstraction and nothingness or vacuum. To a real self one is to be in the society. To accept reality of the 'other(s)' in existential situations is to posit a dynamic view of the external real world. Then the dynamic view of life will necessarily follow from it.

In the existential situations it is very difficult to resolve the dilemma of action in historical time, as it can't be controlled. It can't be stilled either. Realisation of an abstract *akala* (timeless) is not possible. When we try to still or concretise it, it slips away from us and shall be distorted. Hence, every moment is distinct and unique. The Sikh Gurus and the Bhaktas lived in and with the following stream of historical time. It implies that history doesn't repeat itself. The ideal man of Sikhism is required to swim with the rising and falling tides of temporality. The process of spiritual development of moral agent is a dual triumph over the ceaseless flow of real time in which history is moving forwards. The future without return and repletion of the events of the past. Here temporality is transformed into the stilled consciousness. As, for example, *sahaj* in Sikhism and *satori* in Zen Buddhism are the states of stilled consciousness. Einstein also confirms it that when a man can move at a speed of the light (say, 186,000 miles per second) mathematical time becomes motionless. It is called ending of scientific or historical time, but potency of dynamic nature is still inherent in it.

The book, *The Ending of Time* by J. Krishnamurti and David Bohm discusses the issue of ending psychological time by transcending temporality and living with eternity in the mystical time (Arabic, *waqt*). Man has an inward existential urge to become perfect and eternal. He wishes to be immortal. The root-cause is the inner conflicts in the self and without in the society. The inward and outward dichotomy is to be overcome. It is possible when egoistic centre of 'me' is done away with. 'Me' as an entity is too replaced with point-instant activity. When 'me' ends, there is insight into the 'eternal present'. We want a certain permanent historical identity in us to function as a force behind action. The inward psychological time is moving and that is to be transcended. If inner time is stilled, it shall be ending of the psychological or the empirical time. It means that consciousness of the self transcends psychological time and is attuned to the higher mystic time of 'eternal stillness'. It is not ending of historical time, but to be attained to the stream of cosmic becoming. That is living with eternity. Both psychological and cosmic times are reconciled into an eternal universal flux. When there is no movement, even then it is not static. It is not a timeless state of mind. It is plenum of time in eternity.

If mind is not in eternity, we shall have to postulate God as prime mover as self-caused (*sui causa*) Being. The chain of conflict in the empirical time is endless. It is to be transcended that will resolve the conflict. It will be a state of freedom. 'Me' will be transformed into 'I'. It is not denying the very spirit of time by ignoring past as dead and future that is in dark. If inward conflicts cease, then conflicts in the volition will automatically come to cessation. It is rather to recognise time in which past, present, and future, is congealed into the 'eternal present'. We shall live with the stream of time. It is nothing but living with the moving stream of eternity. There is no beginning and end in time. All is in flux. It is to be attuned to the cosmic time (*mahakala*). 'Me' as becoming shall be merged into the cosmic flux. It is realised in a state of *sahaj*. Internal and external conflicts will be done away with.

Since he is initially imperfect, so he wants to become perfect. For this purpose, he requires a larger social universe for attaining perfection. In this sense, eternity in time is realised. This is how the mystic resolves the riddle of time and eternity as two phases of the transcendental and the living existential Being-in-time. The *jivanmukta* attunes to the eternal and simultaneously lives in time in the society. The two processes of identification with the eternal 'Being' and socialisation in the society are realised. The former is a process of acquiring freedom of the self by cutting through the morass of 'me-ness' and attachment with the world. In the second process, the self identifies with humanity. It is a transcended and realised state of the mind.

It is closer to Kantian metaphysical argument and Schopenhauer's voluntarism of the cosmic will. It is independent or inclusive of the contingent world, but it can't be reduced to empirical phenomena. This manifest dynamic world is to be historicised to make it workable in practice. Thus, it will be putting talent to use. Talent without infusion of practicability is sterile and a mere theoretical intellectual construct. In

Sikhism the idea, word and action (*mana, baca,* and *karma*) put together makes a perfect dynamic world-vision. The Gurus gave new ideas and implemented them in history. In due course of time, the ideas became part and parcel of the tradition in history. In this sense, the Gurus were creators of history.

There are many creative innovations of the geniuses of the Sikh Gurus. It is wrong to say that one genius is influenced by another genius. The creative genius can't dance to the tune of another genius. The very distinct mark of the genius is that he branches off a new path that makes a radical departure from the beaten track. His creative mind is a path-breaker. He may agree or disagree to the interpretations of the existing traditions and the scriptures propounded by other geniuses, but his path-breaking articulations create new conceptual patterns and currents of thought in history. He will definitely come out with his new interpretations. This is how the traditions and scriptures are created and recreated by the geniuses for the coming ages. Emergence of a genius's ideas is a rare phenomenon, which opens new 'epochs'. This process rolls down in history till posterity.

Man is finite. He wants to become infinite. He is to overcome his finitude. It can be possible with man's creativity. The philosophical problem is: Can a human creature be a creator? Man has creativity. The creative process is only a comprehensive reflection on all the possible perspectives of the problem that human mind is confronted with the Being. Man is born and is created in time. It is a basic presupposition of Indian religious traditions that man is both creature and creator. He is the creature because he has been created by his parents and is creator because he creates his self and realises his ontic nature. His ontic nature is freedom or autonomy of the self. He, then, proceeds for the freedom of others. This is the societal aspect of man in the concrete existential situations. It is the genesis of morality and values. Man's creativity is comprehension and reflection on all possible perspectives of the problem, which are confronted by the human mind. In some Indian religious traditions man is projected as a concrete being. It is through him idea and action are reconciled. It is the complete self in its perfection that is the main practical quest in Indian thought. It is realisation of real self in the world. Sikhism highlights this aspect in theory and praxis.

It implies that man is in historical concrete time and is finite. He wants to transcend his finitude because he is inherently infinite. Man as a historical agent tries to transcend the transitory world with the help of values, which are created ideals. He is required to overcome ordeals of human predicaments in life. He creates values. So values are not uncreated (*anadi*), but are eternal (*ananta*). Once they are created, they become eternal. These are treasured in the religious scriptures and other books of master minds. Since the conditions change, they need reinterpretation from time to time. The values are eternal. For example, justice, freedom, equality and others are eternal values. The norms of the values change in concrete historical and social conditions, but the values remain eternal.

Therefore, it is only man's creativity, which has created human history. He is living in history and creates it. This is the uniqueness of man that he is creator of history. Just as man is actively creating history, so he is also the creative diviner of future history of mankind. Guru Nanak's ideal man (*gurmukh*) creates new values at every step. Man is to live in the historical present as a station of past and future epitomised in the 'eternal present'. This concept of creativity symbolises eternal becoming of human life. The *gurmukh* of Sikhism is the diviner of past, present, and future through the prism of 'eternal present'. He lives in eternity through lived existential life in the present. In the beginning of Guru Nanak's "Japuji", we find a couplet that the primal Being is eternal. It cyclically pervades through past, present and future. In this way he lives simultaneously in time and eternity

The Sikh movement regained personal concrete identity of man in the society and spiritual social unity, which could adjust to the changing societal conditions as well. It developed into a militant civil society of the Khalsa-panth. The genesis of Sikhism was a bold revolt of conscience against brutality of Central Asian invaders and shameless effeminacy of the indigenous priestly class and the feudal exploiters. It was a movement of reviving sense of sensibility for the welfare of humanity irrespective of any rank, sex, religion, caste, race, ethnicity, and other worldly considerations. The Sikh philosophy was a groundbreaking bold resistance to wage perpetual war against tyranny, atrocities, and injustice. It was a solemn moral commitment and resolution for bearing historical responsibility. Medieval Islamic hegemonic aggression on Indian indigenous culture was actively resisted. Sikhism in the Gurus' period developed a distinct cultural identity. It assimilated essential elements of alien cultures into a composite culture of the land. The Gurus infused martial spirit into the castrated, eunicised, and effeminised subaltern Indian masses. Sikhism was initiated as a social rejuvenation for the achievement of the highest state of spirituality (*sacha-khanda*) and emancipation of mankind (*sarbat ka bhala*). It was more of spirituality (*piri*) and less of polity (*miri*). The socio-political dimension of struggle against tyranny (*ati)* was added in the Sikh movement during the tyrant Mughal Emperors.

Thus, every interpretation either of sacred scriptures or tradition is in flux. Scriptures are not of the age but of the ages because they propound eternal fluxional truth. Tradition stems from the scripture and historical exigencies. We can safely infer from the above discussion that interpreter has to be better equipped to make us understand the ciphers in the 'sacred texts'. He should have developed intuitive insight for understanding the objective truth in the texts. Philosophical hermeneutics with cultural understanding is better because it enables us to draw all the possible logical implications of the statements recorded in the texts. Logical consistency and necessary relationships among the linguistic elements are being reasoned out in the process of understanding the ciphers. Hermeneutical understanding as an objective understanding is directed towards truth and meanings. Such understanding of the interpreter is freed from the original authorial intention and prison of subjectivity and solipsism or scepticism. Philosophically all interpretations are reinterpretations of the original intuitions of the mystics. These are restructured out of the remains or ruins of the past interpretations. This point can be substantiated from the history of the religious traditions as well.

A philosophical question arises: Does the Sikh Canon allow reinterpretation in the changed conditions? My answer to it is 'yes'. Sikhism itself was a hermeneutical reinterpretation of the prevalent Indian and Islamic traditions without repudiating their pristine ontic natures. The contributors of the Sikh Canon had been reinterpreting the fossilised doctrines of the previous scriptures and traditions, and made significant departures from them. Guru Nanak reinterpreted other traditions in the context of his contemporaneous times. He took full cognizance of the historical developments in those traditions. With the same logic we can also argue that the Sikh Canon can be reinterpreted. In the Gurus' period there had been interpretations and reinterpretations in the Sikh Canon itself and the Sikh tradition as well. The Sikh Gurus reinterpreted the hymns of the earlier bhaktas whose compositions are incorporated in the Canon. Guru Gobind Singh apotheosised it as an eternal living guru as perennial source of guidance. He authenticated and finalised the contents of the hymns of the Scripture, but doors of reinterpretation were kept open for eternity (*jugo jug atal)*. If it is not allowed, then it shall degenerate into fossilised dogma. It shall be a make-belief of the past having dogmatism and fundamentalism.

Hermeneutical reinterpretation is a metaphysical necessity from its fluxional ontology. Similarly the fluxional nature of being enjoins upon us to reinterpret the Sikh faith from time to time as to keep up pace with the changing historical events and conditions without deviating from its original essence of truth. We are to restructure the Sikh world-view with the help of accredited collective historical consciousness of the people. We may discard outlived religious institutions without setting aside their essential aspects but inner urge of communitarian solidarity and participatory social contact with the mundane world is to be carried out.

The Sikh movement was a revolt of the *atman* against evil in the society. The martial spirit in Sikhism was a logical and existential necessity for eradicating evil in the society for restoring justice and peace. The supreme sacrifice of Guru Arjunadeva in CE 1606 was a turning-point in the Sikh tradition. The movement turned into a militant upsurge and revolt of conscience.

Mythical identity was congealed into historical identity. 'Me', 'I' and 'Thou' are glued into one *sui generis* groundless identity of the Akala Purakh. In Sikhism the 'me' is first confronted with other fellow beings in the world when it is dominated by 'me-ness' (*haumai*). When 'me' is transformed into 'I', then it identifies itself with the Akala Purakh. 'I' is a microcosm and 'Thou' is a linguistic construct of macrocosm so long as attributive imaginary and historical attributes persist, but at the transcendental level all the attributes get dissolved into the formless Being. All other distinctions are brushed aside. If he does not retain his historical personal identity and cuts off from temporality, he can't affirm societal realities. It is possible only if one simultaneously identifies with the Akala Purakh and is voluntarist in the moral collective struggle of life.

Once man has the transcendent lived experience in a state of ecstasy, he knows the Truth. He can't buzz off from his existential moral responsibilities. Ethical voluntarism is possible only if ultimate ontic reality is dynamic and the external world will necessarily entail from its dynamic ontological nature. It is not to be presumed that intellect is denied. It is given secondary status as compared to will. It is further attuned to the regulative cosmic law (*rita / hukam*) of the dynamic Reality. The voluntarist has no other alternative, but to sacrifice for the cause of humanity and social justice. Aristotelian *akinesia* presumes an existential predicament for the will. It is applicable in the case of an ordinary person who has a weak will power. But free will of a realised person is above it. In the case of a martyr (*shahid*) *akinesia* is Guru Tegh Bahadur's lived mystic experience of the Truth, so they did not have the fear of death. Their sacrifices made them immortal in the annals of history. They created an eternal value of self-sacrifice on the altar of truth. They gave new life to the Sikh faith. In the Sikh history, the Sikh martyrs have been nursing the Sikh faith with their blood. Even a modern Hindu fiction writer Chandherdhar Sharma Guleri confirms the steadfast faith of a Sikh soldier. In his short story "Us Ne Kaha Tha" his main character Lahana Singh, son of Buddh Singh represents true Sikh faith. He dies as a martyr in the battlefield for his faith and the country. He is committed to Amritsar. It is Sikh voluntarism to die a dignified death in the battlefield. It leads us to the philosophical analysis of the Sikh moral conduct.

Restoration of the historical sense is one of the singular contributions of Guru Nanak to the cultural history of medieval India. The Sikh doctrinal world-view is enshrined in the Guru Granth, which is the fountainhead for understanding the Sikh faith. The Sikh tradition in the history emanates from the Sikh Canon. It enjoins upon us to understand the Sikh Scripture in its proper perspective. The doctrines of the Sikh Scripture and the tradition should go hand in hand. Like Goethe's interpretation of the "living nature," *qudrat* in the Guru Granth is a historical world-picture of the Akala Purakh. In culture, history, and religion we are concerned with direction and destiny of man and the nature. History is a continuous progression from uncivilised society to the civilised social order. Guru Nanak envisaged the ideology of the social order (*sacha-khanda*) in the colophon of the Japuji. The Sikh religion was directed towards the destiny of the Khalsa creation. Passage from the *sacha-khanda* to the creation of the Khalsa-panth is a historical progression from the possible to the actual, unfolding the realm of actuality. Unfortunately, the present scenario of the Sikh ideology and the culture are developed from the inner vision of the supreme truth. The triad of thought, saying, and deed (*mana, bacha,* and *karma*) are fragmented. The optimal synthesis of theory and practice is the central theme of the scripture. We do not find dichotomy in the preaching and doing in the Gurus. The Gurus represent quintessence of the doctrinal aspect of the Guru Granth. The gurus demythologised the mythical Indic and the Semitic ideologies, which were prevalent in the medieval ages.

The Sikh faith during the Gurus' period represents the 'Faustian spirit' of history. The Faustian dynamnic spirit is detachment from the objects of the world. By such a treatment is meant that one distances oneself from the world and accepts that the "present" is the only significant for man. None of the personal hopes and fears and other inward impulses, which checkmate practical life, do not influence such detachment.

For the 'Faustian' eye everything is in motion and life means struggle. In the history of the culture, we are concerned with the actualisation of the possible. It is the history of an inner spiritual becoming Being through the lifestyle of the world or region or the nation. Perhaps, for this reason the higher cultures are born in great crisis, upheaval, and turmoil. The Sikh history in the Guru period is full of turmoil. It gave birth to the voluntarist culture that was the motivating force for supreme sacrifice of the fifth and the ninth Gurus. The euthanasiac (heroic) spirit of dying an honourable death is the message of the Guru Granth. It reaffirms the historical sense.

Guru Nanak was seized of secular or historical realities of his times. When Guru Nanak personally met Emperor Babur at Amnabad, he vehemently criticised his invasion on India in CE 1526, but he had not taken resort to sword by that time unlike the Sikhs in later period of history. His tongue was his sharp sword, which could pierce into Babur's conscience. Furthermore, the dynamic metaphysical base necessitates the Sikh movement to develop it into an active resistance. For instance, Guru Nanak's long poetic anthologies, "Babur-Bani" (GG, pp. 417-18, 722-23) is a virulent condemnation of the Mughal Emperor Babur. His utterances, in the form of hymns, are a crusade against tyranny and injustice of the then Mughal Emperor. The word picture presented in the hymns is a portrayal of agony of the poor masses that were victims of the invaders' tyranny and injustice. It shows Guru Nanak's historical sense of duty for the amelioration of the subaltern intimidated masses. It advocates restoration of man's historical action, freedom and self-dignity in the coveted civil society. It sets aside medieval objectivity and absoluteness of truth and the feudal despotic authoritarianism. These are the kernel polemics confronted by the Sikh movement against the medieval philosophies and cruel practices prevalent in the land.

Prior to the birth of Sikh movement Punjabis were not martial. Mutual skirmishes and tribal remarriages for wealth and honour of the women were the common features in the Punjab. The cultural concept of honorable death for the sake of noble cause was the innovation of the Gurus. This is possible only if one has a historical sense and is alive to the societal and historical responsibilities. The Punjabis were revengefully tolerating humiliation at the hands of the marble hearted invaders. They were mostly menial workers and tillers on the land. Brahmins through rituals ruled over the peasantry. Moneylenders exploited them. Landowners dominated the scene of power. Feudal lords had the reins of power in their hands. On the contrary, Rajputs and Marathas had the real sense of history. Guru Nanak infused martial spirit into the morrows of the masses of India. The martial spirit became explicit in the Sikh tradition from Guru Hargobind when he was adorned with two swords of *miri* and *piri*. The Sikh insurgence has the elements of spirituality and temporality.

In the Indian and the Greek traditions, time is cyclic and in the Semitic or Syrian tradition, it is linear. These concepts are presupposed only to explain human life in the world. Therefore, struggle in the world requires either cyclic or linear concept. The singular contribution of Guru Nanak lies in reconciling both the viewpoints within his philosophy. He propounds the concept of 'eternal present', which is without beginning, and end. It is ever living, growing and existentially experienced by progressing human consciousness. The vicious cycle of human life and death are endless phases of the flux of reality. In Sikhism, the reality of the historical events has been given central salience. Time is the very essence of the reality. There is no lease of life in the otherworld. The liberation from the mundane world is sought out. An endeavour is made to overcome death. Death has been treated as an event in life and a step forward is the renewal of existence and not an abrupt end of it. Human life is absorbed into the eternal life, as drop of water becomes one with the ocean.

This can be legitimately applied to the social phenomenon as well. The fact that the historical time was accepted as a reality, Sikhism recognises oscillating seasonal rotation of twelve months of the year (*baran mahan*). It is the cyclic view that is reflected in man's sense of the realistic progress of the historical consciousness. It is in the real historical time that man is to negotiate his narrow vision of the *manmukh* to the cosmic vision of the *gurmukh*. His will becomes attuned to the cosmic will (*raza*). It implies that the cosmic will executes the divine purposes through man's will. Thus, all divinely ordained actions are carried out through man in the real historical time. The *gurmukh* is a free person who attains dual victory over the seamless and ceaseless flux of time and lives in eternity. He is an epitome of theory and praxis because he carries out all actions in society.

Alberuni who came to India along with Mahmood Ghaznavi wrote in his classical work *Al-Hind* that the Indians did not have the sense of history. They were living in the dreamy world of otherworldliness. In the medieval ages people lacked genuine awareness of the historical time. The mythical one shadowed the historical time and, consequently, the phenomenal world was conceived as maya and a magic show. The medieval world-view, overall, was cut off from the stark social realities. It resulted in negation of the empirical life and the world. Sikhism reinterpreted the prevalent negative Puranic and the Qur'anic world-views of the middle ages and revived the ancient Vedic affirmative historical world-view, which is primarily concerned with this world.

The sages of antiquity in India and Greece had a real sense of history and time Gr. *kairos*. In the early ancient history of India they had a historical sense. We might have not recorded the chronology of the historical facts and the events. The notion of the otherworld was not developed in ancient India. It was developed in the medieval ages. Our endeavour is to formulate a syntactical structure that helps discerning real signification of the concept of history and time. The logic weaves the ideas into the coherent whole that mirrors the meaning. It also discerns order in the universe. For finding out cosmic order it is postulated. The word *sansara* signifies point-instant universal flux and the regulative principle is *hukam* that owes its origin from Arabic (*qhalq*).

The mythical events in the whirl of the *aeons* (*yugas*) (Gk. *aion*, age) are not recorded in logically interlaced minute details. These are the mythical conceptual spaces of dynamicity. The cardinal emphasis of the cyclic view of time both in India and Greece has been to transcend from the historical time and the mundane world. On the other hand, the prophetic or linear view of time emphasises advancement towards the goal where time ends at a particular point. It is a presupposition used to explain the processes and functioning the world. This is the basic difference between the Indian and the Greek that is juxtaposed to the Semitic view of linear concept of time.

It is nothing but harnessing energy to action, which culminates in *nishkama karma*. In the Gita the theoretical base of the Sankhya School is reconciled with the practical yogic system. The Gita builds its argument on the mythical matrix of cyclic time. On the other hand, the Gurus articulated their world-view based on the historical time that reflects Eternity. The Semitic linear time and the Indian and the Greek cyclic views of time are blended with the affirmation of the reality of the world and the historical action.

When both are blended into one whole, self-transcendence and advancement can be possible. Guru Nanak tried to reconcile both in theory and praxis. This viewpoint advocates the dynamic view of life and world. Hence, the ideology which is to represent such a view is to be dynamic. The ideology is to be structured and restructured from time to time to be in conformity with the changed social conditions. This phenomenon developed in the Sikh ideology moving from the *sacha-khanda* to the creation of the Khalsa-panth.

The basic philosophical question arises: Can time come to an end or can it have a beginning? It is an 'eternal present' without beginning and end. It is living, growing and existentially experienced by progressing human consciousness. The vicious cycle of human life and death are endless phases of the flux of reality. In Sikhism, the reality of the historical events has been given central salience. Time is the very essence of the reality. There is no lease of life in the otherworld. The concept of the other-world came up in the medieval times. In the Vedic period this concept was not developed. The liberation from the mundane world is sought out. An endeavour is made to overcome death. Death has been treated as an event in life and a step towards continuing of existence and not an abrupt end of it.

For the crude materialist there is no return of the human life after the extinction of the body on the funeral pyre. The

Semitic traditions (Judaism, Christianity, and Islam), however, believe in the concept of resurrection of the body. In the Sikh tradition the bodily death means to glide into the eternal life. In the existential lived experience, transcendence from death is to realise freedom from within. It is a stepping-stone for the voluntarist life '*here*' and '*now*'. While creating the Khalsa, Guru Gobind Singh blended the secular time with Eternity. It was a violent rupture from the prevalent real-*yuga* into the real cyclic and the historical social reality. It means that commitment of the self to the present lies in facing courageously the responsibilities. It was the divine will that was executed by realising the ideal space of the Akala Purakh on the earth.

This can be legitimately applied to the social phenomenon as well. The fact that the historical time was accepted as a reality, Sikhism recognised oscillating seasonal rotation of twelve months of the year. It is the cyclic view that is reflected in man's sense of the realistic progress of the historical consciousness. It is in the real historical time that man is to negotiate his narrow vision of the egocentric self (*manmukh*) to the cosmic vision (*gurmukh*). Man's will is attuned to the cosmic will (*raza*). It implies that the cosmic will carries out the divine purposes through man's will. Thus, all divinely ordained actions are carried out through man in the real historical time. The *gurmukh* is a free person who attains dual victory over the seamless and ceaseless flux of time and lives in eternity. He is an epitome of theory and praxis because he carries out all actions in society.

It denies dimensions of the past ('was') and the future ('will be'). It expresses the concept of eternity. Thus, what is that concept? It denies creation, and destruction of the everlasting ontic essence. Eternity is the 'spacious present' ('eternal now'). The Parmenidean 'Being' lacks point-instant changes. He upholds the timeless interpretation of eternity. But Sikhism's concept of Eternity is closer to the Heracleitean and the Buddhist philosophies of the universal flux. This change is not an "endless recurrence of the same". It is different and distinct at every moment. Guru Nanak ascertains this idea in one of his hymns. With reference to the Kartapurakh he says:

> He is new at every point-instant,
> And He is always benevolent.
> /(1-1) / GG, p. 660.

Nietzsche eroded the Greek myth of the 'eternal recurrence'. It is interesting to note that Sikhism anticipated Nietzsche's concept of perspectivism and creativity in variant ways. The realised self lives in the 'eternal present'! The hero sketches his finer internal *kala* into totality of eternity to view past, present and future through the window of the 'eternal present'. The Greek concept of the 'eternal return or recurrence' is discarded because creativity transcends the repetitive sameness of the static instant-states. The dynamic view implies that to live with the ever-flowing seamless stream of the creative duration is the essence of eternity. This is what the Sikh philosophy means to say. One should live in eternity through the 'now" (present) in history. The realised self, according to the Sikh Scriptures, simultaneously lives in the historical time and eternity.

7

Reconciliation of Time and Eternity

(i) Bhakti to Shakti

The quintessence of Indian Bhakti Movement is to realise truth. Man is not a helpless pawn that can be placed anywhere in the chess game of life. Man has latent freedom that can be aroused. He is, thus, intrinsically free. Every religion postulates his freedom that is to be culled out. For this purpose religion was developed. Religion is a human creation for bringing out the best in man. The founder of every religion often conceives in his mind the ideal image of man. This transformation was carried forth in history. It constitutes a unique phenomenon in the history of religions. We do not come across in other religious traditions the logical process of transforming man in the course of history. It was carried out during the Gurus' period. It is a unique contribution to the world religious traditions.

The quintessence of Indian traditions mostly adopt spiritual discipline for *rarefying* consciousness that gradually transcends from the empirical world. At the same time, consciousness (mind=*mana*) is developed from gross bodily elements and spirally goes up through mandals or khandas of ascension to identity with the supreme truth or consciousness. Consciousness is simultaneously attuned to the eternal truth and is engaged in the empirical world (*sansara*). It was distorted in the medieval ages. The Bhakti movement came into being to revive original concept of Indian metaphysics. Culture is the necessary epiphenomenon of the Indian metaphysics and societal realities are its necessary offshoots. This was the pivotal point which Sikhism continued.

The Bhakti Movement is a precursor to India's cultural revival. The Tamil Siddhas represented the Buddhist tradition which is a distinct stream from the Vedic one. In the Vitthala Bhakti tradition of Maharashtra, Shaivism is mixed up with Vaishnavism. The former dominated the latter. In Pandharpur cap on the icon of the deity symbolises Shaivism. This tradition spread in the North. Sikhism continued it and further developed. From this standpoint an endeavour is made to argue that Sikhism is a reinterpreted continuity of Indian culture. Sikh faith anchors solely on *nama-simran* for achieving the goal of life *here* and *now* while discharging all worldly responsibilities. Guru Nanak, the pioneer of the faith, had in his mind the ideal image of the gurmukh, which was transformed into the Khalsa (militant hero) of Guru Gobind Singh. This transformation was carried forth in history. We do not come across in other religious traditions the process of transforming man in the course of history.

It is believed in the religious traditions that man has the primary "essential" characteristic of *ruh / atman* and a secondary shaping characteristic of the *nafs / jiva*. When both are treated as distinct and independent elements in the human person, it will create diversity in the unity of the self. In respect of the former, every person's ontic identity of the 'I' is identical, but his magnified 'me' is diversified into multiplicities of the 'me,' which have 'I' latent in them. The 'me' is to be developed into the 'I' with esoteric discipline. Anyone who breathes and wears clothes either subsists or exists. In the true sense of the term, what makes his character distinct from other human beings are the spiritual attributes, feelings, instincts, and the singular personality traits, which spin around the 'I'. Once a person develops them, he realises his essential "I" in the existential situations as a fount of categorical imperative (*nishkama karma*). He realises in himself the 'I'.

Despite all these, one is to be vigilant about one's self-respect and independent distinct historical personal identity. In the Kantian sense, he should be treated as a "person," "a kingdom of ends and not means". The Sikh Scriptures advocate the distinct identities of the gurmukh and the Khalsa. His freedom and self-respect are to be safeguarded. If these are not granted to him, the issue of a separate state of consciousness crops up. The problem of the 'Sikh Homeland (*'Khalsathan'*) is not an abrupt political slogan but a natural explicable emergence in recent years. It needs an impartial rational analysis to underline the causes of its appearance. Because of discriminatory attitude of the majority community and fanatic attitude of the youth, this problem has come up. The agonies of the Sikhs are being suppressed through secular principles of democracy. The Khalsa of Guru Gobind Singh is to be governed by the divine principles of the Akala Purakh and secular principles of the state are periphery. Both cannot go hand in hand. This is basic existential dilemma of the Sikhs.

The central focus shall be on the contributors of the Sikh Canon (Namdeva, Kabir, Ravidasa and the Sikh Gurus). They made a radical departure from the prevalent medieval Indian culture and reinterpreted it from the hermeneutical and existential standpoints. They ruled out the hypostatised other-world and restored social realities and the historical reality of human action. For them everything exists in the nature (*qudrat*). They have projected man as a concrete social being in the nature. Man is real and his historical actions are real. At the time of birth man is a *jiva* ('me'). The eternal self *atman* is to be culled from within the *jiva* ('me'). Man creates his 'I' from within and then struggles with it in society to restore peace, harmony, and justice. He is to strive for bliss (*ananda*) and emancipation of humanity.

Man's life is considered a rare opportunity to realise the ontic reality. The human being is the only species that can transcend the empirical world and enjoy the life of intrinsic freedom. His life in the world is not a gross material life or of pure abstraction from the temporal realm. His life is like that of a moth that lives in the garden and enjoys the fragrance of the flowers without being entangled in them. It is simultaneously in the garden and out of the garden; it has the freedom to move out of the garden as well. Similarly, man is to live in the world, but should not be over engrossed in it. Man is to go through the tunnel of spiritual discipline before he enjoys this state of ecstasy.

In Sikhism, man is placed in the concrete existential moments created by the historical situations and the societal life. Unlike the Vedantic concept of incarnation, it is held that the incarnate (*avtara*) is dormant within man. It is to be aroused to make man act in history for executing the divine will as a responsible free moral person. The khalsa should always be ready to discharge his duties for the welfare of all and sundry. Here, the Khalsa means one who is always eager to face any eventuality and risk to life. He is an embodiment of disinterested deeds. Man is the miniature representative and executor of the divine will in history. Hence, he is a doer in history. This is the spirit of the Sikh dynamic view of human culture.

It may be said that negation of the world and the self were prevalent in the medieval ages. The medieval saints reinterpreted and reaffirmed the existence of the phenomenal world and the self. The Bhaktas ushered in the new trend of voluntarism and the Gurus struck the perfect change in the movement. In other words, the Bhaktas dotted the i's and the Gurus crossed the t's. Sikhism propounded the spiritual voluntarist philosophy, which gives precedence to praxis over theory without marginalising the latter. Volition and cognition go hand in hand, and former dominates. Voluntarism means autonomous action as distanced engagement in the temporal world. All ideals of human life are to be realised in the *sangat* of the householders. It stands for the restoration of social realities and repudiation of the otherworld. It is the singular contribution of the Sikh voluntarist view to the global thought. In the social context, abstract ritualism and formalism of the Vedantic tradition is devoid of spirituality. Sikhism restores human freedom that was epitome of all religions in the past. The Gurus preached and practised their ideals in the course of history. This is how theoretical and practical teachings have been concretised in praxis. Eternity has been yoked to the chariot of temporality.

However, this blending does not remain the same. Guru Nanak's philosophy of praxis erodes the Greek myth of eternal return or recurrence. It implies that every moment is new. It is revisiting the Heracleitean concept of 'change' and the Buddhist 'universal flux'. Therefore, only man has consciously created the history of humanity. He lives in history and creates history. He is, at once, a creature and a creator. Man, in praxis and history, is the creator of future. He does not live in the dead past and entertains false hopes of the otherworld. He is to perform his role in the playground of the 'eternal present'. This concept of praxis symbolises an eternal dynamic life. Man becomes man only if he realises his historical responsibilities for the emancipation of man. Guru Nanak's *gurmukh* is never alienated from the social realities. He is always active in the welfare of the real human beings.

Man is intrinsically hedonist. All human actions revolve around the pursuit of pleasure. He seeks *moksha* or *nirvana*, which is a rarefied pleasure—bliss (*ananda*). He wants to achieve this ideal by overcoming the existential problems in society. Thus, the concept of pleasure is an innate phenomenon in man. The genesis of religion lies in overcoming the impediments to life caused by the uncanny natural forces like floods, earthquakes or droughts. Man is expected to eradicate evil that is embedded within man and society. *Nama-simran* is the means for eradicating evil from within man's self. It is practised both in seclusion and in the holy assembly (*sangat*).

The meaning of bliss is changed from private and empirical pleasure or happiness to the welfare of other fellow beings. This disinterested involvement in the worldly life is the ideal of the Sikh ethics. Gurus translated this ideal into practice. He is not to fall a prey to the impermanent empirical pleasures that do not represent the lasting bliss. When he transcends his selfishness, he becomes an altruist in practical life. He sheds the sense of possessiveness and involvement in other selves. He becomes the true *gurmukh* or the Khalsa when he identifies himself with others and is motivated to be kind to the sentient and the insentient beings. His deeds make him realise the purpose of human life and discover the deeper meaning of life.

Each stage of life strengthens the urge to reintegrate oneself with each transcending stage in order to play its part in history and in the recycling of life in society. In Guru Nanak's "Japuji", the *khandas* (created conceptual spaces) from the *dharma-khanda* to the *sacha-khanda* represent the inward journey of the self towards an enriched and sublimated unity of the 'I' ("*atman*"). It is not withdrawal from the world. It is inward dive to merge with the cosmic consciousness and resurrect to life in the world. It is disinterested involvement while discarding worldly desires and the ego-sense. It is a psycho-social development of the self from the 'me' to the 'I' through the inner rigorous self-discipline. The self, thus, becomes an active and voluntarist entity.

The meaning of life is idealized and made authentic by man's creativity. Is there any meaning in life at different levels, ranging from an amoeba to human beings or from neurotic humans to superhuman beings and God? The modern existentialists are preoccupied with this problem. The scientists are engaged in researches to make man happy, but it is the concern of the philosopher and the religious thinkers to work out the solution of human problems. Hence, the problem of meaning and purpose of life is man's articulation for working out the existential problems and their solutions. It is in this context that the exploration of the meaning of life gains ascendance.

Human beings have inherent urge for autonomy, which is present even in lower species. As compared to lower species, man creates the articulated world of his own. Birds and animals construct their nests and dens in accordance with their levels of existence and needs of the specific species to which they belong. They have territorial sense, but they have no higher creativity of linguistic articulation that may help them to have freedom and creativity. Man, on the contrary, knows how to create. He creates his own ideal world to realise autonomy.

He knows how to articulate concepts to the appropriate use. He forges tools in accordance with his will and mind. The realised man wills in tune with the cosmic law. The whole argument boils down to the point that articulation of the concept of praxis is a universal and self-creative activity. It is to be developed as a free and conscious enterprise. It then evolves in peaceful atmosphere, and it must be preceded by intensity of suffering. The genesis of creativity is put to use in the existential situations. From this concept, the affirmation of historicity of social action follows. If man is a self-creative being, then he constantly creates and changes himself and the world around him. In every altered condition, man recreates a new world in order to mirror the Akala Purakh. The Being is always recycling and reincarnates itself in new myriad forms. The Being remains concealed for the ignorant. The creative genius has the ability to project it in the form of ideology (world-view). It is not the Platonic Being that is pre-existent and beyond time and space. Becoming exists in the Heracleitean time of the 'universal flux'.

The well-known Western philosopher Arthur Schopenhauer in *The World as Will and Representation* and Nietzsche in *The Birth of Tragedy* propound the tragic view of life. Schopenhauer in the second part of his work says the power of transporting the audience or reader is peculiar to tragedy. It arises from our sudden recognition that life fails to provide any true satisfactions and, hence, does not deserve our loyalty. Tragedy guides us to the final goal, which is resignation or self-surrender to the cosmic will.

Man is a prisoner in the cave of *maya*, and his feet are chained to societal relations. Schopenhavewr's tragic vision of life is symbolic of the blind alley of the existential human conditions in which he is placed. He has been unsuccessfully grappling with the empirical world. Nietzsche, however, tries to wriggle out of the quagmire of the world with the help of the inherent "will to power". Both end their quests with a tragic note. On the other hand, Indian philosophy transcends the phenomenal world and enters the haven of *moksha/nirvana*. Guru Nanak strikes a balance between the two extremes. This is the essence of the philosophical teachings of the medieval Bhaktas and the Gurus.

The tragic view of life needs to be traced from its primordial cause of misery. It is not sufficient to say that the tragic view of life exists only in art, rather it is also found in literature, poetry, and drama. It emanates from the metaphysical underpinnings of life. In the Indian thought, the tragic effects of the *sansara* are overcome by the hero's dynamic and fearless encounter with existential human predicaments. He delivers himself from the overt and avid thirst for earthly desires and transports himself through his artistic and philosophical creativity and esoteric discipline, to a higher existential space of living in the world. Sikhism, thus, views human life from the existential and socialist standpoints. Its 'groundless ground' or self-existence is spiritual, but that is at once secularised and reversed through *sangat, seva,* Akala Takht, and so on.

The tragic and pessimistic views of life imply that man is eternally condemned to agony and suffering. In Christianity, it is due to the 'eternal sin' owing to disobedience to the divine command. In Islam, the original suffering is caused by the violation of divine law by Iblis. He is the archetypal cipher of disobedience and defiance in the Qur'an. In the Vedanta and Buddhism, suffering is caused by intrinsic ignorance (*avidya*) and in Sikhism, *haumai*, as an individuating force, is at the root of eternal sufferings. The transformation of *haumai* into Thou-consciousness is the central lynchpin of the Sikh faith.

The medieval Bhaktas and Guru Nanak boldly face this ticklish existential problem. They leave no stone unturned to create an optimal balance between this world and the transcendent eternal reality through an overdose of voluntarist optimism and the dynamic life. They try to strike a balance between asceticism and eroticism. According to them, the purpose of life is to attain emancipation from human suffering and misery while living in society.

Guru Nanak's viewpoint advocates the dynamic and existential view of life in the world. He reconciles the Indic and the Semitic religious traditions without suppressing either one. Sikhism assimilates heterogeneous elements of both the cultures. The Gurus strived to eradicate evil and tyranny from India. For this purpose, they exploited the heroic spirit of the multiracial society of the land. Guru Nanak was a different kind of mendicant. He was concerned with the existential social realities and culture of the land. His *sacha-khanda* is an ideal social order, which was concretised through history by the subsequent eight Gurus, and Guru Gobind Singh gave the process final touch by creation of the Khasla-panth in CE 1699. The Khalsa ideology is a concrete viewpoint in history. Guru Gobind Singh apatheosised the script for as living guru till eternity (i.e., *jugo jug atal*). He passed over gurudam to shabad (word). The prophet as charismatic religious leader was ruled out. He rules out the concept of incarnation.

The central problem of the chapter is to highlight the efforts of the Gurus for steeling will of the subaltern marginalised populace so that it could confront boldly the tyranny and rebel against cruelty of the alien invaders. Their approach was existential approach toward societal problems. They successfully unfettered Indians from the alien dominance of the Muslim servility. This was one of the contributions of the Gurus. For this purpose, man is projected as a concrete valiant hero who is ready to stake his life for truth. It is concerned with problematic issues of the medieval ages. It will also enable the readers to have the comprehensive understanding and bird's eye view of the Indian culture.

Bhakti cult was a subaltern revivalist and protestant movement of voluntarism. It was a sharp reaction to the Islamic cultural invasions. In the medieval ages, the socio-religious florescence emerged in the South and it spread into the North like a wild fire. It checkmated the malignant influence of Muslim rulers. Its proponents gathered momentum in India. It rejected casteism and despotism, gender discrimination and hegemony of the priestly class, and dominance of the feudal lords. The priestly class created the myth of the otherworld that resulted in life and world negation. There was a powerful resurgence in cultural revival in India. The medieval bhaktas emerged as a counterforce. To reverse the prevalent trends the bhaktas exerted strenuous struggle. The medieval saints (say, Ravidasa, Sein, *et al.*) motivated regional Indian rulers of principalities for resisting alien invaders.

The Sikh Gurus made a radical departure from the prevalent rituals and inspired the devotees for self-dignified life. The very birth of Sikhism owes itself to active resistance to tyranny (*ati*). They owned responsibility to destroy tyranny on the Indian soil. Thus, the Sikh movement emphasises on active resistance to evil and struggle in life. It fortified will of the Indians. It was a voluntarist movement. The purpose of life of Sikh faith culminates in supreme sacrifice It conquers death and steels will power for executing the goal of human life. It leads to heroic life in the world. It created nation of the khalsa who defied temporal sovereignty of the Mughal Emperors. This kind of life was missing in the medieval India. It was due to weak will power of the Indians that they underwent servility for centuries. The Gurus strengthened will of the orphaned masses. They developed steadfast faith in their leitmotiv—the supreme Deity. This is a dauntless religious conviction to offer for supreme sacrifice for the sake of higher values. The Gurus evolved cultural and militant concept of martyrdom. Thus, militant element was infused into the subaltern people.

In the medieval times, the priestly class separated this world from the concrete social realities. The Gurus concretised the abstract world that was to be lived heroically *here* and *now*. They sharpened the edge of revolt against the prevalent morbid social order. The Sikh Gurus made supreme sacrifices and struggled hard to revive essence of ancient Indian spiritual and heroic culture. It led to heroic life in the world. The masses successfully realised their coveted goal of self-dignity and autonomy.

Guru Nanak, also, considers man as concrete unit in historical time and propounds dynamic view of life. In order to strike reconciliation between eternity and temporality, the ten Sikh Gurus from Guru Nanak to Guru Gobind Singh (CE 1469-1708), carried forth their crusade for revivification of the ideal of fluxional stark social reality.

Whatever, Guru Nanak preached and practised in his life was carried forth by eight Gurus and Guru Gobind Singh gave to it a finishing touch. Guru Nanak tried to reconcile theory and praxis, which is the central linchpin of almost all developed religions. They wanted to put in to 'use' their ideals into practice. Sikhism deals with concrete social life in history from the existential viewpoint. There was no contradiction in their *saying*, and *doing*. Guru Nanak sums up in one of his hymns in the Guru Granth (p.62) that truth is higher than all kinds of truth, but truthful living is higher than those. Guru Arjundeva pronounces attitude toward 'power' as under:

> Seek I neither kingship nor liberation,
> My mind yearns for reposing at Thy lotus feet.
>
> Guru Granth, p. 534

(ii) Passage from *Sacha-Khanda* to *Khalsa-panth*

The Medieval Bhakti cult in India initiated the process of desacralising and socialising religion that culminated in the hands of Guru Gobind Singh. He concretised the dream of ideal of *sacha-khanda*. The religion which had been cut off from the social life was given a new orientation and brought closer to the society. Thus, the term desacralisation stands for the process by which a religious faith — overshadowed by superstitions, rituals, absurd commands, and beliefs — is emancipated from the dogmatic and exegetical exposition, and — its understanding is based on the rational interpretation. The Gurus contributed a lot in this respect. Their teachings did not have an aura of the cultural and religious superiority. On the contrary, the Gurus propounded catholicity of truth and promoted human virtues that could unite mankind.

The process of restoration of the social realities was emphasised by the Gurus. Guru Nanak created centres of preaching in India. These were called the *manjis* (dioceses): the centres of preaching the Sikh tenets to the *sangats*. When we have a bird's view of the Golden Temple and the Akala Takht, both reconcile eternity and temporality. The erection of the Akala Takht at Amritsar, adjacent to the Golden Temple (Harmandir Sahib), represents the response to the historical and the political challenges. The tyranny let loose by the Mughal Emperors forced the Sikh Movement to assume the militant form. The erection of the Akala Takht (throne of the Eternal) by Guru Hargobind was not just an extended architectural structure, adjacent to the Golden Temple. The Golden Temple symbolises the deep-roots of the ancient heroic cultural heritage of India.

The Golden Temple, immersed in water, is symbolic of spirituality (*piri*) and the Akala Takht is its martial (*miri*) dimension. It was an addition of the martial dimension to the devotional dimension. It needed deep insight into the history of the land and understanding of the culture, and sensibility and moral commitment to humanity. The architectural structure of the Golden Temple and that of the Akala Takht symbolise the inseparable dimensions of *piri* and *miri* respectively. Guru Hargobind's understanding of the Indian culture was the coeval necessity. He created the values for the coming generations that had been derived from the martyrdom of Guru Arjunadeva.

The martyrdom of Guru Arjunadeva and Guru Tegh Bahadur embraced the supreme sacrifice for the sake of truth and moral values. They were fully attuned themselves to the divine will of the Akala Purakh. The instances of martyrdom reaffirm the societal relationships and the living social responsibilities. Their supreme sacrifices gave new lease of life to the Sikh movement and paved way for the deliverance of humanity from the suffering and the cruelty of the then Mughal Emperors. Their sacrifice became the icons for the emancipation of the suffering human beings. They are the shining steadfast pole stars that guide the distracted selves from the path of Truth and the moral obligations.

The '*takhts*' and their *Jathedars* (custodians) in the Sikh tradition occupy a very significant position. The Sikh *sangats* often seek advice from the Jathedar of the Akala Takht as if he were the supreme authority of the Sikhs. In the Sikh tradition the Akala Takht occupies the pivotal position.

Leadership of the Gurus continued till the tenth mentor Guru Gobind Singh's demise in CE 1708. At that time the Guru did not nominate the custodian (*jathedar*) to take care of the Akala Takht. Guru Gobind Singh discontinued the personal guruship which in turn came to be represented by the five beloved ones (*panja piare*). Bhai Mani Singh was sent from Anandpur Sahib, along with five Khalsas, as in-charge (*sevadar*) to look after the Golden Temple.

Thus, individual responsibility was transferred to the collective responsibility of the five khalsas. It shows that the collective leadership was developed by the Gurus. It was based on Guru Nanak's maxim of the supremacy of the collective will of the wise persons (i.e. *panncha parvan, panncha pardhan*). The underlying idea of the collective leadership is that an individual can err, but the five persons will not commit an error. The erection of the Akala Takht at Amritsar adjacent to the Golden Temple was a historical step in the direction of evolving collective responsibility and the martial spirit.

The collective responsibility of the *panja piare* was a historical necessity. Church, a social institute, grew after the tenth mentor's demise. Immediate coming up of the *jagirdars* and the *jathedars* was a deviation from the fundamental tenets of Sikhism. The centralised power of the mighty Mughal Empire collapsed and it was usurped by the feudalist forces. The maxim of "might is right" was order of the day. The country was divided into splintered feudalities. In the post-Guru period the Sikh confederations (*misls*) came into being. It was revisiting the feudal system. The militant Sikh confederations were headed by the *jathedars*. Historically the Gurus were the rallying central charismatic personalities. When the Book was replaced by the *shabda-guru*, personalities of the feudal leadership emerged. Then social institutions emerged and social and political aspects overshadowed the Book and the church. Feudalism revived in the form of *misls* (confederations) headed by the *jathedars / sirdars*.

The emblem of the saffron flag on the Akala Takht is the sign of freedom of the self and the synthesis of the temporal and the spiritual. The Akala Takht is the result of the Guru's deep sense of the existential project. The dormant *shakti* in the *bhakti* became the manifest *shakti* with the erection of the Akala Takht. It was an expression of the Guru's deep vision of Indian culture and history. Guru Nanak sowed the seed of the militant theocracy which with the passage of time was developed into a sapling that grew to full glory in the creation of the Khalsa-panth. Thus, the two concepts, the martial and the spiritual, were blended into one on the earth. The Gurus had intuitive understanding of the ancient Indian culture. They could feel the pulse of the people and the meaning or purpose of the human life. In short, the Akala Takht is the true architectural symbol in bricks and mortar of the Akala Purakh's will on the earth. The sign of *khanda* signifies reconciliation of *miri* and *piri* in which sainthood is the domineering spirit.

In the hands of Guru Hargobind, the spiritual power was supplemented with the temporal power and polity. His active resistance to injustice and cruelties reflects his spiritual voluntarism, coupled with the temporal voluntarism. From the existential standpoint, it stands for complete commitment to the emancipation of humanity. For instance, Guru Hargobind's four battles in Punjab against the Mughal armies signify his historical sense of moral commitment to his people. Gobind Rae's appeal to his father (Guru Tegh Bahadur) for laying down his life for the sake of justice also signifies his historical responsibility. The young Guru Gobind Rae was fully conscious that his father was sure to be beheaded, but he could not turn his back on the moral commitment to the victims of fanaticism of a despot. Subsequently, he engaged himself in perilous battles that had been thrust upon him.

His *khanda*-baptism is the complete identification of his will with the collective will of the Khalsa-panth, the societal reflection of the eternity. The collective will of the *panja piare* represents the whole humanity and the eternity. And the wills of the individuals receive inspiration from the Akala Purakh. The Khalsa, thus, reconciles spirituality and temporality with the grace of the Akala Purakh.

The Sikh movement transformed the personal identity of the gurmukh into the khalsa who mirrors the Akala Parakh on the earth. The peaceful *sangat* turned into the militant society of the Khalsa-panth. The spiritual militant unity could adjust to the changing societal conditions. And it developed into the militant civil society of the Khalsa-panth. It was the movement of resurrection of the fortified will for the welfare of humanity irrespective of any rank, sex, religion, caste, race, ethnicity, and other worldly considerations. The Khalsa-panth, was the ground-breaking bold resistance to tyranny, atrocities, and injustice. It was the solemn moral commitment to the resolution for discharging the historical duties. The medieval Islamic hegemonic aggression on the Indian indigenous culture was actively resisted. Sikhism, in the Gurus' period, developed the distinct militant ideology and cultural identity. It assimilated the essential elements of the alien cultures into the composite culture of the land. The Gurus injected the martial spirit into the castrated and the effeminised Indians.

The Gurus' period in the Sikh history is the period of reinterpretation of the scriptures and the religious traditions. Thus, every interpretation either of the sacred scriptures or of the tradition is in flux. The scriptures are not of one age, but of all the ages because they propound the eternal truth. The tradition stems from the scripture, the historical and the political exigencies. We can safely infer from the above discussion that the interpreter has to be hermeneutically equipped to make us discern the ciphers in the 'sacred texts'. We should develop the intuition for understanding the contemporaneous rational truth in the texts. The philosophical hermeneutics, enriched by the cultural understanding, is better because it enables us to draw all the possible logical implications of the statements, recorded in the sacred texts. Logical consistency and necessary relationships between the linguistic elements are being worked out in the process of understanding the ciphers. The hermeneutical objective understanding is directed towards truth and meanings. Such understanding of the interpreter is freed from the original authorial intention and the prison of subjectivity, solipsism and ethnocentrism. Philosophically all the interpretations are the reinterpretations of the original illuminations of the mystics. They are restructured out of the ruins of the past interpretations. This point can be substantiated from the history of the religious tradition. The Sikh tradition, from Guru Nanak to Guru Gobind Singh, is the continuous process of interpretation of the existential socio-political situations.

With a view to emancipating people from suffering, the Sikh movement was the revolt of the *atman* against evil and atrocities in the society. The martial spirit in Sikhism was the logical and existential necessity for eradicating evil and atrocities in the society for restoring justice and peace.

We are confronted with a question whether there was a deviation in the Sikh movement from Guru Hargobind to Guru Gobind Singh because the dimension of the martial spirit was added to the spiritual. When Guru Hargobind met Samrath Guru Ramadasa (spiritual mentor of Shivaji) at Shrinagar Gadwall in U.P. (India), he replied to him that the real sainthood lies in inward piety and outward regality is its manifestation. Guru Hargobind justified the martial spirit to Samrath Guru Ramadasa. He meant that one should be internally spiritual and outwardly martial (i.e. *batin faqiri zahra amiri*). The point I make is that there was no doctrinal deviation in contending transformation in the Sikh movement. Rather it was continuation of the original Bhaktas' and the Gurus' implicit message that was made explicit. The original message was to resist atrocity boldly.

Our understanding of the Sikh religion from the standpoints of social, economic and political standpoints introduce the existential socio-political problem of power. This is the concrete interpretation of Sikhism in history. Sikhism accepts neither overindulgence in the temporal power nor does it favour cowardly withdrawal from the historical commitments and the active resistance to tyranny.

The ideal of renouncing (*sannyasa*) from the temporal power and shunning the active disinterested struggle in the world for righteousness was reinterpreted. With this interpretation the Gurus continued their crusade in history. It was fully realised in the Dasam Granth. Now it is self-evident that in Sikhism power is not to be exploited for worldly lucrative gains and to harm the enemies. Violence is to be used for the eradication of evil in society. In the Sikh faith the use of force for the welfare of humanity is the highest form of *ahinsa*. The use of the sword as the defensive weapon is used for restoring social justice in the society. It is not used for encroachment on others' territories and grabbing their wealth and property. This was the *sui generis* contribution of the Sikh Gurus to the social thought of India. So violence is the defensive tool or force for giving a new life to the depressed and the deprived masses. It is manifestation of the voluntarist view of life.

In this context, the most important point to note is the simultaneous self-surrender and retaining of one's historical personal identity. It means that self in the historical time and space is real and action in history is also real. It is the philosophical interpretation of Ramanuja's doctrine of self-surrender (*sharnagati*) and the Tantric reaffirmation of the reality of the human person. The human body is the instrument for discharging the moral and the voluntarist deeds. In Buddhism and the Vedanta the human body was negated. Earlier we also find that practically Buddhism and the Vedantists negated the historical personal identity of the self as an active agent (*karta*) in the temporal world.

Sikhism has positively reinterpreted the concept of the *sannyasa*. It gave birth to confirm involvement with the mundane world. Guru Nanak reinterpreted the cipher of the Indian concept of the *sannyasa*. It is the key concept in the Indian social philosophy which has been reinterpreted by the Bhaktas and the Gurus. In the medieval times this concept had created a chasm between the visible and the invisible worlds. This chasm does not fit in the pronounced dynamic non-dual onto-theology of Sikhism. It does not permit negation of the human body and the external world. The self realises its true ontic nature in the world. The human body is the raft (*beda*) which helps him to realise the coveted goals of human life. There is no need to aspire for the otherworld. It is true that consciousness is the precondition of all knowledge and judgements. Consciousness with the help of the word moves from the ego-consciousness to the cosmic-consciousness. It is how the *manmukh* is transformed into the gurmukh. If the external world is negated, the historical reality of the human action cannot be accepted. As a result, the people would start withdrawing from the societal realities and the arduous responsibilities of the human life like those of the medieval ages.

Guru Nanak in the *mulmantra* (creedal statement) of the Japuji used a hyperbole of two terms '*nirbhau nirvair*', meaning thereby absence of any extraneous control that implies freedom from the fear of death. It warrants freedom of action and solidarity with other fellow beings. When any type of cruelty occurs against any person(s), it is our moral duty to resist the cruel person. Thus, the idea of active resistance to overcome evil and tyranny was already existent in the Sikh Canon. The VIth Guru and the subsequent Gurus only accentuated it. It was the Khalsa-panth and, further, to the khalsa. It was transformation of the *manmukh* into the *gurmukh* that actively fought against evil forces. In other words, it was the development from the society of saints (*gurmukhs*) to the militant civilised society of the khalsa.

The khalsa is an ideal man of Guru Gobind Singh who is above the sectarian and parochial outlook. He is the guarantor of justice and destroyer of evil and tyranny in the society. The khalsa an individual and social order mirrors the supreme Reality. The khalsa, an emancipator of mankind, is the representative of the Akala Purakh on the earth. He is expected to live up to this ideal in the practical life. It is the institutionalised form of the militant Sikh society.

The above development in the Sikh tradition signifies the dynamic nature of the Sikh faith. The very essence (*tat*) of the illumination remained unchanged, but the tradition was transformed. With the culmination of this development the charismatic personality or personal guruship was dispensed with and replaced with the *shabda-guru* as the divine monarch and the Khalsa-panth is the militant democratic polity. Both are inseparably intertwined with the domineering note of the former. It is called *gurmata* in the Sikh tradition. It developed in the post-Guru period.

From the point of view of the socio-political milieu, the concept of the true king-guru (spiritual-king) in the Sikh tradition in the times of Guru Arjunadeva was an internal development within the Sikh social thought. This phenomenon is unique in the Sikh tradition as well as in other Indian traditions. We do not find any such historical development in other religious traditions. As a rebuff to the tyrant Mughal Emperors the Sikh *sangat* started calling Guru Arjunadeva as the true king (*sacha-patsha*). The Mughal Emperor Jehangir was ignored and Guru Arjunadeva was accepted as the true king or *raj-guru* like Janak of ancient India. The concept of the true kingship was transformed into the *shabda-guru*. It was conceptualised by Guru Gobind Singh and the holy Sikh Scripture was raised to the status of the supreme Deity. It is the connecting link between the Akala Purakh and the Khalsa (individual) and the Khalsa-panth (militant society) of the Khalsa. Thus, the idea of the Sikh polity is embedded in the Sikh Scripture and the tradition. It is deep-rooted in the psyche of the Sikh folk. This concept became more pronounced after the martyrdom of Guru Arjundeva.

The Sikh voluntarism stems from the individual's free will. The divine will (*hukam*) carries out its purposes through the realised person's will. The medieval Bhakti cult formed a prelude to Sikh voluntarism. The first five Gurus had prepared the background and their successors actualised it in history. Till the last breath of their earthly sojourn, they wrestled with absurdities of the existential life. The philosophy of negation of life and the world in the medieval ages was in vogue world over. The Gita is a philosophical treatise on the spiritual voluntarism, but the laity and most of the scholars have misinterpreted it. As a result of it, they withdrew from the worldly responsibilities. The medieval Bhaktas again revived the voluntarist trend that was reinforced by the Gurus' and consummated in the khalsa creation.

Sikhism being a concrete realistic and idealistic system should be interpreted from the standpoint in which the spiritual values are given priority over the empirical facts. The dynamic ontology of the Sikh Gurus reflects the societal structure (*sangat*) constituted of the individuals who are the miniature representations of the Akala Purakh on the earth. Man, a unit in the social network, is projected as the concrete person in temporality. His historical actions are real and the societal relationships are based on the principles of equality, fraternity, and freedom. The Sikh Gurus critiqued the prevalent Hindu social order which was based on the hierarchical, caste based social structure. The subalterns were marginalised. The common masses were deprived of the spiritual values in theory and practice. Thus, the voluntarist philosophy of the Sikh Gurus lays more emphasis on the societal relations and the *sangat* and the 'Khalsa'. Revival of the spiritual and the historical identities is the *leitmotif* of the Sikh Canon.

The *sangat* is the holy assembly or social group in which the holy name is recited. Guru Nanak created the *sangats* in different parts of India to disseminate the Sikh tenets. The institution of the *gurudwara* is a recent development from the *sangat*. The *gurudwara* is an abode of collective worship under one roof in a building. It was not the innovation of the Gurus. In fact, Guru Nanak created the small and the big *sangats* for preaching the Sikh tenets in the very beginning the Sikh faith. The Sikh Scripture and the Gurus had been striving to put an end to the personal guruship since its inception. There is no room for the priestly class in Sikhism. In the first quarter of the twentieth century the institution of the *gurudwaras* came into being. The mushroom coming up of the institution of the *gurudwaras* is accompanied by the resurrection of the personality cult of the personal guruship. The priestly class, which is non-existent in the Sikh faith, stealthily crept into the Sikh tradition. It leads us to the discussion of the Sikh moral conduct (*rahit maryada*).

The moral conduct of the khalsa is obligatory for the baptised persons. It developed gradually in the Gurus' period, but it was institutionalised in the period of the tenth mentor. The contemporary devout Sikhs and the scholars articulated it in the form of written manuscripts on moral conduct (*Rahit Namas*). In order to authenticate the documents citations from the scripture were given. Some "Rahit Namas" assert that Guru Gobind Singh himself laid down the moral prescriptions. These utterances are called "*Shri Mukh Vaka Pashahi-10*". The authors of the *Rahit Namas* were contemporary associates of Guru Gobind Singh. They had the privilege to have the blessings of the guru. The main writer of the *Rahit Namas* is Bhai Chaupa Singh, Bhai Prahlad Singh, Bhai Nand Lal, *et al.* Morality should emanate from the scripture itself. It also evolves from the life events of the originators of the faith. When the pioneers disappear from the scene, many deviations and digressions crop up into the faith. The fundamental principles of morality remain, but the norms and modes change with the changing conditions. Thus, the moral conduct has been changing in the Sikh tradition according to the changed social and political exigencies. The follower of the Sikh faith is required to work in the field as the farmer and the tiller of the land. Honest hard labour is the very spirit of the Sikh moral conduct.

The Gurus had been using the conceptual or imaginary attributes (*kirtam namas*) of the Divinity ('That') borrowed from the Indian scriptures and the Qur'an, but Guru Gobind Singh used *kirtam namas* that could affirm the historical reality of the mundane world and the historical human action. One's historical action can unfold itself simultaneously in the eternity and temporality. In the Dasam Granth the Sikh doctrines are put to execution in praxis. Perhaps, this is one of the most important factor for the institutionalisation of the Sikh *rahit maryada*.

The mythical identity was congealed into the historical identity. The 'me', the 'I' and the 'Thou' are telescoped into one groundless identity of the Akala Purakh. In Sikhism the 'me' first clashes with other fellow beings in the world when it is dominated by the *haumai*. When the 'me' is transformed into the 'I', it identifies itself with the Akala Purakh. The 'I' is the microcosm and the 'Thou' is the linguistic construct of the macrocosm. The attributive imaginary and historical attributes are valid in the phenomenal world, but in the transcendental realm they disappear. If man does not retain his personal identity and is cut off from the temporal world, he cannot affirm the societal realities. It is possible only if he simultaneously identifies himself with the Akala Purakh and acts as a voluntarist in the moral collective struggle of life. This is the gist of Sikh dynamic view of life.

(iii) Akala Takht: Concretisation of Eternity

The Akala Takht gives precedence to spirituality over temporality, but over the time the relationship between *piri* and *miri* has been reversed because of over dominance of politics and orthodoxy of the clerics and the politicians. It means that politics (*miri*) dominates religion (*piri*). It is contrary to Guru Hargobind's interpretation.

The '*takht*' is a Persian word which means a seat or plank for sitting. Takht is a throne of the temporal emperor or king. The kings used it for sitting on a cushion. In Sikhism eternity is concretised in the Akala Takht—an embodiment of eternity (Akala Purakh). Its meaning was transferred into 'throne of the king'. Thus, in the Persian tradition the '*takhat*' assumed connotation of seat of temporal power of the king. The Sikh tradition radicalised the meaning of the concept of the 'takht'. It has a central or a very significant position. It is not throne ('takht' of the temporal emperor or king. It is throne of the Akala Purakh who controls functioning of cosmos. Here temporality and spirituality are blended into one and the spirituality dominates temporality. Both are inseparable from each other. The role of the Guru was executor of the divine will. The will of the Guru and the cosmic will were interchangeable. From the philosophical point of view the Akala Takht is concretisation of eternity in time. It was the singular contribution to the Indian culture and the world thought. The Gurus lived unto their ideals. There is no contradiction in their coveted ideals and practical life.

The Sikh *sangats,* often, sought advice from the *jathedar* (custodian) of the Akala Takht as if he was the supreme authority of the Sikhs. In the Sikh tradition, the Akala Takht at Amritsar occupies the central position. The other four takhts are at Anandpur Sahib, Damdama Sahib, Patna Sahib (Bihar), and Nanded Sahib (Maharashtra). The Akala Takht as 'Akala Bunga' came into being during the period of Guru Hargobind. He constructed it at eight-foot high mound facing Harmandir Sahib. Initially it was raised on a basement and Maharaja Ranjit Singh added the present three storeyed building to it during the confederation (Persian, *misl*) period. Its height was kept two feet higher than the temporal Mughal throne at Delhi. Here Guru Hargobind at the age of eleven was adorned with two swords of *miri* and *piri*, instead of traditional "*seli topi*" (woolen cord and cap), worn by the earlier Gurus and

Bhaktas of the Sikh Canon. He also wore a turban adorned with an aigrette (*kalgi*) and held a falcon (*baj*) in his hand and rode a horse as emblems of royalty. He sat here and held court to discuss and decide common community problems. The Guru issued edicts (*Hukamname*) from it to the Sikh congregations (*sangats*).

When Guru Gobind Singh was besieged in the fortress at Chamkaur Sahib he obeyed the order of the five baptised khalsas. When Guru Gobind Singh bowed at Narayana (Rajasthan) to Pir Dadu's grave, the five Khalsas imposed fine (*tankha*) on him. When Banda Singh Bahadur was dispatched to Punjab, he was accompanied by five khalsas as his advisers. Here I want to argue that the collective leadership of the *Panja Piaras* from the sixth to the ninth Guru evolved. The underlying idea of collective leadership was that an individual could, but five persons' collective resolution (*mata*) will not commit error. Hence, there was erection of the Akala Takht at Amritsar adjacent to the Golden Temple. He created a new consciousness for humankind for the coming generations that were derived from the particular event of the martyrdom of Guru Arjunadeva.

The Sikh movement regained concrete identity of man in the society and spiritual social unity, which could adjust to the changing societal conditions as well. Logically it developed into a militant society of the Khalsa-panth. The genesis of Sikhism was a bold revolt of conscience against brutality of the Central Asian invaders and shameless effeminacy of the indigenous priestly class and the feudal exploiters. It was a movement of resurrection of the righteous sense for the welfare of humanity irrespective of any rank, sex, religion, caste, race, ethnicity, and other worldly considerations. The Sikh philosophy is a ground-breaking bold resistance to tyranny, atrocities, and injustice.

The Gurus' sense of history, manifested in the concrete form of the Akala Takht (eternal throne), is an epiphany of the Akala Purakh. Unlike the Vedantic and the Buddhist standpoints, the manifestation is real. In other words, eternity descends on the earth for emancipation of humanity. The Akala Takht mirrors eternity in history. It, therefore, enjoins upon us to discuss the institution of the Akala Takht, which transformed the Sikh insurgence to a militant movement.

My attempt is to focus on the essence and its appearances that are its epiphanies. The phenomenological method investigates the religious phenomenon that is devoid of any ontology. The phenomenological significance of the Akala Takht lies in its temporal and spatial categories, which at once signify eternity and spirituality.

When we have a view of crow flight the two magnificent buildings, from above the Harmandir Sahib or Darbar Sahib (Golden Temple) and the Akala Takht, we find that the pavement bridges both. The architectural structure artwork is such that the pavement between the two signifies that both constitute an integrated unity of eternity and temporality. It gives the impression that the Akala Takht and the Darbar Sahib is a ship that can take us across the mundane world (*bhava sagar*). It signifies that both constitute telescoped together unity of eternity and temporality. The complex may be likened to a raft (*beda)* that takes travelers from the mundane world to a higher realm of *sacha-khanda*. It symbolises epiphany of the Akala Purakh. The Darbar Sahib immersed in the blue water signifies its universality and immanence of the Divine.

From the aesthetic viewpoint, the blue shade of the water signifies its vastness. The floating Harmandir Sahib in the tank reminds us that Guru Nanak's metaphors of the lotus (*kamal*) and the duck are in the water but both remain dry. It is an eye-opener for us to become an ideal person. The gold-plated dome-shaped structure of the Harmandir Sahib and *shabda-kirtan* of the holy hymns from the Guru Granth elevates the devotees to a state of equanimity (*sahaj*). One feels as if a self is ascending to eternity while standing in the precincts of the holy complex. It takes man's consciousness to higher and higher realms of spirituality. While listening to kirtan from the Guru Granth, we have a peace of mind. We have a glimpse of spirituality through the dome-shaped architectural structure. It radiates multi-coloured sounds of spirituality through recitation of the divine word (*shabda-kirtan*). The environment is resounded with hymns of the *gurbani*. It is a perennial source of solace for the distressed souls of the devotees.

It is a living faith of the devotees that a dip in the holy tank at the Darbar Sahib cleanses all of their sins. A visit to the complex makes one oblivious of the mundane worries and sorrows. It is healer of human sufferings and ills. The four doors signify omnipresence of the Divine. It also signifies that all doors are open to all castes without gender discrimination. Persons of other religious are also welcome to the Golden Temple. The emblem of two ochre (*kesri*) flags, fluttering in the blue sky in front of the Akala Takht, is a sign of triumph of spirituality over temporality. The ochre is the blending of two primary colours, yellow and red.

Generally yellow symbolises spreading, defusing, and pervasiveness of light. In religion, yellow colour signifies renunciation and spirituality. It also signifies sacrifice for higher values. Guru Arjundeva's attire was yellow. Bhagat Singh Shaheed wore yellow (*kesri,* coloured cloths before proceeding to the gallows. Moreover, red symbolises intensity of emotions, passion and it also symbolises martial spirit.

Both are to be blended harmoniously. Thus, the semiotics of two ochre flags is synthesis of spiritual and martial spirits. The unfurled flags are the signs of freedom of the self. It may be pertinent to point out that the saffron colour in the yogic and the Vedantic traditions are symbolic of renunciation from the world. Kabir in one of his hymns criticises the spurious yogis that they have dyed their cloaks with dark saffron colour, but not their minds. The Gurus have reinterpreted the saffron colour. For the Gurus the red colour is symbolic of martial spirit and the yellow represents renunciation. When both are mixed, the resultant colour is *kesri*. Their harmonious blending coheres with the ideal of human life.

The Akala Takht was built at Amritsar in CE 1609. Bhakti was transformed into the manifest shakti with the erection of the Akala Takht. It was a sign of Guru's creativity and sense of historical commitment to humanity for eradicating suffering. Guru Nanak sowed the seed, which developed into a sapling of the militant spirit. The martyred two Gurus irrigated the plant of Guru Nanak's faith with their blood. They revitalised the Sikh insurgence. It blossomed in the creation of the Khalsa-panth. Thus, two swords of martiality and spirituality are complementary to each other. The sixth and the tenth Gurus, thus, created history of martial spirit on the earth. The Sikh tradition has been embedded in it. The Sikh tradition records that B[1]aba Buddha ji a companion of Guru Nanak, adorned the Guru with two swords of *piri* and miri. Henceforth, the Guru always girded around his waist two swords of *piri* and *miri*. The Guru fought all the defensive battles against the Mughals with the sword. This is the innocent quintessence of the Sikh faith. The Gurus had deep full understanding of the ancient Indian culture. Its significance of the Akala Takht is the necessary existential and *logical outcome* of the political and historical exigencies. Earlier the temple was called the Harmandir Sahib, but after the construction it was renamed Darbar Sahib, the exalted court of the Akala Purakh. The genesis of the Akala Takht is a gradual process of historicisation of the development of the Sikh movement. The combined architecture of the Akala Takht and the Golden Temple complex signifies the hidden meanings of martiality and spirituality. Both are bridged with a pathway, which is a symbol of the Akala Purakh in the world. The architecture is a symbol of custodianship or trusteeship of the Akala Purakh and authentic existence of the truth. It hinges on the Guru's creative response to the historical atrocities of the Mughal Emperors. The sixth Guru divined it in ecstasy and concretised it on the earth, turning it into a symbol of sovereignty (*miri*) and spirituality (*piri*). He made a violent rupture in the Sikh movement. The erection of the Akala Takht was a siren of active resistance to the bigot and tyrant Emperor Jahangir. It was a red alert to the state's despotic sovereignty.

The Guru prepared a garrison to house his voluntary brave fighters. The fort of Lohgargh at Amritsar is symbolic of militancy in the Sikh insurgence. After taking over the spiritual throne of gurudom (*gurgaddi*=spiritual throne), the sixth Guru sent *hukamnamas* (edicts) to the devotees through the masands (deputies) that in future they should come to Guru's court (*darbar*) with offerings of horses and arms. It was an experience of the integral reality. It is a grand symbol of commitment to the eradication of the suffering of humanity and protection of the saintly persons. The Gurus drew authenticity of the unique innovation from the Akala Purakh. Thus, the Darbar Sahib and the Akala Takht constitute the haven of safety and protection for the suffering humanity. Guru Gobind Singh further developed it into a double-edged weapon, khanda. It was an experience of the integral reality of the Sikh Faith. It is a grand symbol of commitment to the eradication of suffering of humanity and protection of the saintly persons. The Gurus drew authenticity of the unique innovation from the Akala Purakh.

The Akala Takht is the manifestation of the Guru's deep sense of existential history. Guru Arjundeva sacralised the Sikh scripture and Guru Hargobind sacralised the institution of *piri* and *miri* in the concrete form of the Akala Takht. He was a *raj-yogi* at the exalted court of the Akala Purakh for decree of justice. He sat at the Akala Takht as impartial representative of the Akala Purakh. He was trustee of voluntary offerings (*bheta*).

From the existential standpoint, the historical time involves entails social life. It would be wrong to turn our back towards its spiritual significance. The Akala Takht is a manifestation of eternity on a particular space consecrated by the sixth Guru. In the present scenario, politics has apparently overshadowed and muzzled its spiritual import. Politics of the sacred is not the truth. It is criminalisation of divinity. We should not be disheartened because every cloud has a silver lining.

The concept of true king-guru (spiritual king) in the Sikh tradition was an internal development within the Sikh movement. This idea was conceived in the *swayyas* of *Bhattas* (bards), which are incorporated in the Guru Granth (pp.1378-1409). The Guru was worshipped by the Sikh sangat as a true king and spiritual guru, a *raj-guru* like king Janak. The concept of true kingship was transformed into *shabda-guru*. Guru Gobind Singh materialised this concept when the holy Sikh Scripture was elevated to the divine status. The Sikh tradition has a faith that the tenth Guru ordained to the Sikhs that the holy granth be revered as of the Akala Purakh.[1] It implies that the physical bodies of the Gurus are insignificant as compared to the eternal message that is embodiment of the Akala Purakh. The tenth Guru sealed the scripture. It precluded any kind of interpolation in it. However, reinterpretation is permissible in the coeval context without deviating from the eternal message. It means that the Guru transformed the granth into the canon. It became an embodiment of the Akala

Purakh's will. *Shabda-guru* is a living Guru in the Sikh tradition. It is a connecting link between the Akala Purakh and the Khalsa (individual) and the Khalsa-panth inherent. Thus, the idea of the Sikh polity was embedded in the Sikh Scripture and the tradition. It was deeply rooted in developing collective psyche of the Sikhs. This concept became more pronounced after the martyrdom of Guru Arjundeva in CE 1606 at Lahore.

The martial spirit in Sikhism was a logical and existential necessity for eradicating evil in the society for restoring justice and peace. With the passage of time, the movement grew into a militant upsurge. The sixth Guru Hargobind's practice of wearing of two swords of *miri* and *piri* signifies the synthesis of temporal polity and spirituality respectively. Thus, two swords of martial spirit and spirituality are complementary to each other. Both constitute the concrete truth. The Guru infused a new martial spirit. It synthesises spiritual and martial strands in which the former dominates. It doubtlessly rejuvenated the Sikh movement and infused life into it. The Akala Takht became the property of humanity. It is a ubiquitous symbol of identification with the interests of the humanity, and a guarantor of justice.

Guru Hargobind, as part of his education, got training in horse riding, swordsmanship, and warfare at the hands of Baba Buddha. Guru Arjundeva initiated Hargobind into military training. The fifth guru could divine the future turbulent events. To me Guru Hargobind introduced militant trend. He replaced the cord belt (*seli*) by the sword and cap (*topi*) by turban (*dastar*). The plume (*kalgi*) and eagle (*baj*) are signs of regality. The sword is the sign of self-defense and martial spirit. Turban (*dastar*) represents self-respect. And *kalgi* and eagle complement both sword and dastar. The Gurus created a new value system of reconciliation of the ideals of moral and social commitments to society. From this standpoint, the martyrdom of Guru Arjundeva was regarded as the most significant event in the Sikh history. It was a radical departure from the past Bhakti and spiritual practice in Sikh history.

Note

1. Narbud Singh Bhatt—a, son of Keshc Singh Bhatt—a, recorded it in a "Bhatta Vahi". He was at Nanded when Guru Gobind Singh was attacked with a sword at dark night by grandson of Paide Khan. On the request of devout Khalsa the Guru passed over personal gurudom to the Pothi Sahib.

8

Ideology of Sikhism

The Indian epics, the Ramayana and the Mahabnarata have been rendered into many regional languages with variant readings because of mingling them with regional traditions and creative interpretations of the writers. Originally the present epics were written in Sanskrit. Their renderings into regional languages and dialects were necessitated because of common people's understanding of Sanskrit. One point is clear that the central spirit of the epics has been kept true to conflict between good and evil and final victory is of goodness.

With a view to explaining the unending seed of life, philosophers presupposed that in the beginning there was all darkness. This idea we come across in the Ramayana and the Mahabharata and other religious traditions as well. Valmikah and Vyasa reduced past, future and present into the eternal present. They churned out the cosmic vision of human life as an eternal principle for ages to come. Both the epics are true mirrors of Indian philosophy and culture. The teachings of the epics have gone deep into the marrows of the collective psyche of the Indian masses. Their eternal message is still relevant in the modern times. For understanding them, philosophical reinterpretation is needed. Their meanings are to be given in the modern idioms.

The hero of the Mahabharata, Arjuna confronted the existential dilemma which awfully paralyzes foreseeing destruction of his kinsmen. Krishna's divine message purges all his fears and doubts. He finds solace in sacrifice from higher plane. Krishna always urges allegiance to a higher

Truth which synthesizes temporal and the eternal realm. The Mahabharata was fought for higher moral values for restoring peace and justice. This is the undercurrent of the epics. The Vedic idea of sacrifice and surrender is at a higher plane. Surrender of one's ego and sacrifice of the lower self is the central idea of the epics. This is the spirit of the concept of sannyasa (renunciation) in Indian culture.

Kurukshetra symbolizes the quintessence of Indian philosophy of culture. This is the soil where decisive war of the Mahabharata was fought between the Pandvas and the Kaurvas. Krishna is the mouth-piece of Vyasa. He is mediator between the warring cousins and is at once above good and evil. He does not take sword against either one. He is advisor to the Pandvas. When Krishna was returning from his embassy without the five towns, without as much land as could be balanced on the point of needle, he failed in his mission. He tried to resolve the problem with dialogue but was of no avail. Sword is the last resort to cleanse earth from the evil forces. Krishna's objective is to restore peace and justice. For this purpose he reconciles *dharma* and *karma* in the doctrine of *nishkama karma* (disinterested action) which is discharged without any selfish motive and worldly desires. In the words of a Western philosopher, Immanuel Kant, it is a categorical imperative. Kant's doctrine is a theoretical paradigm of moral action. The Mahabharata's *nishkama karma* reconciles theory and praxis which is the *sine quo non* of every religion. Optimum reconciliation of theory and practice is the spirit of the two epics (the Ramayana and the Mahabharata). It projects the existential view of human life. The Gurus continued message of the epics and Guru Gobind Singh gave a finishing touch to it. Guru Gobind Singh in his letter to the Mughal Emperor, Aurangzeb (the Zafarnama), continues the same message of peace through dialogue, but was disappointed. He had to take sword for annihilation of evil forces. The sword was a defensive weapon for restoring peace and justice.

Language as tool plays significant role in creating ideology. The talented ideologue creates interconnected world-picture of concepts, values, ideals, beliefs, and so on. The creative writer through his different genres creates the world of literature. He projects true picture of society of the author's times. The realist writer presents the social ideology which is useful in the existential world. The idealist creates an ideal picture of the society that is to be actualized as a living reality. He idealizes his future world through his creative writings. His works give insight of life and society. He projects the ideology for the future society. This kind of ideology we find in Guru Nanak's writings. These are related to the human life, society, and value systems. It also deals with social, political, aesthetic, and other institutions or polities.

Ideology, thus, mirrors culture that is the way of life of the people including their attitude towards other people and the world. Attitude implies values, beliefs, arts, aesthetic sense of sensibility, vision of social ideals, or values, habits and various customs, ethos, conventions, and other societal activities. Cultural pattern of action is acquired and cultivated in society. These patterns are mirrored through values, beliefs, and religious ways of living.

Formation of culture through religion plays a very significant role. Religion is often mistaken for a fashionable institutionalized substitute of the prophetic faith and beliefs. Such a religion cannot emancipate humanity from suffering. It keeps man at a formal and customary level. Religion and culture are lived experiences. Role of religion is to emancipate man from the clutches of the mundane world. It aims at making man happy and creating conditions for harmony in the society.

The fundamental purpose of dignified life is autonomy and justice. For this purpose, the talented genius creates the ideal to live life of freedom and self-dignity. The Sikh Gurus ushered in new ideology anchored on equity of societal relationships. They represented Guru Nanak's ideology of *sacha-khanda* that culminated in Guru Gobind Singh's ideology of the khalsa. It does not approve of a parasitic life of renunciation from the worldly duties and leading life of a recluse. It persuades us to remain in the lap of the nature and live a natural life in society. It may be pertinent to point out that without sangat of other fellows, one cannot be a perfect man. Hence need of ideology arises for taming human being with rules and regulations. As a seed needs water, manure, etc., to become a healthy plant, similarly society is necessary for developing a healthy ideology. The rules are devised with a view to evolving an ideology for introducing an egalitarian social structure for yielding peace and justice.

When man is born, he enters into definite relationship with others that are independent of his will. His birth in a particular family or caste is beyond his control. The baby is born with its ego sense. He finds a definite cultural environment around him. It also marks a definite stage of development of civilization. When these relationships are formulated into law, they are turned into their fetters. These are necessary for developing its personality. Then, an epoch of social revolution in history sets in. Chronological and historical development of human relations in history changes the epochs. It is not only material revolution. It is a cultural revolution inclusive of spiritual, moral and other values. Religious and political leaders initiate new ideologies, which transform the social structure.

What is the status of norm in formation of ideology? Stone hewer, for example, cuts the stone for carving out a statue. His chiseling process starts when he has clear idea of norm of a statue in his mind. The lawmaker has in his mind the statute as a guiding line —norm of society in practicing and performing action. Then the question arises: how to implement norms of equality, liberty, and justice. Some times without proper rules of implementation, the coveted target is digressed and the individual is lost in the desert of suffering and miseries. Caste system as device for division of labour was introduced for good of the people but the priestly and the feudal classes have abused the norms. Then, how to control abuse of rules of the covenant?

In Sikhism contract or agreement is between Akalapurakh (God) and the khalsa. The Sikh tradition holds that creation of the khalsa id due to the decree of the Akalapurakh (i.e., agya bhai akala kl tabhi chalaio panth/ sahje rachio khalsa). It is a divine creation. In religion the contract is posited as a divine agreement between the Divine and the community.

Paulo Freire says, "Ideology is doctrine or theory which is changed administratively preserved and transmitted." Ideology has prescriptive character, which directs to abide by some principles for achieving the goal of peace and justice. New ideology often prescribes to revolt against the existent social structure because social conditions change with the change in time. Revolutionary ideology breathes the spirit of struggle against oppression and dehumanization for replacing with new just social order. Ideology transforms societal relations and configurations through new ideas and action. In the 'culture of silence,' the marginalized persons are prohibited from creativity. They cannot take part in transforming society. To transform society is to humanize social relationship that is sympathizing for other men and living beings. Medieval epochs' transformation of society was nothing but humanizing the dehumanized masses. It implies that ideology is to be kept abreast with the changing social conditions.

Every religious philosophy offers an ideology to create an ideal man. The Bhaktas came with new egalitarian ideology for transforming the corrupt social structure. The new egalitarian social ideology of the saints and the Gurus was ushered in for steeling will power and reviving the heroic culture of India. It was a movement for steeling 'will' of the horrified masses. The movement created a nationality with strong desire for self-dignity and independence. The new concept of the medieval world-view (ideology), along with multi-dimensional aspects of social affirmation and restoration of historicity of human action, had a healthy impact on Indian society. The Sikh faith got a clue from the Bhaktas that introduced a new ideology knitted in societal relationships, and avoids leading life of a recluse. It persuades us to remain in the lap of the nature and live a natural life of a householder.

Then the question arises: What is the meaning of ideology? Any wide-ranging system of beliefs, ways of thought and categories provide the basis for formulation of ideology for programming political and social or cultural actions. An ideology is an ideal conceptual scheme that should mirror social order in theory and executing in use. The systematic analysis of the term ideology has been done in the West. The underlying idea of the ideology is to embed it in the socio-cultural realities and it should motivate people for moral and fearless action.

Again, we can ask a question: Why is there a need of ideology? The term has been variously used to characterize patterns of cognitive and moral ideas, belief-systems, and values pertaining to man and society. New ideology is the outcome of the ideologue's creativity from the cultural milieu that mirrors corporate collective consciousness. When the ideology alienates from the dynamic social realities, it becomes rigid and fossilized. It loses its vitality of usefulness and outlives its social utility because of the lack of diachronic social relationships and inherent dynamic nature of the ideology. If it does not change, it becomes dogmatic, reactionary, and conservative. It generates communalism and ethnocentricity. Terrorism is the natural result of it. It is a misconceived babe of religious fanaticism. Will to lord over the minor cultures by the super-powers cannot be justified on moral and human grounds. Lust for power is to be avoided. The super-powers should open eyes to this burning global existential problem. Today the problems of the Taliban and the 'Khalisthan' (Sikh Homeland) cannot be easily dubbed as crazy fantasies. The Taliban leader Osman bin Laden tried to check such evil designs of the U.S.A. and the British. We should go deep into the root-causes of such grave problems and try to find out the realistic existential remedies. The super powers are to be made conscious of their evil designs. Hence, love for humanity is the basis of it.

Then a question arises: Why should we create an ideology? It is because man is intrinsically free and he wants to be free in the society. He desires to be ethical voluntarist as an autonomous self. His freedom is curved when he is born in the society. Rousseau in the "Introduction" of the Social Contract says, "Man is born free but he is everywhere in the chains for being a member of the society." It is a check on anarchy and fascism or despotism. Ideology is a guarantor of freedom and not a check on man's liberty. Society is not a check on man's freedom, but a necessary means for security and freedom. For this reason, ideology is necessary. His chains are due to societal relationships. The ideology is formulated to come out of the fetters that curve man's freedom. In the society, absolute freedom is not possible. It is relative freedom. Man is to live in the society without encroaching upon freedom of other fellow beings. The Kantian maxim can be applicable here, "Treat others as kingdom of ends". It means that 'others' are to be treated as persons having freedom. Freedom is the final goal in the East and the West. Ideology ensures autonomy of the will. Self-determinism is the essence of human existence. Modern existentialism is a staunch advocate of human autonomy. Man cannot be free till he comes out of the cocoon of his the clutches of the ego and worldly attachments. So long as man's ego is not dropped and developed into an autonomous self, his actions cannot be disinterested voluntary actions.

The great ideologues have projected their ideologies for transforming the existing social orders in their countries. If any obstacle comes on the way, the hero stakes his life for the supreme sacrifice. All the ideologies are built on the precondition of foundation of human autonomy and the societal relations. To withdraw from the worldly responsibilities is a suicidal streak. The suicidal streak lies in running away from moral, political, and social responsibilities. To flee from moral commitment and the nature (Arabic, *qudrat*) is negation of the life and the world. This was in vogue in the medieval ages. Mercy killing comes closer to suicidal streak, which cannot be equated to martyrdom. The suicidal streak is an expression of morbidity in the human personality. It is associated with an escapist person who has a weak will power.

Ideology is a set of principles that determine the whole gamut of societal relations. It provides direction for transformation of social order. It is concerned with this-world and the eternity tampers it with dynamic spiritual continuum.

If the social structure does not change with the changing social conditions, it will become a frozen reactionary, dogmatic, and conservative ideology. It should be changed without deviating from the core. Welfare of the masses is ignored and the feminine identity is suppressed. If an ideology does not cohere with the present changed conditions, it will collapse.

The ideology has its own inner inherent contradictions, which can be resolved by reconstructing them. Reconstruction of an ideology requires acute critical, analytical, and sound theoretical understanding of the concept in the coeval context. It requires interpretative articulation in agreement with the existential socio-political situations.

Guru Nanak was the pioneer of the Sikh ideology. He formulated the cultural concept anchored on his dynamic onto-theology. The concept was articulated within the context of contemporary medieval societal conditions.

Ideology is to be restructured in accordance with the contemporaneous outlook and needs of the people. It should give new direction to society. The ideologue may be a great genius, but he cannot create a new ideology in the vacuum. Logically he has to derive his ideas from the culture of the land. Man's social relations are always flexible. New ideologies are needed from time to time and place to place. The form of the ideology may continue, but contents are reformulated in accordance with the changes in the socio-cultural milieu. Therefore, ideology is the outcome of the crisis between the tradition and the coeval outlook of the people. In order to overcome this crisis there is genesis of a new ideology. Human creativity plays significant role in it.

Thus, it is a hermeneutical necessity to restructure ideology with sound theoretical doctrines. Then a philosophical question arises: Is there a rational justification for creating an ideology? My answer to it would be 'Yes'. It is because of the fact that man wants to be free in the society. He cannot be free till he is imprisoned within the cocoon of his narrow ego (*haumai*) and worldly attachments (*mohmaya*). The self in Sikhism is like an 'entelechy' (Gr.) of Aristotle, which has the possibility to become perfect or realize its autonomous essence.

In Sikhism, it is attained with strenuous practice of *shabda-yoga* and the divine grace (*kirpa*). Therefore, the self ('me') has the possibility to become actuality ('I') with the grace of shabda-guru. Ideology is a logical construct or mechanism devised by the genius to ensure freedom of man for realizing his ideal and real self from within the human person (*deha*) and without in society. It is synthesis of ideal and actual. It is to be put to test in the existential situations to test its viability. Ideology, thus, is a necessary means for emancipating man from the worldly clutches. Without ideology autonomy of the self is impossible.

Then, a philosophical question arises: How to articulate a sound theoretical structure of ideology? It should be objectively analyzed and workable in the practical use in the society. It was done in the Sikh movement. The ideology should have sound theoretical foundation according to the changed social conditions. The Sikh ideology is the natural outcome of Guru Nanak's 'cosmic vision'. The gist of the problem of ideology is that all practical problems can be solved only if we have a sound theoretical structure that is viable in society. It implies that there should be no muddling of theory and praxis. In the modern context the Sikh ideology is in crisis. There was a wide gap between theory and praxis. It needs a radical transformation.

Every interpretation, either of the sacred scripture or the tradition, is in flux. The scriptures propound eternal dynamic truth. The message of the scriptures is eternal for posterity. The tradition stems from the scripture, holy sayings of the celebrities, and the historical exigencies. We can safely infer that interpreter has to be vigilant and better equipped to make us understand candidly the ciphers in the 'sacred texts'. The reader should have developed intuitive insight for understanding the objective truth in the texts.

The philosophical interpretation is the best technique of understanding the ineffable in the sacred scriptures because it enables us to draw all possible logical implications of the statements recorded in the texts. Logical consistency and necessary relationships interlocked in the syntax are reasoned out in the process of understanding the ciphers. The hermeneutical understanding as an objective is directed towards truth and meanings. Such understanding of the sacred texts is candid and freed from the prejudices of the interpreter's preconceived ideas and the cocooned subjectivity and solipsism or skepticism.

Philosophically all interpretations are reinterpretations of the original intuitions of the mystics that are creatively restructured out of the debris of the past interpretations and the texts. In the Guru Granth, the Gurus kept the doors of reinterpretation open for eternity. In the Islamic tradition, innovation (*bid'ah*) is a grave sin. It does not mean that new interpretations are not possible. It means that the basic creed of the Qur'anic revelation is not to be disturbed. It logically implies that the Gurus left the Scripture open-ended for reinterpreting it. However, it implied that spirit of the text is not to be distorted. The hermeneutical reinterpretation is a logical necessity from its fluxional onto-theology. This point can be substantiated from the history of the Sikh religious tradition. There was a transformation from a peaceful religious reformative movement to militant insurgence and active resistance to tyranny.

Culture is a reservoir of ideals of the people. Ideology is articulation of new social order, beliefs, values, norms, and the alike. It imposes checks and constraints on instinctive actions of man and social groups and their inter-group relationships. The cultural elements refine beast in man. It is a means of refinement of collective psyche of human beings. It is a mirror of the belief systems. It mirrors collective memory and oral traditions, collective beliefs, and ethos. It represents ethnic gods and their mutual habitats. The gods of the ethnic cultures live on common mountains. The Kailash parvat is rendezvous of Shiva and Baikuntha is the abode of Vishnu in seclusion. The havens of the Indian gods are the Kailash Mountain (*parvat*) and the Greek gods live on the Olympic Mountain. Thus, culture is a process of putting old wine in new bottles. Ideology constantly refines or reformulates beliefs, values, and norms. These are the functional ways of cultural life.

The Bhakti cult made a radical departure from the morbid and outdated traditions of the past and introduced new socially oriented healthy trends. It ushered in the trend of reaffirmation of social realities and historicity of human action. From the existential standpoint, it projects man as a concrete unit in the society struggling for human freedom. It tried to make man perfect as an emancipator of humanity and guarantor of social and political justice.

One should enjoy '*qudrat*' as a manifest attire of the Divine. It should be enjoyed in a state of equanimity, which is the essence of the Sikh. The exponents of mercy-killing may argue that it is heartless and immoral to allow a patient to suffer more when the doctor may suggest terminating of his life. For the moralist it is a complex dilemma. In some religious traditions, killing or mortifying the body is not the euthanasiac way of living. The body is to be yoked for achieving the goal of life. Self-mortification is a kind of withdrawal from moral commitment to higher life. The sannyasis, yogis, and sufis falsely thought that by killing or mortifying their physical selves they could realize the goal of human life. They consider the body insignificant. To die with dignity is the real basis of euthanasiac life. In this sense, Sikhism uses the euthanasiac way of the life of a hero. The true Sikh and the khalsa should die in the battlefield, fighting for the cause of righteousness. Mercy killing and suicide are regarded a blasphemous in Islam and Sikhism. The ideal persons of Islam and Sikhism prefer to die in the battlefield than show a clean pair of heels in the thick of the battle. Instantaneous dignified death is preferred to cowardly death of humiliation and slavery.

The common person accepts the unreflective world. It is naïve realism. However, for a mystic the intuited world or 'formless form' (*arupaloka*) is significant. The mystic's vision of the world is a subjective realization. His ideology is the resultant of logical constructs. The first kind of world may be dangerous for humanity. The whole biosphere and the animal world are excluded. Such exclusive world-views (ideologies) have shown their catastrophic effects in the history of mankind. Sikhism, on the contrary, is a critically resuscitated ideology of sacha-khanda, which is exclusive of utopian ideologies (e.g., Thomas More's *Utopia*, Plato's *Republic*, et al.). Marx lacks universal and Hegel's rational structure lacks particulars. Sikhism rejects the unreflective world-view for abandoning ratiocination. Pure reflective abstraction and mythical activity end in pure rational ratiocination and skepticism. It limits the practical efficacy of virtues and values. Therefore, the ideal state of existence (sacha-khanda) is to be realized in history. Guru Nanak's ideology was actualized in the Khalsa-panth.

The ideology should have been based on the sound interpretative foundation according to the changed social conditions. The Sikh ideology is the natural outcome of Guru Nanak's 'cosmic vision'. The gist of the problem of ideology is that all practical problems can be solved only if we have a sound theoretical structure that is viable in the society.

The Ramayana and the Mahabharata are real mirrors of Indian culture. Besides *mukti* or *moksha* dharma is the central doctrine around which Indian culture revolves. The concept of dharma is a complex term which has been interpreted in different ways. It refers to the voluntary action that autonomous and *nishkama karma*. It clubbed with wisdom and will; human will dominates man's autonomous actions. In the Western terms it is called voluntarism. Thus, activity dominates Indian philosophy. In the West main exponent was Author Schopenhauer, a German philosopher. He was an idealist thinker. His philosophy is idealistic and lacks practical dimension. The epics of Indian and Guru Gobind Singh's philosophies are practical. These can be applies in the existential situations. The Gita summarizes three-fold objectives of human life: continuity of righteousness; protection of the saints and destruction of the evil doers. The same ideas have been reiterated by Guru Gobind Singh in the Dasam Granth.[1]

There are some special features in Guru Gobind Singh' ideology of the Khalsa which are to be highlighted. These are as under:

(i) Autonomous Action (Dharma)

The purpose of human life is achieving the autonomy of the self. Man is to be allowed to have freedom. Continuous striving and struggle in the world constitutes the essence of the dynamic view of life. Man should have freedom in every walk of life and should not run away from the moral and the societal responsibilities. The essence of human life is to create balance between the two. Man's personal resolution determines the criterion of his autonomous voluntary actions. The personal resolution implies that there should be no clergy, and no imposition of the moral *rahit maryada* (moral code) by the priests. The 'other' is the real but transcending the negative aspects of the person is to be pursued ceaselessly. The other persons and the *sangat* are real. The *sangat* and society are parts of man. Evil is real and struggle is also real. *Seva*, voluntary service without conceit, is real. These are products of the societal life. The *sangat* can be useful in checkmating the *haumai* and the enticements of the world. Man is to be a cultivator and not a parasite or only consumerist and hoarder. He can be a mendicant but not a *sannyasi*. Every person is to be a householder and not a priest. It means that the collective responsibility and the will prevail over individual will. The Bhaktas and the Gurus revolt against monasticism and the temple life. Sikhism is a cultic faith and a revolt against the church. It advocates social progress. It is a religion of the workers, the peasants and the tillers of the land (cp. Gandhi, Tolstoy, Martin Luther, *et al.*).

Man has the sense of manhood. Self-awareness of the self that "I am man" is the unique expression of man's creative nature. He is the crown of creation and the lower species are devoid of creativity and language of the signs and the symbols. The awareness that he is man makes him distinct from the animals. Then a philosophical question arises: why is man better than the animals and other lower species? Why is man capable of self-awareness (i. e., identity/morality)? Man has memory which helps him to keep track of the present and the past. It is learned through the languages (e.g., Sanskrit, Punjabi, Marathi, etc.). Culture is an escape from the beasthood of the lower animals, the barbarism of the tribal people, sheep, and the animals. Sheep only bleats *"main, main, main"*. Man has the potentiality to transcend his limitations through creativity and language. He can go from the jive to the realized self. He can realize his personal identity. In every religion, the central objective is to create distinct identity of man. In the medieval Bhakti cult the Bhaktas had divergent identities because of their caste distinctions and hailing from different regions. The

Bhaktas of Maharashtra have their distinct identity from other denominations. The Kabirpanthis are different from the other denominations. Similarly, the identity of the Sikh is different from that of the Khalsa. In the Sikh tradition there are different sects (*sampard[1]yas*). Each sect lays emphasis on different aspects of the Sikh ontology and voluntarism.

The Sikh faith is treasured in the Sikh Scriptures and the tradition. The Sikh Gurus and the contributors to The Sikh Canon made a radical departure from the religious and philosophical thought of the Indian and the Semitic philosophical systems that were prevalent in the medieval period. It was a powerful philosophical endeavour to reinterpret the Buddhist and the Vedantic thought along with the Islamic world-view without repudiating their primordial truth. It has been argued that the earlier medieval religious philosophies were devoid of voluntarist import in the practical life. The existent philosophies practised the abstract ideas least concerned with the social realities, which have always been the basic concerns of the religious ideologies of the world.

The Sikh voluntarism represents the radical individualism. There are no intermediary deities or prophets/gurus between the supreme Deity (Akalapurakh) and the personal conviction of man. Faith in the Akalapurakh is a matter of personal and subjective conviction. His relation with the supreme Deity is personal and direct (i.e., *guru* is *chela* and *chela* is *guru)*. The strength of the personal conviction is preferred to the dead man-made rules and laws. Man's actions get direct inspiration from the Deity. It strengthens his will. It is to be borne in mind that the individual will and the Divine Will are interchangeable terms and not acosmic.

The killing of a snake/hen/cow is paradoxical if all is Brahman, but for a man of action (voluntarist) it is neither a contradiction nor a paradox. Guru Gobind Singh and Gandhi were celebrities of action. The latter used to assert that that there is no scriptural sanction of unsociability. What he understood in the scriptures there are no untouchables. In making this categorical statement, he transcends the religious scholarship, and the exegetical interpretations of the scriptures.

He does not accept the prevalent stock interpretation of the scripture. One cannot be an activist in the real sense of the term till one's will transcends the phenomenal world. Gandhi did not accept the exegetical interpretation of the Gita regarding *svadharma* as an obligation of his caste (*varana*). He accepted what his conviction validated. It is a form of radical individualism, animated by what one embraces as his firm conviction. No rules, books, and formulations will guide us. It is solipsism of the individual's personal conviction. His concepts ahimsa was based on his conviction. His personal and subjective conviction will be the deciding factor for determining the course of his action. Sikhism does not believe in the Hindu *varanas* (castes). It is the dynamic religion in theory and praxis. It changes its signification with the changed social conditions. Genuine faith is always dynamic and the meanings are diachronic. Men of religion and scholars of religion lack creativity and real scholarship. The Sikh religion did not grow after Guru Gobind Singh. The Misl period was the period of religious decadence which continues till today.

In Islam *fana* is the state of dissolution of the empirical self (*nafs*). In Sikhism there is dissolution of the *haumai* (egoity), but not the personal identity and the will. Evil is real which is the basis of voluntarism. And the *sangat* and the society are part of man because all the voluntarist historical actions are carried on the in the society. In the case of the *raja-jogi* (say, King Janak) there is no dissolution of the will. Bhishanpatama, in the Mahabharata, got boon from the Deity of his self-willed death (*svaiccha mritu*) which was the highest form of autonomy and martyrdom. It is the highest form of the martyrdom when a person has full control over his will and death. It is said that Ravan had tied up 'Death' (*jama/kala*) with one leg of his bed. It was a mythical make-belief that Ravan claimed to have conquered death. The world does not dominate him, but he dominates the world and death. Baba Ajit Singh and Baba Jorawar Singh two elder sons of Guru Gobind Singh laid down their lives in the battlefield at Chamkaur Sahib. When they saw from the fortress of Chamkaur the legion (army) of thunderstorm they plunged into action and fell fighting in the battlefield as the valiant warriors. This is the highest form of voluntarism of the Sikh martyrs.

In the modern times the martyrs of 1984 Action Blue Star were seized in the four walled precincts of bricks and mortar in the Golden Temple Complex. The Indian army laid siege to the Akala Takht and the Golden Temple Complex. All supply lines were cut off, food and water ran out and ammunitions were exhausted. Sant Bhindranwale and his *marjivdas* followers plunged into action amidst thunderstorm of bullets and air attacks. There was a fierce fight between the khalsa and the army. They fought to the last until spectre of death over powered them. The staked their lives for their faith, but did not show the Indian army a clean pair of heels which was equipped with the latest war weapons and ammunitions. They infused blood into the very marrows of the Sikhs for living life of self-respect and self-dignity. With their mortal death they removed the dross of opacity and entered the kingdom of heroes of faith.

In Islam the 'other' is real as manifestation of Allah. In Sikhism all multiplicity is manifestation of Hari. Islam also upholds the validity of the manifestations of the Numinous. In Sikhism will is not an illusion. In Sikhism there is no passivity and quietism either. In Buddhism and Hinduism the will (*samkalpa*) is illusory and thereby follows inaction and passivity. And the categorical action is not possible till one transcends the contours of the phenomenal world with his invincible will. Transcendence from the world does not mean negation of history. Struggle will continue. Hence, it upholds voluntarism.

There is infinitude in the Sikh onto-theology. Sikhism accepts pluralities or 'other' as the real (*niche kar apni jit karun*). The historical action is not possible unless the 'others' are accepted real.

In the Vedanta and Buddhism, the 'other' and the 'differences' are not real. Man's personality and will are ultimately dissolved. The Boddhisattva of Buddhism does not retain the will at the end. In Buddhism will (*samkalpa*) is illusory, so there is inaction and passivity at the transcendental level of nirvana. There is negation of history and the empirical world. Hence there is no struggle in history.

In the traditional idealistic traditions the will is subjugated to the divine will and it is treated as the *maya*. Self-surrender does not mean passivity and annihilation of the will. It gains infinite autonomy. The individual will is not dissolved; rather it is transformed into the Cosmic Will that executes all the voluntary actions. In the Gita and Sikhism individual will mirrors the divine will and execute the message in the world.

Guru Gobind Singh highlights the role of the invincible will in the existential situation as the social and moral responsibility. This is the essence of the Sikh spiritual voluntarism. For this reason the khalsa, led by spirituality, had to defy the temporal state or rule. According to Guru Gobind Singh the Khalsa is not purely created by history. It is a natural creation by the Divine Will (i.e., *sahje rachio khalsa*) for the realization of the eternal freedom of the self. The Dasam Granth reiterates the voluntarist thoughts *passim*. The concept of voluntarism derives its sustenance from the concrete self. Now the question arises: What is the origin of the ego in the world? The root-feeling of the longing for its goal motivates the search for the fulfillment and actualization of the inward possibilities that unfold the idea of the individual being. It is the child's longing, which pervades the consciousness more and more clearly in the form of a feeling of constant direction and finally confronts the mature spirit as the enigma of Time. The birth of the ego (*haumai*) rebounds from the awareness of the external world. It emerges to impart order to the external world. From this point of view the inward journey of the self starts. The self traverses through the vicissitudes of self-discipline and grapples with the oddities of the mundane world. The inward journey consummates in self-illumination. The self realizes its identity mirrors the Akalapurakh 'here' and 'now' in the world.

Ideology of the Gurus does not come under the philosophical systems of the East and the West. It is a *sui generis* system which has elements of idealism, realism, pragmatism, radicalism, solipsism, voluntarism, and so on. One point is clear that Sikhism has a holistic approach which excludes nothing from its all-inclusive vision. The Gurus and other contributors have cosmic vision. We interpret their hymns with narrow perspectives. For instance, there is no fixed connotation of idealism either in the East or in the West. Idealism is primarily a metaphysical system and its epistemology is dependent on its metaphysics. On the other hand, realism is an epistemological system lays emphasis on theory of knowledge. Both idealism and realism have assumed different shades of connotations. Idealism in the metaphysical sense is the theory of the ultimate reality which is spiritual in nature. And epistemological idealism broadly maintains that the observed objects are modified and dependent upon the observer. It is opposed to epistemological realism which holds that the observed objects are not modified and is independent of the observer. The external real objects have their independent existence. The Absolute, according to idealism is the precondition of all the multiplicities. Idealism gives precedence to the whole whereas in realism the particulars are independent of the whole.

Sikhism reconciles the perennial controversy of idealism and realism. Metaphysically it is idealism and epistemologically realism. It is idealism because the supreme reality is spiritual and it is realism because the external world is real. In Sikhism the particular mirrors the universal. In idealism the particulars are the moving shadows of eternity. Sikhism is a practical religion of this-world which has nothing to do with the otherworld. It advocates social involvement from the altruistic standpoint.

Like the Buddha, the aim of the Gurus and the Bhaktas was emancipation of the suffering subaltern masses and reform of the exploiting classes of the feudal lords and the religious masters. The dynamic philosophy may be called the dynamic idealism because it starts with the inquiry of the dynamic *Ik* (One) and ends in it. It is because the principle of the 'becoming' of time (*kala*) is latent in it. The *Ik* is the primordial cause of all creation. The *hukam,* the dynamic principle, is latent in the *Ik*. Being the precondition of all the pluralities, it cannot be reduced to the illusory appearances because they are cemented by the cosmic principle of the *hukam* that is inherent in all the animate and the inanimate pluralities. Therefore, the cosmic identity and the pluralities are both 'identity-in-diversity'. Both are ensconced in the cosmic law. Thus, the creation is in the Creator and the Creator is in the creation because their essence is the 'becoming'. In the former consciousness dominates and in the latter the conative aspect dominates. It follows that both consciousness and the creative energy are inseparable from each other. There exists a difference of degrees and not of kind between the two.

The Guru Granth points out that the universe has been created by blending the five gross elements (i.e., earth, water, fire, air, and ether). During the time of the Sikh Gurus, these five material elements were well-known, but in the modern times the concept of innumerable chemicals has come into being. It means that the Sikh Gurus used only the five elements because they were prevalent in the medieval period. They were primarily communicating their ideas to the medieval masses. If we are to interpret it in the modern times, we will have to take cognizance of the modern concept of these elements. Spirit and energy are taken as interchangeable terms.

After Einstein modern science has ceased to contend that matter is different from energy. Both are interchangeable or inter-convertible terms according to the Law of Conservation of energy and matter. Einstein's equation of $E=mc^2$ is often quoted to justify it. Experiments have been conducted to demonstrate matter can be created out of energy. In the modern science there is no exclusive concept of matter. Matter can be converted into energy and energy into matter. This is an open-ended question whether consciousness is matter or is different.[2] The gradation of these elements is ranging from gross to subtle. Out of the five elements 'ether' is the subtlest one. It is invisible to the naked eye. Some scientists identify it with empty space. It definitely belongs to the universe. It is not acosmic. Human brain is evolved of these elements. When they are combined together in a particular pattern, their functions produce certain activities. This is the animated state of the human brain. These brain activities are converted into mental activities. The neurogenetics has not come to any conclusive view as to what happens as a result of this conversion. It is envisaged by the Guru that the sixth element (mind) is the creation of man's creativity. The mind further develops into self-consciousness. Guru Nanak's five *khandas* in *the Japuji* delineate the progression of the mind to the apex of self-consciousness (*sudhi*). The Guru envisages this scientific fact through his mystic vision. It implies that 'consciousness' (*surati*) is inherent in the inanimate elements. It is latent in the elements.

The human mind, the dynamic principle of creativity, is taken as the blank slate at the time of birth in the mundane world. Though man inherits certain hereditary traits, yet consciousness is to develop itself *de novo*. Experiences of the external real objects have the creative potency. Even the modern neuroscientists, on the basis of their experimental data, say that the human brain holistically functions as a mystery. Localized functions of the brain are qualitatively different when they function as a whole. The brain activities are qualitatively different from the mental activities. This is the neurological basis of human creativity. It is systematically worked out in the Sikh Scriptures. And the development of consciousness is symbolic of the human creativity which is kindled by wonder and curiosity, the distinct qualities of man.

Guru Nanak, in one of his hymns, categorically says that he sees everywhere a combination of the *shiva* and the *shakti*. Both are in the process of becoming. When the *shakti* is rarefied, it assumes the status of the *shiva*. In the Samkhya System, the *purusha* and the *prakriti* are two co-eternal principles which never interact with each other. While the former is passive, the latter is active. The impregnation of the *prakriti* through reflection of the *purusha* causes evolution. The term '*prakriti*' does not appear in the Sikh Canon. The Gurus, on the other hand, do not accept the metaphysical dualism of the Samkhya School. In order to dismantle the dualist standpoint of the Samkhyaites, the Bhaktas and the Sikh Gurus hold the view that both *shiva* and the *shakti* have the dynamic nature. Instead of *prakriti* the Arabic term *'qudrat'* has been preferred in the Guru Granth.

From the philosophical standpoint the *'qudrat'* is self-creating; the essential creative power (creative energy) of the dynamic *Ik*. It is created self which encompasses the manifested creation. Again, from the standpoint of ethics the world is a living reality because it is the base for realization of the 'I' which has the numerical identity with the 'Thou'. The ethical endeavours are made here in the world. The objects of the world help the 'me' to survive and serve as the means of self-realization because they sustain the human consciousness (*surati*), inherent in the human body (*deha*). The body provides energy to consciousness (mind). It will be pertinent to point out here that in Sikhism the manifest world is regarded as the real 'other'. It has degrees of reality. The ephemeral world is, therefore, relatively real. The 'me' is to wade through these degrees of realities. Consciousness has also degrees of realities which are represented through the *khandas* in Guru Nanak's Japuji. It is through the intuitive experience of the self (*atam parbodh*) that the identity of the 'Thou' is realized in the *sacha-khanda* in which all distinctions and differences are dissolved into the concrete identity of the 'Thou' wherein the 'me' is transformed into the "I' or 'Thou'. It is a non-conceptual absolute state of consciousness (*aphur avastha*). The "me' (*haumai*) and delusion (*maya*) fade away into nothingness. They existed due to divine ignorance (*avidya*). In this context, Guru Nanak says that he has realized the identity with the 'Thou. Now he has no doubt about it. His individual will is attuned to the *hukam* (i.e., *chakhi chodi sahasa nahi koi ... karta kare karavai soei* / GG, p. 796). His historical actions stem from the 'Thou'. It marks the beginning of voluntarism.

Sikhism lays emphasis on the problem of the *haumai* because of its dynamic onto-theology. The concept of the 'Thou' is the Creator (*karta purakh*) of the manifest world. The *haumai* is the distorted form of the will which is individuated from the cosmic will. When the individual will is identified with the cosmic will, it is attuned to the *hukam*. Hence, the 'me' (*haumai*) and the 'it' (objects) are the epitomes of the individual self (*jiva*) and the universe is the outcome of ignorance and the divine will respectively. Firstly, the individual self (*jiva*) is born with the *haumai* and then dies in the *haumai* (see, /GG, p. 466).

The *hukam* (divine will) is the ground of all creation. The cosmic will manifests itself through the creation. Due to *hukam* the world comes into being. The divine will 'wishes', the world to come into being. The 'I' manifests itself as the word (*shabda*) commands 'to be', it comes into being. The 'me' gets emancipated with the ethico-spiritual efforts and the divine grace. The individual will is required to negate its 'me' for perfect attunement with the cosmic will. It means that the individual will surrenders to the divine will. It is a continuous volitional effort to attain oneness with the 'Thou'. Once the self realizes the divine will, which is within the self, it always acts in accordance with the divine will. The self realizes, from within itself, the true nature of freedom and creativity (*hukami razai chalana nanak likhia nali*/ GG, p. I).

The Sikh philosophy starts from the base of the mind. Kabir explicitly explains that the mind (*mana*), at the initial stage, is dominated by the *Shakti.* And when it is rarefied (tinned) at the highest stage, it becomes the self-luminous consciousness, inclusive of the *Shakti*. The *Shakti* is transformed into pure consciousness that is potentially active. This progression takes the shape of a spiritual voyage into the interior self. The five gross elements are given in the graded forms, ranging from the gross to the subtle elements. Consciousness, that is dormant in the matter, surfaces. When it ascends to the highest state, it traverses three divine regions; i.e., nether (*patala*), heavens (*akasha*), and the earth (*prithvi*). Kabir has expressed this idea in the following words:

> his mind is energy, [and] the consciousness,
> It is born of five gross elements.
> By taking it to the highest state of self-consciousness,
> It unravels the truth of the entire triple world (33).
>
> /GG, Kabir, p.342

The realized self, attuned to the cosmic law, transcends the limitations of causality and temporality without actually withdrawing from the existential socio-political responsibilities. This disinterested involvement in the historical events brings about the restructuring of history Eternity is harmonized with praxis of the historical action.

It is interesting to note that the Bhaktas and the Gurus neither solely secularize nor spiritualize. Rather they try to synthesize the processes of spiritualization and secularization or the sacred and the profane. The efforts of the Gurus are directed towards spiritualizing the temporal. It is a practical technique of yoking consciousness of the individual self to the transcendental consciousness of the Akalapurakh. It is a process of self-transformation of the 'me' (first person singular perspective) into the 'Thou' (third person singular perspective). From the lowest state of consciousness is developed into the highest state of the Thou-consciousness. It culminates in the absolute state of the mystical identity of the 'I' and the Akalapurakh. The human action in history is restored. It is the form of realism because the reality of the external world is accepted. For this purpose, the self is to pass through the tunnel of history that entails the social realities. It is just like striking a ball against a wall. The ball rebounds and comes back to its original source. Similarly, consciousness is 'intentional' because it is directed towards the others, apart from the subject. When it transcends the 'me,' then it cuts across all the phenomenal categories (i.e., space, time, causality, etc.) and the self realizes its oneness or mystic identity. It realizes its intrinsic autonomy.

There are no innate ideas of the previous life. Free will in man is not innate as an inherited given fact. If innateness of the ideas is presupposed, the concept of freedom of the will becomes redundant. The concept of the 'innate' means, fixed entity, inherited from the previous life. Free will is nurtured through the dynamic process of the point-instants. The development of man is carried out with the help of the guru's grace (*guru-kripa*). For this purpose, articulation of the concepts regulates the human conduct. All the created words act upon the human mind (consciousness) and activate it. Human consciousness is transformed from individual consciousness into the self-consciousness. 'Me-consciousness' is transformed into the 'Thou-consciousness' after wading through the inwardly ascending degrees of consciousness.

An individual is granted free will though he has inherent devilish elemental traits in him. The *shabda* assists man to subjugate the evil in him. This incessant struggle within man gives birth to radical dualism between the *manmukh* and the *gurmukh*. In Sikhism the *manmukh* is egocentric 'me'. He travels toward the 'Thou'. The prophetic instructions of the religious master minds have more effect than those of an ordinary person. Continuous esoteric efforts yield the desired result. The prophetic words create feelings of respect and reverence.

The fundamental dictum of morality is that: "as you sow, so shall you reap". The ideal of the human life, based on the new model of morality, is not to be realized through ecstasy and meditation in the solitary jungles, but it is to be attained in the societal world while living the life of a householder. Regeneration and transformation in the society is to be consciously ushered in. Every person is to contribute his might to the cause of amelioration and transformation of the existing abnormal conditions in the society. Everyone is required to carry on incessantly the duty of redeeming the pangs of the human beings in accordance with the divine will. The individual will is the executor of the divine purposes. Thus, the cosmic law functions through the individual will. He is capable of carrying out the mission. No other lower species is capable of doing it.

In spiritual voluntarism there is decisively the primacy of spirituality over materiality. The material way of living is no more than the life of an animal and the materialist (*sakta*). Man has to strive to bring out the spiritual from within and to respond to the call of the transcended state of consciousness. He has to live the life of a hero. Here the spirit (consciousness) comes prior to the matter or energy. Thus, the consciousness or mind is a transformed cognitive energy because it has its roots in the five gross elements. The phenomenology of the mind gives precedence to the consciousness over the energy.

The real voluntarist philosophy starts with the stabilized consciousness. Guru Nanak reiterates this idea in his *Japuji* when he says victory over the mind is the victory over the world, "*...mani jite jaga jiti* (28) / GG, p. 6). In many vital ways the *Gurbani* makes a radical epistemic departure from the six orthodox systems of the Indian Philosophy.

(ii) Voluntarism and Karma Theory

In this context the problem of the karma theory is to be studied. The following problems are vital: (i) free will, (ii) scientific determinism, (iii) theory and karma, (iv) transmigration of soul and immortality of the self (*atman*). The Day of Judgement in the Semitic traditions is the negation of transmigration of the soul and of the eternity of the soul as an entity.

In Buddhism *shunnya* is not emptiness, but a state of consciousness that transcends all the mental and the intellectual constructs. And in Sikhism the One (*Ik*) is not a mathematical numeral, but it is the cipher of the ontological dynamic Being. It is not by chance that the Indian savants discovered the concept of the zero (cipher) or that it was conceived simultaneously as the mathematical concept and the metaphysical reality. It was inspired by their passion for the lived ontic identity of the 'Thou'. The sign of the zero in the Arabic, placed on the left side of the numeral, is valueless. But in the Buddhist metaphysics it is not emptiness or devoid of the metaphysical reality. It is a 'cipher' in the religious sense. It has its mystical signification that means the ontic reality which is beyond the concepts (*vikalpas*). The *shunnya* is without concepts and linguistic or symbolic constructs, yet it is the matrix of the reality of time and Eternity. In the Madhyamic School of Buddhism it has been called *shunnya*. This meaning has been accepted in Guru Nanak's "Siddha Goshti" in the Guru Granth. Guru Nanak says that '*Shunnya*' pervades everywhere.

For the Bhaktas and the Gurus both identity and 'other' are real. Unlike the Heracleitean or the Buddhist concept of 'Becoming,' they see progression in the social reality. The zero represents the sign of the circle of perfection in the Greek thought, but the Bhaktas and the Gurus make a radical departure from it in order to reconcile eternity and temporality for reaffirming the social realities. It is the beginning and the end of reality. The zero is the sign of the eternal motion of the terrestrial and the celestial bodies. The point-instant moments advance towards the eternal becoming and return to the original beginning. It is the process of recycling of the 'Being' in time without 'eternal return'. Every-instant moment appears as 'new'.

(iii) Sikh Moral Conduct (*Rahit Maryada*)

Religious belief is politicized, personalized, and privatized. When these beliefs are expressed through public speeches, and practised, these are institutionalized, and become stringent and static. Our emphasis is on inner spirit of religious faith. The mystic emphasizes on his personal visionary experience of truth whereas the priests and politicians anchor their statements on fossilized beliefs. The followers often distort the mystics' genuine faith into dogmas that are stringent and static rules. There is, thus, always a gap between religious faith of a prophet and the followers. Moreover, the faith of the followers depends on the development of their minds .Guru Gobind Singh says in one of his compositions that one utters according to the development of one's mind (i.e., *api apani bhadi hai jeti barnat bhin bhin tohe teti*) explains the Divine. The truth is eternal, the expression in thought and practices change with the changed situations. The new mystic comes with new morality that emanates from truth. Truth is eternal, but moral code of conduct is contingent and relative (*rahit maryada*).

For realizing the social ideal of unity there is a need of ethico-spiritual discipline. Man is required to do honest earnings (*kirat karna*). Guru Nanak was a mendicant, but he was not an ascetic. His personality and philosophy are synthesis of asceticism and domesticity of a householder. Before he undertook his spiritual sojourns (*uddasis*), he was employed in the provision-store (*modi khana*) of the Sultan at Sultanpur in the district Kapurthala (Punjab). And after his *uddisis* to different parts of India and the West-Asian Islamic countries, he tilled the lands at Kartarpur (now in Pakistan). He is against exploitation and hoarding. There is no room for hoarding and drones like feudal lords and exploiters, celibates and ascetics in the Sikh faith. As a voluntarist it was incumbent on the part of a true Sikh/khalsa to earn his hard-earned bread and share with others. For this reason the Gurus evolved social institutions of free kitchen (*langar), pangat, seva*, and sharing one's earnings with others. In the khalsa society man's personal identity is recognized as a free person with a social and moral commitment for the amelioration of mankind. The Gurus tried to descend the so-called mythical otherworld on this earth. The Gurus preached and lived up to this ideal.

Therefore, trio scheme of meditative remembrance of the divine *nama* (*nama japana*), honest hard earnings, (*kirta karna*), and sharing goods with others (*wanda chakna*) are well known in the Sikh social philosophy. He says (*ghala khahai kichu hathahua dei / nanak rahu pachanchi sehu* / GG, p. 1245). Therefore, *nama-simran* and *kirat-karna* should go hand in hand. *Mama-simran* has been democratized and secularized in the medieval Bhakti cult and this wave was continued in Sikhism. There are no caste and gender barriers in Sikhism.

It implies that mere spirituality and meditation will not do. One must do hard and honest labour with the sweat of one's brow. One is to work in the field as farmer or tiller of the land. One should produce for others and share with them. One should not be only a consumer but also be a producer for others. One should lead an optimistic and dynamic way of life with altruistic ethical values (*nanak nama chaddi kala, tere bhane sarbat ka bhala*). *Guru ka langar* (free kitchen) and *pangat* are based on the principle of equality, which are practised in the Sikh tradition irrespective of caste, colour, sex or gender, creed and any other discriminatory considerations.

The underlying idea of human life is to attain bliss and autonomy. Indian philosophy endorses this viewpoint. It does not lay exclusive emphasis on bodily pleasures but bliss (*anand*) of the *atman* that is the subtlest aspect of human existence. At the same time it does not negate bodily pleasures. These are to be satisfied in a regulative manner. It, rather, lays emphasis on sublimation of bodily pleasures. There is reconciliation between *nivrati* and *pravriti* in the Sikh Scriptures. There is a qualitative difference between the pleasure of a pig and a realized self. Our concern is with the bliss of the realized person.

It is true that man always hankers after hedonistic pursuits. He does not want to exert himself to swim with the tide of problematic dynamic life unless he develops the habit to do action. Thus, the concept of pleasure is a natural phenomenon in man. Not to speak of human beings it is present even in lower species. The only difference between lower species and human beings lies in the fact that man is at advantageous position because he can create the articulated ideal world. The Gurus tried to balance bodily pleasure and spiritual bliss. They steered a middle path between two extremes. Yogic practices tried to arouse *kundalini,* but the Gurus made *surati-shabda-yoga* as means of transforming consciousness with the help of meditative remembrance of holy names (*nama-simran*) of Akalapurakh. The genesis of religion lies in overcoming oddities of life caused by the uncanny natural forces like floods, earthquakes and shortage of rains, etc. Man is expected to eradicate evil that is within him and in the society. *Nama-simran* is a means to eradicate evil within man. It is practised in seclusion as well as in the *sangat.*

The ultimate aim of Sikh way of life is to make the world an abode of peaceful and blissful living in the society. The meaning of bliss is changed from private and empirical pleasure or happiness to welfare of all and sundry. This disinterested dynamic involvement in the worldly life is the ideal of the Sikh ethics. He is not to fall prey to impermanent bodily pleasures that are not lasting states of bliss. When he transcends his selfishness, he becomes altruist in his practical life. He gets rid of the sense of possessiveness and identification with the bodily self; he is a true Sikh or khalsa. He rather identifies with others and is motivated to be kind to sentient and insentient beings. It is his deed that makes him realize the purpose of human life. He discovers deep meaning of life in the world. He becomes saviour of all beings.

There is a gradation of values that man creates to achieve

his coveted goals and purpose of life. The values have hierarchy among themselves. If there is a cow, it should be killed to save human life. Among gradation of values higher values are to be preferred. For this reason the concept of non-violence (*ahinsa*) has been reinterpreted. In Sikhism violence is *ahi÷s*[1]. If all rational arguments fail, it is justified because sword is the last resort to restore peace, social equilibrium, and justice in the society.

At the end it can be said that the essence of the Sikh social Philosophy is development of identity of the self in the world. It is committed to social and moral responsibilities toward humanity. It is an endeavour to create an ideal man who could mirror eternity on the earth. Hence social philosophy of the Gurus is a ratiocinated world-view that retrieved the existential Indian culture in their conterminous times.

(iv) *Panja Piare* (Five Beloveds)

The voluntarist philosophy of the ten Gurus is the translation of their ideals into praxis. They justify sword as a defensive weapon for restoring justice.

The numeral five is very significant in the Punjabi culture. It replaced the myth of miracle (*karamata*). It signifies victory achieved through one's own efforts, a feat performed with one's own hands. Guru Gobind Singh made this point explicit when he personally administered the sacrament of *khande-ki-pauhal*. He said that the five beloved ones, who would baptize the new converts into the fold of the khalsa-panth, should be able-bodied baptized khalsas. For instance, if a man's right hand does not have five fingers intact, he cannot get full grip on the hilt of the sword. He cannot fight in the battlefield, either. Full grip of the hilt on the sword is possible, only if one has five fingers intact. His body should in a position to fight in the battlefield. If he is not a fit person, he should voluntarily withdraw from it.

The assembly of the five beloved ones constitutes the micro-unity of the macro-society of the Khalsa-panth. The numeral five is very significant in the Indian culture. The Guru Granth makes use of it in the spiritual context. The context of the creation of the Khalsa-panth is symbolic of the socio-spiritual unity. The digit five is applicable to the collective will of the masses. The collective will of the five beloved ones replaced the despotic kings and the charismatic personality of the prophet and the Guru. The collective will mirrors the cosmic will of the Akala Purakh that reflects through the five beloved (*panja piare*). It also reaffirms significance of the societal relationships.

Guru Nanak envisioned an ideal social structure of the *sacha-khanda* and Guru Gobind Singh further restructured the existing hierarchical social scaffolding and brought into being the egalitarian militant social order (khalsa-panth) that represented synthesis of the indigenous, the Semitic, the Vedic and other religious traditions of the prevalent medieval, and the global cultural milieus. As a religious genius, he was the creator of history. His role in the history of humankind was that of the emancipator and crusader for justice against tyranny and evil. It was the struggle for the rejuvenation of human conscience, revitalization of human freedom, and restoration of self-respect. This innovative endeavour was to introduce egalitarian social structure and humanitarian values that were imperative for the restructuring of the healthy social order. In the times of Guru Nanak, the religious dignitaries had cowardly withdrawn from the existential historical responsibilities. In such a state of oppression and suppression, Guru Nanak was deeply concerned with secular and historical commitments. He advocates historical action oriented philosophy that has glow of spirituality.

The khalsa attains sovereignty of the autonomous self. He moves in the world as a free citizen of the eternal sovereign state of the Akala Purakh. It was not the intention of the Gurus to imbibe sense of independent and separatist ideology from other fellows of India. The Gurus' cut across the narrow limits of caste, gender, and regionalism and so on. For them the entire humanity is to be strung into the unity of the Khalsa Brotherhood provided they stray beyond the cocoon of the ego and the worldly enticements. Guru Gobind Singh's khalsa is intrinsically and extensively a global citizen. In this domain the universal and democratic values prevail. The elect five (*pañca*) in the Sikh tradition is the select social group of the enlightened persons.

The charismatic personality of the Guru paled into insignificance in the Sikh tradition. The Guru, as the redeemer was executing the divine will. Guru Gobind Singh was the existential voluntarist in discharging the moral and the historical responsibilities. After creation of the khalsa, the Guru dissolved his historical personality and identified himself with the khalsa-panth. Then everybody became both the redeemed and the redeemer. Consequently, the charismatic personality of the divine incarnates (*avataras*), the *messiah* and the Semitic prototypal prophets (*nabis/rasuls*) as the divine intermediary forces were demolished. Guru Nanak had initiated the process of demolishing the charismatic personality of the religious dignitaries. He finalized it. Guru Gobind Singh concretized the doctrine of the *shabda-guru* when he himself besought baptism from the *panja- piaras*. In this unprecedented historical event, the tenth Guru defused his personality into the subaltern khalsa. He drove a nail into the coffin of despotism and clergy.

With the initiation of the *khanda*-baptism the medieval feudalism and the absolute autocratic monarchy were brushed aside. Instead, the temporal power was spiritualized. It was a radical transformation of the existent social structure of the medieval hierarchical social world-view *shabda-guru* of the Guru Granth. It transformed the despotic temporal kingship into the spiritual democratic militant society of the khalsa-panth. Thus, the Sikh movement is the bridge between the medieval autocracy and feudalism and the modern democratic subaltern trends. It is anchored on the crossroads of medievalism and modernity. The modern Indian democratic structure is governed by the secular principles and man-made laws. However, the democracy of the *panja piare* is controlled by the divine *hukam* that is enshrined in the Guru Granth. Guru Gobind Singh, therefore, did not abolish the institution of monarchy. He rather sacralized it. He formulated ideology of the divine monarchy of the Akala Purakh, and transformed its pure secular character into a blend of the secular-cum-spiritual monarchy. The tenth mentor reinterpreted Guru Hargobind's concept of *piri* and *miri* as one unity.

It follows that the *khanda*-baptism was the simultaneous twofold identification of the individual wills of the masses with the divine will. Verticaliy it is the process of identification with eternity and the horizontal identification with the collective will of the khalsa-panth, which is reflected in the collective will of the five beloved ones. The collective will of the five is the will of the Akala Purakh. This idea was current in theory during other Gurus, but it was concretized in the hands of the tenth master. Thus, a spiritual dimension was added to the secular dimension of the five elects. So *khanda*-baptism is the synthesis of spirituality and secularity in which the former dominates. It opened doors for modern democracy. We will take it up in the twelfth chapter.

Nobody can be a spiritualist without overcoming the fear of death. One is required to transcend the historical time and at the same time to remain attached with the cosmic Time (*Mahakala*). The creative cognitive will in man arouses the desire to overcome the human suffering and evil. Inherent freedom is existent in man. It goads him to go beyond the spatio-temporal limits. It also kindles a yearning for continuity after death. It forms the crux of the Sikh philosophy of the voluntarist action. The Sikh tradition strikes an optimal synthesis between theory and practice. It resulted in the restoration of validity of the social realities and historicity of the human action. With the creation of the khalsa, the caste system became redundant. The hereditary hierarchical social structure of the Hinduism was replaced by an egalitarian social structure.

Note

1. *yahi kaja dhara hama janamam* /
   samajha lehhu sadhu sabha manamam//
   dharma chalavana santa ubaran/
   dust-a sabhana ko mula uparina//
   (chaupi-43) /// "Bichitra Nat-aka," *The Dasam Granth*

9

Sikhism: A Subaltern Movement

"The world you see that is form of *Hari*;
Nothing but *Hari* is visible everywhere."[1]

(i) Introductory

The genesis of Sikhism is attributed to Guru Nanak (CE 1469-1539), the founder of the Sikh faith. The Indian society was on the crossroads of medieval ages. It emerged at a time when medieval period was ending and modern era was setting in. The Sikh movement ushered in modern trends of inter-faith harmony. It was a vanguard for restoring social justice, self-respect of man and freedom of the depressed masses and the women. It reaffirms the social realities and historicity of human action. From the existential standpoint man or woman is projected as a concrete unit in the society struggling for self-dignity and freedom. The Gurus tried to make man perfect as an emancipator of humanity and guarantor of social and political justice. The Sikh movement came as a robust revolt against the existent social and political malpractices. The Sikh Gurus tried to put to 'use' their ideals into praxis. They preached their revolutionary ideas and practised them in their lifetimes.

I shall analyze and validate the Sikh Gurus' philosophical activities from the standpoint of their socio-cultural ideology. Their activities culminated in the creation of the Khalsa-panth when Guru Nanak's ideals were concretised in the hands of Guru Gobind Singh. It shall be analyzed how long the social relations are useful in guaranteeing freedom, human dignity, and other human virtues and values. In this connection some analytical questions about ideology of the Gurus are to be critically analyzed and validated with reference to ratiocination of the social ideals of *sacha-khanda* to *Khalsa-panth*. Basic issues for the Gurus were social and moral responsibilities, solidarity, virtues and values, *sangat* and *pangat,* free kitchen (*langar*), *seva* (voluntary service), and synthesis of theory and praxis. All these are offshoots of the Sikh social thought, which was envisaged by Guru Naṇak and developed by other Gurus.

Sikh faith is reinterpretation and reaffirmation of the societal realities that were negated in the medieval ages in the false hope for the otherworld. It was a social revivalist movement of conscience for ushering in societal harmony based on egalitarian social order. The classical caste oriented hierarchical social structure was ruled out. In the new social ideology human beings were projected as concrete units of this-world in the society and the historical time. Their actions in the history are real. They are expected to be detached from the worldly seductions. His actions are to be free from dogmatism, fanaticism, and fossilised beliefs. The Sikh faith represents catholic and tolerant attitude towards other genuine religions and healthy traditions, but it was critical about the degenerated forms of religious practices. The underlying idea was to yield social harmony in the composite religious culture of India. It propounded the ideology of tolerance and co-existence of the faiths on the Indian soil. 'Live and let live others' is the motto of the Sikh faith. Welfare of all is the creed of Sikhism (*sarbat ka bhala*). It advocates reinterpretation of other religious scriptures without digressing from their fundamental truth. It has adopted liberal attitude towards other scriptures and persons of other faiths.

It is a concrete idealistic and realistic system. It is spiritualism because ultimate nature of reality is spiritual in nature. It advocates idealism because it is grounded on the transcendent consciousness. It is realistic because the external world is considered real. Sikhism being an idealistic and realistic system it should be interpreted from the spiritual standpoint in which spiritual values are given priority over empirical facts. The dynamic ideology of the Sikh Gurus reflects societal structure (*sangat)* constituted of individuals that is a miniature representation of the Akala Purakh on the earth. Man as a concrete unit in the social network is projected as concrete person in temporality. His historical actions are real and the societal relationships are based on the principles of equality, fraternity, and freedom. The Sikh Gurus critiqued earlier prevalent Hindu and Muslim societies, which were based on hierarchical caste, based social structures. The subaltern masses and women were marginalised. The common masses were devoid of spiritual values in theory and practice. Thus, social ideology of the Sikh Gurus is based on the societal relations and the holy assembly (*sangat*) and the militant social order (Khalsa-panth). The revival of human dignity was the objective of the Sikh Gurus.

The sangat is the holy social group where *nama* is recited. Guru Nanak created *sangats* in different parts of India to propagate Sikh tenets to the Sikhs *sangat*. *Wadi* and *choti sangats* were created by Guru Nanak, and *manji* system was introduced by the third Guru Amardass. Further, *manjis* (dioceses) in which the experts of the Sikh doctrines were appointed to explain the Sikh doctrines to the *sangats*. Guru Arjundeva supplemented the *masandas* to the *marjidars* whose duty was to preach the Sikh tenets. And *masand* system added by Guru Arjunadeva had been centrifugal force for the devotees. The *masands* (deputies of the Gurus) were intermediaries between the Guru and the *sangat*. Their duty was to collect voluntary offerings (*daswanda*), one tenth of their honest and hard earnings from the Sikh *sangats* and to make over to the Guru on the auspicious festivals of Baisakhi and Diwali at Amritsar.

Till the last tenth Guru, charismatic personality of the gurus had been source of forging unity among the Sikhs. By introducing juristic moral conduct (*rahit maryada*) the Sikh *sangat* was knitted into the Khalsa militant social order. The world mirrors the Akala Purakh. It is certain that the Guru accepts the societal relations as stark reality. It analyses the social phenomenon as a living fact.

New world-view is built on the foundation of old traditions with new articulations. New ideologies are formulated that are put to use for their viability. Here our concern is with knowledge of the antiquity, the sacred scriptures and philosophy of Indian and Sikh cultures. Philosophy is a critique of the past knowledge. The emphasis is on desacralisation and socialisation of religion for restoring peace and justice in the Sikh Movement under the guidance of the Gurus.

The archeology of knowledge is to be reconstructed in the form of ideology. Knowledge of the Sikh scriptures and the tradition developed thereof are to be reformulated in the contemporaneous context. It is wrong to assert that any truth can be absolute. All truth is partial and relative because contexts are always in flux. New issues crop up in new contexts. It needs chiseled analysis of the problem. Debris of the past truth is to be carried forth, but it is to be reformulated in the context of the new scenario. This is the present problem of Indian philosophy. We have been living in the traditional medieval world from the standpoint of methodology.

The term social philosophy does not have a fixed connotation in the philosophical circles. What is philosophical activity? Philosophical activity is a rationally chiseled critique of feeling, emotions and passions for working out vivid perspective man, world and others. The process of critiquing through regional languages will be more authentic and rational. Language is a medium of philosophical reflection for digging out hidden meanings. Guru Nanak after survey of philosophical and religious traditions of Indian regions and the Arabic countries of West-Asia expressed his ideas in the regional language of the Punjab. His language has shades of Indic languages as well as Arabic and Persian words though sounds of the words were modified. Regional language is the best medium for philosophical reflections. We should think and express in our own language. It will help free and spontaneous expression of our thoughts. It is accomplishing self-consciousness, collectivity, solidarity, and identification with humanity. It reaffirms relationship between the visible and the invisible.

Feeling is passive because it is derived from the sense- data. And intellect is active. It articulates and ratiocinates to construct concepts. It is the privilege of the person that he articulates language for having dialogue with others. He deciphers and constructs concepts, which are images of the external particular point-instant events. Last intuition is assertive and passes judgement. Kant used in German language in these senses.

Guru Nanak was the progenitor of the Sikh faith. Till the last Guru, Guru Gobind Singh, charismatic personality of the gurus had been source of forging unity among the Sikhs. *Wadi* and *choti sangats* created by Guru Nanak, *manji system* by Guru Amardas and *masand* system had been centrifugal force for the devotees.

It will be pertinent to point out that the primary sources of the Sikh social philosophy are enshrined in the Guru Granth which was authenticated by the Sikh Gurus themselves. The tenth mentor, Guru Gobind Singh in CE 1708 apotheosised the Sikh scripture as a living *shabda-guru*. It is for eternity for the welfare of humanity. It is an eternal fount of the holy sayings of the contributors of the Guru Granth. The Sikh social order is derived from the dynamic ontology of non-dual Akala Purakh. The reality of the fluxional social phenomena is a logical necessity of the pronounced dynamic onto-theology of Sikhism. It is to be seen how far their social order is capable of reconciling eternity and temporality. The social philosophy of the Sikh faith is a development from Guru Nanak's ideology of *saca-khanda* to creation of the Khalsa-panth.

Sikhism evolved all-comprehensive concrete metaphysical system. It derived dynamic view of life from its fluxional ontology. It agreed to the Buddhist ontic view of a dynamic impersonal flow of momentary point-instant (*kshanaka*) events. For the Gurus time (*kala*) is not mythical, but a historical and real time. Akala in the Sikh onto-theology is not vacuous of temporality but plenum of time. Thus, the Akala Purakh signifies eternity inclusive of temporality. It justifies dynamic ontology of the Sikh faith. It will also imply that societal dynamic relations are real because social phenomena are real. This was done by the Gurus through their philosophical activities in the society and validated them through confirmation in praxis.

Sikhism tries to reconcile the controversy between the universalists and the realists. In Sikhism the external world is in a real universal flux and the particulars are its manifest momentary events. It is based on the sense perception (*pratyaksha*) of the real objects. For Guru Nanak universal and particular are intertwined with each other. *Jiva* (consciousness) is universal and *shakti* is particular manifest creative energy. Both are inseparable fluxional units. Like Aristotelian 'form' and 'matter' they are two extremes of the transcendent Reality. And the universals encompass the particulars. The particulars mirror the universal (eternity). Sikhism goes beyond the universals and the particulars and realises ontic identity of "That" ('isness') through mystic identity. It is a mystic sentient experience, which is difficult to explain with discursive reasoning (*...nanak kathana kardaha saru* / GG, p. 8).

Indian metaphysics encompasses both eternity and temporality. Consciousness is a transcendent reality that can't be reduced to empirical reality because it is a metaphysical ground and precondition of the essence and existence. It is simultaneously transcendent and immanent. On the contrary, in the Indian religio-philosophical scene the *Shramanic* tradition of Buddhism is considered to be opposed to the Brahmanic eternalism or essentialism that tried to restore social realities through its theory of *apohavada*; a dialectical process of exclusion or negation. It implies that reality is beyond the linguistic contours. The concept of *apoha* (significance) was conceived by the Buddha himself and the Buddhist logicians Dingaga (6th cent. CE) and Dharmakirti (7th cent. CE) developed it. It is an epistemic and logical tool for articulating and validating through cognitive conceptual constructs (*vikalpa*). These thinkers based their philosophy on the eternal metaphysical flux. Mere logic is a lopsided epistemic tool to comprehend the all-inclusive fluxional reality. Had reason been the sole epistemic tool of comprehension of reality, the Buddha at the end of his earthly sojourn would have not pronounced that reason is incompetent to explain reality.

The Madhyamikas carried his silence to the metaphysical queries forward. He advised the seekers of reality', 'be a lamp to thyself' (*atmo dipo bhava*). It was the profound spirit of Indian metaphysics that was also upheld in the Upanishads. The Sikh voluntarism is revisiting the Vedic and the Buddhist philosophies of the eternal flux.

In the Indian metaphysical scenario of early Buddhism and Vedanta for giving precedence over the universal *nirvana* and *Brahmana*, the particulars were minimised and were reduced to delusion (*maya*). The social realities were ignored. The real world was replaced with otherworld (*svarga*) in the false hope of idyllic happiness or bliss. It also took cognizance of the Semitic ontology of Islam. And Averroes (Ibn Rushd, CE 1126-98) a philosopher of the *Qur'anic* legacy and commentator of the Aristotelian metaphysics also emphasised reality of the particular objects. Greeks and Indians believe in cyclic view of time. The cyclic view has the tendency to transcend the phenomenal world and build an ideological otherworld.

Guru Nanak reconciled historicity of the prophetic or Syrian historical real linear time with the Indo-Greek cyclic time, which is the basis of dynamic view of human life. Guru Nanak places man in the existential concrete historical time. In simple words, it was reaffirmation of the micro-reality of the *homo sapiens* as concrete individuals in the societal space in history. Personal identity is to be developed from the matrix of *jiva* ('me') through esoteric discipline in the historical time. Guru Nanak used *shabda-surati-yoga* as a tool for it.

(ii) Critique of Otherworldliness

In the early Vedic times the concept of the otherworld was not effectively developed. In the Vedic period search for reality was from articulation of gods and goddesses, which were signifiers of the natural forces (say, *agani, vayu, jala, etc*). People used to worship forces of nature to achieve their desired worldly objectives. The concept of *moksha* was not yet developed in the Vedic period. These articulated supernatural deities were considered eternal and distinct from the mundane human beings. The innovation of the otherworld may be attributed to mystical trend that developed in the Upanishadic period. It was a movement of reification of one's experience that culminated in the mystic identity and the Brahman. In the Upanishada it was asserted, "I am *Brahaman, i.e., aham braham asmi*"). In the Upanishadic period inwardisation resulted in realisation of the supreme transcendent Reality (Brahaman). Gradually, it snapped its relation with the temporal world. Consequently it gave birth to the concept of the other-worldliness.

So idea of the otherworld was developed in the medieval ages due to various reasons. Later the concept of otherworld (*baikuntha*) the transcendental abode of the Vedic deities was developed. It was an abode for living of the deities who determined human destiny. It was aspired by all. It was believed that the liberated self (*atman*) is granted eternal abode in the otherworld (heaven). Guru Nanak was critical of the otherworld because it negated social realities. Sikhism made a *sui generis* contribution in the field of social philosophy from Guru Nanak. It reaffirmed social realities that were negated in the medieval ages in the false hope of the otherworld (heaven or *bahisht*).

Guru Nanak was also very virulent about the Siddhas, yogis, and *sannyasis* who withdrew from the social responsibilities. When Siddhas asked from Guru Nanak the cause for his wandering about, he replied that he was in search of an ideal man (*gurmukh*) who can discharge social responsibilities. His *gurmukh* is a householder. He was deadly against asceticism and celibacy for the simple reason that *Siddhas* and *sannyasis* withdrew themselves from the social, moral, and political responsibilities and became parasites on the society. For their food they had to beg from door to door with beggars' bowls in their hands. In this context Guru Nanak castigates the ascetics who called themselves *gurus* and *pirs*. One should not bow at their feet because they were parasites (...*guru piru sadae mangan jai / ta kai muli na lagiai pai)* (GG, p. 1245).

Social philosophy of Sikh Gurus steers a middle path between the otherworld and this-world. It steers clear of gross materialism and Vedantic abstract idealism that negate the phenomenon world as illusory (*maya*). Sikhism is an idealistic and realistic system. It is spiritualism because ultimate nature of reality is spiritual in nature. It is a concrete spiritual system, which emerged at a time when medieval period was ending and modern era was setting in. It is idealism because it is grounded on the transcendent consciousness. It is realistic because the external world is considered real.

With this background the Sikh Gurus envisaged an ideal man and social unity which could be concretised in the course of history. It is based on ontic intrinsic human nature. At the initial stage man is incomplete. He requires continuous development from within and without. Man is the only species, which can become perfect with his creative and rational faculties. His helplessness needs help of his parents and other members of the society. He is not born free, but is to become free. He develops human values and virtues in the family and in the holy social group (*sangat*). He is the concrete unit in the social structure.

(iii) Personal Identity of Man

Man is not a machine devoid of freedom. Machine deprives man of freedom which is intrinsic in human nature. Thus freedom is intrinsic value that man is required to develop. If we reduce man to a machine, then we are to postulate a superior agent that regulates its functions. In Indian philosophical traditions man has latent potency of freedom. He is to develop from within with spiritual discipline. The objective is to achieve personal identity of the self.

What is identity? What is personal identity of man? Personal identity is concerned with single person at a time. 'I' of *gurmukh* or a realised person is beyond time-space limits. He survives change, as lotus remains dry in the water. In the modern times, a French philosopher Descartes started this problem of personal identity. Kant restores unity of the self as a unifying principle of the multiplicities. Wittgenstein reduces it to a point of activity without extension. There is no solipsism of the 'I'. "I" is manifestation of the cosmic Being. Solipsism is transformed into activity.

With the help of practical discipline consciousness ascends from the aggregates of amorphous pregiven facts (both within and without). In Sikhism word-yoga is used as a tool for carrying out development of the self from gross to self-consciousness. In the process of spiritual discipline of (*sadhana*) and philosophical reflections, facts of amorphous consciousness transcend the spatio-temporal world. This is the process of involution that is to be sublimated (identified). It is developed with *shradha* that is an attitude of faith or conviction towards the Ineffable.

My concern with the world is not only as the seer (*drishta*) but also as agent (*karta*) in praxis. I struggle in the world to bring out my own transformed self-identity. My self-identity would be of a *sanyasi* who identifies himself with the cosmos and humanity. This would be a meaningful world for me. The meaning of the world is in my mind and not in the world. It leads us to explain nature and ontology of man as a concrete person being who continues living in the world from laps to grave. He is an epitome of freedom.

Solipsism is often considered egocentric having an eternal soul-substance. Pearl is a flux from within, but it is controlled by the cosmic regulative law (*hukam*). In the dynamic ontology of the cosmos there is no such eternal and static soul. In the Indian culture, like Buddhism, Sikhism dispensed with self as a fossilised entity like a soul or an *atman*. It is an activity that is to be developed into a point-instant historical, real and personal identity. Man himself posits it. Self is an activity. Wittgenstein says it is "limits of language" (*TLP*: 5.6).

In the present section, I am trying to justify that mystical experience can be expressed though language of metaphors, symbols or signs that can arouse our religious sensibility. This is the justification of the religious scriptures as means to arouse contemplator's consciousness to direct experience of the Numinous. For this reason in the Sikh tradition, the word (Guru Granth) is revered as a living guru or word. It is the perennial source of inspiration to the suffering humanity (*jugo jug et al.*). The scripture is a means to truth and not truth (end) in itself. The moment the contemplator realises truth, the scripture disappears. There is the state of *anahadnada* that is complete identity or atonement with the cosmic law (*hukam*). In a nutshell, language is not a simple tool but a complex network of signs or symbols and rules used in practice for finding out correct meanings/signification.

But an epistemic problem arises when we are to express (*kaha*) the inexpressible (*akaha / abola*) in words. No doubt, it is subjective experience of identity with the Being, but there is identical experience. All these may occur interdependently in the coeval epochs. In the beginning, it hinges on 'first person singular perspective'. When 'me' is transformed into 'Thou', then solipsism as an individuating category is changed into 'cosmic-consciousness'. In the philosophical terms it is experience of 'God intoxicated philosopher'. His utterances have universal import of meaning. 'I' then acts as representative of 'cosmic-consciousness'. It is a universally accepted fact that mystic experience is trans-linguistic experience of ecstasy. It is manifested through ciphers in written words (scriptures) in divergent scripts (characters). We are not concerned with phonetic, philological or psychological and other neurological linguistic phenomena that are concerns of linguistics. Linguistic analysis in the philosophy of religion encapsulates the ciphers and their decoded meanings, and articulation of knowledge with spiritual disciplines.

The concern of decoding the ciphers revealed through utterances of the seers and mystics is the epistemic problem of philosophy. The philosophers could not express it through language. The seers made efforts to experience the "Beyond" and express through dusk language (*sandhya bhasha*) which encompasses horizons of the empirical world and (visible and the invisible). The recorded verses of the seers were expressed through spoken language of their times. It was either spoken dialect of the common masses or the language of the elites. Many philosophers have said that where ideas can't be expressed in words, one should keep silent. Since our vision is limited, so our understanding is limited. It is to be developed. We are required to increase the limit or range of our consciousness for understanding the meanings. Our vision does not end. It can be increased with meditative spiritual development and study of vast classical literature--intuitive and critical understanding. It pales into invisibility. It may be an illusion for an ordinary person. The mystic rarefies his consciousness and increases scope of vision of comprehension. We find that with the help of a telescope our visual horizon is increased. For this reason the Tamil Siddhas have evolved dusk language that at once comprehends the visible and the invisible. At the time of dusk, we see the meeting of two horizons. It only indicates that our vision is limited. At the meanings that we get from such a twilight language we are of two types. The first is concerned with the phenomenal world and the second one discerns the hidden ciphers.

Can historical identity in the third person experience be retained? In the Semitic religions, the self retains its identity distinct from the 'Holy Other". Prophet Muhammad approximates Allah but doesn't identify with Allah. In the

Islamic tradition identification with Allah is a blasphemy (*shirak*). Mansur's Allah is *haqq* (creative truth). When he claimed identity with Him, he was put to death. For instance, a fish in the water does not lose its identity, yet it is inseparable from water. Similarly the iron files become red like fire in the furnace, but the iron files don't lose their identity of iron. In Sikhism, the sun and the rays and water and ocean are interchangeable identities (i.e., *suraj kiran mile jal ka jalu hua rama / joti joti rali sampuranu thia rama /* GG, p. 846). Semitic flight is to mediate non-absorptive experience. On the other hand, Indian immediate absorptive experience (Buddhism, Sikhism, Vedanta) makes no difference between identity of the micro-self and macro-Self. For instance, the Buddha, Bhaktas, Gurus, *et al.*, realised this ideal. It is encounter with the authentic Being. Guru Nanak asserts when he identified with the transcendental Being he became "That" (i.e., *atmu chinhi bhae nirankari /* GG, p. 415). Despite these differences all religions lead to one truth.

In order to adhere to the dynamic view of life, historical action was reaffirmed. For discharging moral responsibilities for the emancipation of humanity, the 'personal identity' of the individual self as a free subject in the society was restored. Without freedom of the self, voluntarism can't be rationally upheld. Without freedom of will it shall be a contradiction in terms. Hence, 'personal identity' for the restoration of social realities is the key concept in the pronounced non-dual dynamic onto-theology of Sikhism. If it is set aside, then discharge of moral responsibility is impossible to perform. In order to make man a responsible person toward other fellow beings, his self-developed personal identity and free will were upheld in the existential situations. Both are not given facts. Personal identity is to be developed in the society from within the undeveloped self (*jiva*).

Different religious traditions have propounded different means and ways to reach out this goal. Once personal identity in its fullness is realised, the self starts living the eternal life and enjoys ontic freedom. Ravidasa's concept of *begampura* is an ideal social structure in which the self is free in the true sense of the term (GG, p. 345). The narrow 'first person singular perspective' of the self ('me'=*jiva*) is transformed into the 'third person singular perspective' of cosmic consciousness ('I'=*atman*), which transforms 'me' and subsequently his 'I' is directed toward personal identity of 'Thou'. Furthermore, the 'I' merges with the cosmic consciousness (Akala Purakh), which is basis of the ontic existence. It is the fount of knowledge and moral judgements. The Sikh voluntarism emanates from the freed and transfigured state of consciousness that culminates in the unity of consciousness that is the primordial cause of plurality of the manifest world. This is the Sikh theory of voluntarism, which asserts that intuitive volition is to be developed from within. This point has been mentioned in the *karma-khanda* of Guru Nanak's "Japuji". It has been emphasised that mind *(mana)* reconstructs and *budhi* makes an assertive judgement. And Kabir in one of his hymns says that when he approached the sanguine One, he himself became red. Here personal identity of Kabir mirrors the transcendent macrocosmic reality. Guru Gobind Singh's *khanda*-baptism is complete identification of his will with the collective will of the Khalsa-panth, the societal reflection of eternity. The collective will of the five beloved ones (*panja piare*) represents the whole humanity and eternity. And wills of the individuals are mirrors that derive inspiration from Akala Purakh. The Khalsa, thus, reconciles spirituality and temporality with the grace of Akala Purakh. The creation of the Khalsa is the concretised eternity in history.

The recycling mythical *yugas* of the Indian religious philosophy (*satya-yuga, treta-yuga, dvapara-yuga*, and *kali-yuga*) was the Puranic concept. It implies that timo vanishes with the ending of a yuga. But a new mythical epoch (*yuga*) brings new life after the old one. So the universe spins ever without end. In the beginning truth is pure and it declines. In the last phase of *kalya-yuga* it comes to its original pristine truth. In the Sikh movement these yugas were demythologised and historicised into *satya-yuga* as a living historical reality. It was yoking eternity with the chariot of temporality. In the shoes of the khalsa, Akala Purakh writes his autobiography on the footprints of history.

The myth of beheading the five beloved ones was not a historical phenomenon. It was just a make-belief to change the attitude of the baptised Sikhs towards life. Guru Gobind Singh wanted to do away with old beliefs, which had become fossilised dogmas. He wanted to infuse martial spirit in them. The cipher of beheading the five beloved ones was a make-belief. It can be substantiated from an example from the computer. When any file becomes corrupt, it is removed from the computer and new one is replaced. Similarly the Guru removed old beliefs and replaced those new ones.

What is realisation of personal identity? It is to restore pristine identity of consciousness that was fragmented into multiplicity. It can't be reduced to empirical self. *Nama-simran* is a means of creating unity-in-diversity, and identity in multiplicity. Personal identity is the outcome of *nama-simran* and reason supplements the spiritual process. The cosmic ontic identity reflects the micro-identity of human consciousness. This identity shall be crystal clear provided man's consciousness is developed to the state of self-consciousness. For instance, the indolent (*marjivada*) is immunised against the empirical world and is awakened to the transcendental ontic identity. He is conscious of eternity but his feet are on the earth. He is simultaneously in eternity and temporality. For the realised self there is no past and future. He transcends past and future and lives in the 'now' or the 'eternal present' that instantaneously encompasses past, present, and future. Sleep is symbolic of death for the realised self. Death is eternal sleep and awakening of cosmic consciousness is to live in eternity that is 'That' (*nirankara*). 'That' is simultaneously immanent and transcendent everywhere at the same time and space.

The aim of Sikh philosophy is to arouse consciousness that is in deep slumber in the *shakti*.

In the Western and Indian religious traditions there are different approaches of creation and development of the self (*atman*). In the Western model 'I-Thou' contradiction is not resolved because chasm between the two remains at the highest state of understanding and realisation. In the Semitic traditions difference between the Creator and creation is never bridged. On the other hand, in the Indian religious traditions realisation of the pristine *natura naturans* of the self which is ontologically free transcends the dichotomy of 'I-Thou". There is complete ontological identity between the microcosm (*pinda/deha*) and macrocosm (*brahmana*). But the Guru Granth asserts that *nama-simran* is the only esoteric means of transcending the dichotomy of 'I-Thou' (*keval namu dio guri manu* / GG, p. 183).

Within this dichotomous ontological and epistemic paradigm, Sikhism strikes a hermeneutical reconciliation without suppressing the Indian and the Semitic ontology. In Sikhism *hukam* is a regulative principle of the *natura naturans* and individual's will is dominated by *haumai* (me-ness) that is a *natura naturata*. When the individual will be attuned to the cosmic will (*hukam*), *natura naturata* and *natura naturans* are identical, and the Akala Purakh is a mirror through which we peep into our 'I'. It is through *surati-shabda-yoga* the creative process is simultaneously carried out from within and without. Inward journey of human consciousness is from the 'me' to the 'I' and outward process is identification with the whole humanity. It culminates in realising its ontic identity with the cosmic law. Then, there are no extraneous restraints and constraints and the self will be free.

Realisation of this state is a matter of ethico-spiritual progression. It is simultaneously both theoretical (epistemic) and practical (ethico-spiritual) development. It is a continuous process of enrichment of human intuitive insight through internalisation and externalisation. It is carried out so long as attributive personality (*saguna*) of the Akala Purakh continues.

'Thou' is to continue till the mystic realises his ontic identity with the Akala Purakh. After realisation of the mystical identity between 'That' (*nirankara*) and 'I' all the logical constructs disappear. When there is complete existential and mystic realisation of ontological identity between 'That' and 'I', then the projected 'Thou' as personified linguistic construct is transformed into an impersonal 'That' because personality of the Numinous is dissolved. Hence, the Numinous is ineffable because there is no reason to explain it.

The personality of the self ('I') is absorbed into the formless Being (*nirankara*), but personal identity of the self ('I') as doer (*karta*) is developed and retained and the macro-unity acts through the micro-unity (*pinda*). Pipa bhakta has reiterated this idea in one of his hymns in the Guru Granth. He says that whatsoever is contained in the macro-body (*brahmanda*) is also present in the permanent miniature form in the micro-body (i.e. *jo brahmande soi pinde* /2-3/ GG, p. 695). It is evident that in Sikhism moral agent (*karta*) does not annihilate his personal identity, but destroys his conceit of the 'me' (*khudi*). *Khudi* is an impediment in the path of realising the mystic identity with the Numinous. As pointed out above man retains his historical autonomous existence so that he could be active in the world and carry out his historical responsibilities. The personal historical identity is carved out in the course of historical time in the world.

On the other hand, in the Gita we do not find dichotomy between the seer (*drishta*) and the experiencer (*bhogta*). It does not follow that the Gita dissolves the personal historical identity of the self. In the Gita, Krishna categorically asserts:

(i) Fix your mind on me, Arjuna surrender all deeds to me.
/ xviii: 57

(ii) Throw away your dharma, have faith in me,
Take refuge in me and do not fear, you will be saved.
/ xviii: 66

It may be pointed out that Arjuna whose mind was blinked with ignorance was motivated towards 'cosmic consciousness' (*vishavrupa*) that was shown in the 11th chapter. Now it is clear that the Gita projects lord Krishna as teacher and guide in the battlefield. Here the executor and the teacher are two. In the Gita Krishna's advice to Arjuna in the critical juncture of the war was that his will was "dead from within" owing to blinked fear of death and attachment with his kith and kin. Here Krishna as an essentialist did not take part in the battle at Kurukshetra, but his will is executed through Arjuna.

Guru Gobind Singh, on the contrary, reinterprets such critical predicaments from the standpoint of an existentialist. The Guru in his poetic compositions of the Dasam Granth is seen in the battlefield involved in the moral struggle (*dharma yudha)* for vigorous movement against cruelties and injustice. It was crusading for the marginalised suffering humanity. It is interesting to note that in the longish composition of the "Krishana Avatara" Khadak Singh is one of the heroic characters who is the idealised saint-soldier (*sant sapahi*) of Guru Gobind Singh. He transcends the fear of death. With Guru's grace he prefers to fighting in the battlefield to the last breath for the cause of righteousness. He seems to have concretised the theoretical ideals of the guru in praxis (see, 448 *chandas* from 1369 to 1817). When trinity of the Hindu deities (Brahma, Vishnu, Mahesha) approached Khadak Singh that they would grant him *mukti*, he declined their offer and preferred to fight and die a heroic death (*euthanasiac*) in the battle field.

'It' and 'Thou' are transient phases of the Akala Purakh. Guru Arjunadeva explains it: "*nirankara nirguna sarguna eka* / GG, p. 250". This is a simultaneous trekking of the self's identity. It culminates in 'mystical identity' of 'I-That'. It, then, dissolves ontological, epistemic, moral and other forms of dichotomies of eternity and temporality, through inward flight of the self for chiseling out its personal identity and external existential identification with humanity at large. It is a process of self-transcendence from the cleavage of the 'I-Thou' and outwardly identifying with other human beings. This is an existential process of transcending the contradiction of theory and praxis.

It is a state of transcendental freedom (*mukti/nirvana*) of the self. When one realises one's ontic identity of the self and becomes self-conscious (*atma giana*), one becomes eternally free. To be free is to have the 'third person singular perspective'. The Upanishadic seer claims: "I am brahman: i.e. *aham brahma asmi*". It means that the realised self transcends this worldliness and regains eternal freedom. Similarly Mansur al-Hajj declares in his epigrammatic statement '*an ul-haqq*' that he has attained in ecstasy eternal freedom by transcending this-world. He identifies himself with the self-creative Truth (*haqq*). He affirms non-duality of the metaphysical fluxional One.

In the colophon of Guru Nanak's philosophical treatise "the Japuji", it is said that the word (*shabda*) fashions in the mint of consciousness incomparable forms (i.e. ...*ghadiai sabadu sachi taksala/ pauri*-38) to become *natura naturans. Surati* (creative energy) is aroused from its slumberous state with the word (*shabda/nada*) that is to be transformed into cosmic resonance (*anhadanada*). The '*khandas*' (created spaces) of "the Japuji" signify an inward journey of consciousness (*surati*) from its slumberous state to the awakened intuitive volition. It is not an accidental and contingent progression. It must reinforce human will to create a new structure of values and translate them into a living reality in praxis. So internal projection is to contemplate for a bettered perfect world and human will is to carry it out in praxis in the societal relations.

This positive attitude towards the world enjoins upon man commitment for moral, social and political responsibilities for the welfare of others. It is argued out in the Sikh Scriptures that the phenomenal world is a battlefield (*dharmasala*) for culling out one's essential self. It is concerned with the '*now*' without dittoing the past. It, however, continues in the form of a tradition which determines to some extent the present. Man's creativity can revitalise the past in a restructured form. And the future is all in the dark. It is only the mystic who transcends entices or seductions of the mundane world and peeps into the future and the past. From the point of view of philosophy it is difficult to do its rational justification. However, man can create a space of his ideal world and strive to actualise it through the vicissitudes of history.

Matrix of human self is not a finished static product at the time of birth that an individual inherits from the parents. There is *jiva* and not identity of *atman* that is perfect in all respects. The Buddha did not postulate any personal identity of the individual excepting the material elements (*skandhas/pudagals*). It is to be carved out by man himself with the help of esoteric discipline and grace of *shabda-guru*. Personal identity is fashioned out of the improvised given materials of the body (*shakti*). Will and intellect are significant ingredients in the human creative consciousness, which play a vital role in molding *shakti*. *Shakti* is kinetic creative energy and cognitive consciousness, but it is potentially dormant in the gross *shakti*. Consciousness and *shakti* can't be separated from each other. There is no difference of kind but of degree. Consciousness is developed from within *shakti*, but Sikhism lays more emphasis on its conative aspect. Development of the personal identity culminates with *karma* at the top though other dimensions of consciousness are also present. It is necessary that optimum balance between intellect and will is to be actualised. Intellect is primarily concerned with theoretical analysis and will in the praxis. Both are to be reconciled and should constitute concrete identity of the self in temporality.

With the realisation of ontic identity of the 'self', the charismatic hallowed personality of the personal guruship was demolished in the Guru Granth. The higher classes in Sikhism are no more recognised as gifted and chosen offspring of God. The subaltern (*dalit*) masses were motivated to regain equality and self-dignity in the society. Medieval Sufis, Bhaktas, Sikh Gurus, *et al.* have been instrumental for the uplift of the sons of the dusty soil. The wretched people of the earth had been victims of atrocities of the upper strata of the society. Guru Nanak has gone to the extent of identifying himself with the *dalits.* He refuses to have any truck with the higher castes (see, *nicha andari nicha jati nichi hu ati nichu / nanaku tina kai sangi sathi vadia siu kia risa* /GG, p. 15). For instance, in the hagiographic tradition (*janamam sakhi samparda*) Bhai Lalo is a poor carpenter who earns his livelihood with the sweat of his brow. On the contrary, Malik Bhago is a feudal chief who exploits other poor and socially marginalised people. Hence, wrenching of blood from the bread of Bhago and milk from Lalo's bread are symbolic of the exploiter and the earnest person respectively. Guru Nanak's hermeneutics would contend that all experiences of truth are dynamically interpretative in essence.

Guru Nanak and other Sikh Gurus practically identified themselves with the subaltern masses. The creation of the Khalsa is the micro-identity of the Akala Purakh in the micro-identity of the individual realised self in history. He is likened to Kierkegaard's "knight of faith" on the earth. He is above all the parochial grooves of communalism, casteism and sectarianism. Principle of love as a cementing force of mankind is the essence of the Khalsa identity. The social structure of the Khalsa-panth is built on the matrix of individual Khalsas (others).

It is possible through *einfühlung* (Gr.) that is identification of feeling or empathy. It is a flight of *atman* to *atman.* As the Buddha says that with one candle other candles are enlightened, similarly one realised self enlightens other selves. Guru Gobind Singh identified himself with the entire Khalsa both individuals and the social order of the Khalsa. It was complete identification of feelings with entire humanity. Third person singular experience is not timeless (*anadi*) but is eternal (*ananta*). The self creates it, but it becomes eternal when one attains the state of indolence (*sahaj*). Thereafter, one is always in that state of eternal experiences (*sahaj/baqa*). Existentially this is authentic or *dharmic* life attuned to truth (*satya*). When the self is one with the creative cosmic truth (*hukam /rita*), the *atman* consummates its flight into the Numinous (*nirankara*).

This is how 'I-Thou' contradiction is resolved through continuous goal directed self-transcendence. The ultimate goal of self-transcendence is mystic identity with the transcendent consciousness. It is a dialectical creative process of going beyond the clutches of the world withdrawing from the responsibilities of the world. This is the quintessence of Sikhism. The Numinous is reflected in the heart of the individual self. Guru Nanak proclaims that in his immediate absorptive identification with the Akala Purakh, he assumes consciousness of the 'Formless Form' *(atam chinha bhai nirankari* / GG, p. 415). It is realisation of one's intrinsic ontic identity.

With the creation of the Khalsa, Guru Gobind Singh identified with humanity. In his poetic composition "Khalsa Mehma" he eulogizes the Khalsa as the true image of his real self. He goes on praising them that with their help he won many battles and bestowed charity on the [subaltern] with their grace. With their help he could demolish enemies and destroy evil. Due to them he became a scholar and assumed guruship though crores of others are present in the world.

The 'others' are as real as 'I' am. They become 'me,' yet remain also 'not-me'. It implies distinct and independent nature of 'others'. When the 'I' remains a distant observer, the 'I' sees only the manifest behaviour in society. Nevertheless, when the 'I' identifies itself with its inner Self, the 'I' becomes perfect. From the mundane point of view, it is distancing oneself from others. The 'I' identifies with myself with others' anxieties, greed, or their whole 'self'. I could not understand myself in forlornness, aloneness, alienation, hope, or love. However, if 'I' is to be true to my authentic and unique self that needs to transcend the illusion of the 'me' (empirical self).

My 'I' becomes attuned to the very essence of the real self. This is realisation of the 'personal identity' of man and his autonomy. Authentic self mirrors freedom that is the central linchpin of man in the world. The personal identity is not a given fact. It is to be cultivated with meditative continuous striving both from within and without. From within he advances to autonomy of the self and from without he socialises in the society. Man identifies himself with others. The inward journey of the self terminates when the 'I' experiences that I am drop of water on the crest of the oceanic waves. I am concerned with others not as an observer sitting on the fence, rather as an active participant and co-traveler in the existential predicaments. This is the existential approach of the Medieval Bhaktas and the Sikh Gurus. They brought Cultural Revolution in India and prepared the nation to confront any alien incursions. They identified themselves with the subaltern for their emancipation. They formulated egalitarian ideology for the welfare of the subaltern populace.

Note

1. *ehu visu sansâru tum dekhde ehu hari kâ rûpu hai hari rûpu nadri âiâ.../36/3* GG, p. 922.

10

Restoration of Woman's Identity

Only when man and woman both live above body and mind as freed souls, they represent the culture of live freedom Live freedom is freed also of sex differences.

/Puran Singh, *The Spirit Born People*

This chapter is philosophical, critical, and hermeneutical analysis of the Sikh concept of feminism from the standpoint of comparative perspective because the Sikh Scriptures and the Dasam Granth have made use of comparative methodology to reinterpret the existing Indian and Islamic religious and philosophical traditions. The objective of Guru Nanak was not to repudiate other sacred scriptures and traditions but to retrieve their essential philosophical tenets. His philosophical treatise the Japuji, the epitome of the Sikh philosophy, was finalised after his survey of other religious traditions of India and the West-Asian countries. In the Japuji he categorically states that he has perused hundreds of Semitic and Indian Scriptures and has found that ultimate ontic reality is an essence (*sahas atharah kahani kateba assulu iku dhatu...* / GG, p. 5). The Sikh Scriptures evolved viewpoint of woman with transformed semiotic signs and signification having identical metaphysical, mystical, existential, and socio-ethical implications.

Guru Nanak critiqued the *Shramanic*, and Brahmanical traditions of India and Islamic traditions from the standpoint of reconciliation of theory and praxis. For this purpose he undertook odysseys (*uddasis*) to far and wide in India and the Islamic countries. He researched that there was a serious feminist identity crisis. If she does not perform her essential social role, it would be sterile. Hence, there was birth of Sikh faith.

(i) Ontogenetic Issue of Gender Disparity

The modern feminist movement originated in the West. The term *'feminine'* has its origins in the French word, which was coined by Charles Fourier a utopian socialist thinker. The first recorded use in English was in the 1890s, when the word was used to vindicate equality and status of woman, and legal and political rights with man. Earlier in the West some feminists might have opposed the subjugation of woman, but the present chapter concentrates mainly from the Indian standpoint with special emphasis on the Sikh perspective. It is to bring out identity of woman, which was in practice in ancient India.

The medieval movement of emancipation of woman had its beginning in the 6th century in the land of Tamil Nadu and later the vanguard of the uplift of woman culminated in Sikhism. The Gurus infused new spirit of 'fearlessness' in the woman and man to breathe life of freedom and self-dignity. The voluntarist ideas of the Sikh Gurus galvanised weakened will of the subaltern masses of India.

Before the advent of Sikhism the status of woman in the society was deplorable. My aim is to highlight the basic causes, which were responsible for the suppression of woman in the medieval period of the Gurus. Sikhism has many facets, but it can itself be termed as a liberation movement of humanity and the woman from the male dominance. From the conventionalist viewpoint she was looked down upon as intrinsically defile creature and much inferior to man. Male dominated fantastic stories about woman's frail nature were concocted to establish man's superiority. He has exhausted his dexterity to portray the mystery and insanity of the women folks.

In the ancient Vedic Indian society male and female as complementary were symbolic of dynamicity and division of labour. This specialisation does not rob of her femininity nor does it destroy the male and female relationship. She has a sense of tenderness, meekness, and self-sacrifice. She is an incarnate of self-sacrifice for her children and husband. She derives pleasure in the suffering of birth pangs for the sake of creation of a new babe. She forgets all pains in due course of time when she rears her babe in her hands and feeds from the breast. She is the invisible hand behind the creation of her child's personality. She is fount of tender virtues, love, and noble values. Man and woman are procreators of progenies of human race. Mother is producer and man is creator of progenies.

Brutal violence, anger, and cruelty are not her intrinsic feminine personality traits. Male dominance is not natural and it is the result of cultural conditioning. Genes of males and females have significant impact on the offspring. Gene is a unit in cell, which controls particular personality traits of man and woman that has been passed on from its parents. It is mainly environment, which creates gender differences. It was a sort of "sexual apartheid". With one excuse or the other she was kept down in the fabric of social structure. However, she enjoyed respectable and dignified status along with man in the Vedic age of India, but later it was reduced to an utterly subordinate status by the lawgivers (e.g., Manu's *Manusimriti*), and the feudal and the priestly classes. The fourfold hierarchical stratification of Indian society kept women and shudras at the lowest ladder in the societal structure. In the *dharmashastras* the codes and injunctions kept her was practically at par with the shudras. In the Guru Granth we find arguments with cogent logical vigour to carve out complementary, distinct and self-dignified identity of the fair "second sex". The awakening of feminist awareness is the *leitmotif* of the present concern.

In medieval India of Guru Nanak's period, oppression of woman was a universal phenomenon. Suppression of feminine consciousness was at its peak. Feminine consciousness was a victimised consciousness. Woman was a silent sufferer from womb to tomb. She had an alienated state of consciousness due to blatantly unjust maltreatment of males. It was to be fortified or strengthened. The suppressed effeminised will of woman and the weakened will of the subaltern masses needed to be steeled. Guru Nanak was a staunch feminist. He made all efforts to fortify will of the marginalised masses. He tried to fortify it. When from the existential standpoint the feminine consciousness required to be transcended from the fear of death. Guru Nanak and other Gurus tried to steel the effeminised will of the masses that was facing all sorts of atrocities (*ati*) inflicted by the males and the upper strata of the Indian society.

The present chapter focuses on centrality of the feminist Sikh idea and shows that the Sikh Gurus reinterpreted femininity with their innovative intuitive insights. Her mysterious soul clothed in the universe has been sought after since eternity. She is as mysterious as the *qudrat*. The principle of femininity (*shakti*) pervades the whole essence of all creation and diversity of life-forms. The utterances of the Sikh Gurus have been philosophically interpreted from the standpoint of existential, social, and political realities. I have tried to highlight the hermeneutical diachronic semiotic significance of the feminist philosophical dimensions (i.e., ontological, physical, spiritual, social and *et al.*) of the Sikh faith and tradition within complex interpretative cultural milieu of Indian and Islamic traditions.

We are trying to emphasise the feminist sensitive problem of social justice of the female folks and to focus on gender differences and restoration of the respectful distinct feminine identity in the society. Sikhism came forward as an emancipatory revolutionary feminist movement for the amelioration of status of the *homo sapiens* and dignity with its unique innovations. It has heralded the fundamental issues of the ontic nature of woman. Her ontic status is cosmic creative energy. It has tried to give a dignified status to woman in political and social and other walks of life. Sikhism advocated her emancipation from the clutches of male predominance and prejudices.

Guru Nanak confronted the crisis of unity-and-diversity of the gender-paradox current in the medieval society of India and in the Semitic religious ecology. He thoroughly dealt with the problem of femininity. He researched in-depth that there was an existential gender disparity and identity crisis of woman. He identified the feminine problems and tried to remedy them both in theory and praxis. Other nine Gurus re-identified woman's existential predicaments and made all efforts to eradicate them from the Indian soil. Perhaps, no other religious dignitary raised heartfelt voice of revolt to ameliorate her pitiable condition. His critique of the medieval religious ecology was replete with ambivalent orientations towards the distinct gender and sex identity crises and complimentarity because he upheld his viewpoint about identity-in-diversity of life forms within the transcendental phenomenology of the non-dual dynamic *Ik* (lit. one). So man as micro-unity is real unit.

In the dynamic process opposites are in reality identical and that all differences are in essence one. This is the logic of Guru Nanak that diversity of masculine and feminine implies identity. The concrete transcendent One brackets together female and male principles at transcendental level. He articulated a synthesis of the identity crisis of the feminine with his intuitive insight by creating a mystical space (*sacha-khanda*) of the transcendent One. It encompasses the eternal and the temporal, the transcendent and the immanent or identity and difference. Both are real. The Sikh Scriptures have ontological basis of identity-in-diversity of the life-forms, which manifest themselves in the gender-dichotomy in societal network. It sets aside medieval pessimistic view of life and world negation. Its positive attitude towards the world and life reaffirmed their reality. As a result of it, it restores social reality and historicity of human action (*karma*) in the concrete societal relationships. With the reaffirmation of the feminist consciousness the householder's life was restored. This was one of the singular contributions of Sikhism in the medieval India to the pool of religious and philosophical world-views.

The Sikh Scriptures focus on the feminine dimension replete with ciphers having semiotic signs, symbols and concrete folk female imageries, metaphors, and epithets with transformed meanings. Woman has been projected as a complementary equal co-partner of man on the ethico-spiritual path of self-realisation.

Both yearn for spiritual union with the supreme Being through the spiritual co-journey of two souls' continuously longing to immerse in the Akala Purakh. In philosophical terms it is called non-differential mystical identity.

Guru Ramdasa, IVth Sikh Guru, in one of his poetic *Chants* known as *lanvan* (lit. circumambulation) in the Guru Granth explains this spiritual union (marriage) of the self with the transcendent One, the Akala Purakh. This *Chant* is chanted in solemnising the Sikh wedding celebration of the boy and the girl. Both are initiated into the householder's life (*grihasta*) (see GG, 773-74). The attitude of Sikhism on femininity is not negative, which may belittle and downgrade woman's status. Souls of both male and female are also effeminised and juxtaposed with the Akala Purakh who is self-existent (*saibhan*) masculine creator (*kartapurakh*). Fourth Guru says that all women and men, and all humans are women before the transcendent One (GG */5-5/* p. 983). It is the transcended state (*sunamandala*) wherein there is no woman and man (*sunna mandali ka jogi baise / nari na purakhu kahahu kou kaise* / GG /4-1 / p. 685*)*. When the soul attains union with her bridegroom (*kanta*), she is called bride (*suhagan*) and the separated one is *duhagan.*

It is contrary to the earlier negative and derogatory view that she is hindrance in the way of man for realising meaning or purpose of life. A woman who is not attuned to the divine husband is condemned as bad one. Such woman leaves her own husband and is engrossed with other men. Similarly men are also condemned who have sexual relations with other women. It means that Sikhism strictly upholds monogamy *(manmukha maili kamani kulakhani kunari / piru chodai ghari apana para purakhai nali piaru /* GG, Guru Amardasa, 89*)*. The steadfast wife has been projected in Sikhism as a paradigmatic complementary co-partner who facilitates in opening the way towards spiritual union (*sahaj ananda*) with the Divine bridegroom (*kanta*).

The basic biological sexual urge of human nature is a necessity. Failure of biological gratification of sex leaves traces of neuroses or psychoses and instability in the human personality. As a general rule the fact remains that sex gratification is a necessity for the development of human personality. Infinite matrix of primordial energy *(shakti)* can be briefly classified into the following philosophical dimensions:

(ii) Ontological Dimension

(a) Ontology of Identity-in-Difference

According to Indian philosophy all creation is due to twin point-instant genes of the feminine and the masculine. The underlying current in both is dynamic energy, *shakti*. Nature *(prakriti)* is symbolised as the embodiment of the dynamic feminine matrix. *Shakti* is the primordial energy (*adi shakti*) and fount of diversity of life-forms. The equivalent symbolic term of *shakti* is *lila* which is derived from Sanskrit. It's general renderings are amorous playful sport, appearance, and disguise, but its philosophical significance refers to spontaneous creativity of the Brahman. And its semiotic significance refers to causes of the myriad life-forms, which have been perpetually created and destroyed. It is a fluxional creative principle of creation and destruction or contraction of the manifest forms in the world. The essence of the Brahman is an eternal flux having transitory and ephemeral forms. In some systems differences are unreal, but Sikhism treats both difference and identity as real epiphanies.

In order to explain the ephemeral aspect of the world, the term *lila* has been latently posited in the Brahman. Without it the Brahman will be a hermaphrodite or non-productive. It is, therefore, *lila* is a fluxional element coupled with Brahman. In the Bhagavata tradition *gopis* (feminine) are Krishna's creative *lila*. This idea of *lila* is derived from the concrete and the fluxional concept of unity of the Brahman. It was symbolically carried forth in the Sikh Scriptures and the tradition as well.

According to philosophical hermeneutics it refers to complementarity and not subjugation of either one. This concept was wrongly applied on the Indian hierarchical social structure. It smacks of biased intention of the masculine upper strata of the elite class of the Brahmins. It resulted in inequalities between man and woman. In contradistinction to this misinterpretation, Sikhism envisaged egalitarian social structure in which woman and man enjoy equal opportunities and are complementary social and spiritual units. When Guru Nanak states that he sees everywhere *shiva* and *shakti*, it implies that both male and female principles are inseparably interlaced twin co-eternal male and female point-instant dynamic ontic units in the manifest world. It implies dynamic metaphysics of Sikhism and social reaffirmation as its logical and metaphysical necessity. In order to transcend this gender dominated dichotomy, Guru Nanak postulates an impersonal metaphysical principle of non-dual unity of the *Ik*. When this concept is applied on the social structure, the *homo sapiens* will enjoy equity of status in all walks of life. Identities of both men and women folks shall be retained without subordinating woman to man and *vice versa*. This is the equal ontic status of woman in the Sikh philosophy.

Diversity of forms of life is manifestation of the primordial power *(shakti)* immanent in the universe. Creation and destruction are due to the dynamic nature of energy. *Purusha* is a dynamic masculine causal principle of creation of the world. It will be pertinent to point out that in the Sikh Scriptures the term *prakriti* has not been used to mean the Nature. This term, perhaps, has been avoided because in the Sankhya System the *prakriti* has been used as recessive principle and the *purusha* though static is the primordial cause of evolution in the *prakriti* is active one.

The ontological identities of the self (*atman*) and the Absolute (*brahamanda*) are transcendentally latent and neutral, but they become diversified into feminine and masculine sexes at the manifest level. It resolves the paradox of male and female. Guru Arjundeva explicitly says the supreme Being is at once both male and female (*ape purakh ape nari* /GG, 1020). It emphasises that both sexes are simultaneously implicit in the supreme Being. It is true in the case of males and females. Androgynous explicit pre-occupation is not accepted in the Sikh philosophy. The final *sloka* of Guru Nanak's Japuji emphasises equivalence of the two sexes. Here it seems as if the infinite matrix of *shakti* reverberates with the ethical objective for the feminist concern for freedom and justice of womanhood. Similarly we come across in the Guru Granth where consorts of the male incarnates (*avataras*) always come before them;

like, Sita-Rama, Radha-Krishna, Shiva-Parvati, Lakshmi-Narayana, and so on. It is a sheer honorific precedence rather than a metaphysical priority.

Guru Nanak puts this concept that *shiva* and *shakti* are both inherent in the micro-body (*siva sakti ghari vasa paia... /* GG, 1027). Guru Arjundeva (V[th]. Guru) further crystallises this binary opposition in another way. The macro-Creator (*karta*) Himself creates male (*shiva*) and female (*shakti*) from Himself and regulates their functions through cosmic Law (*hukam*) (*siva sakti api upai kai karta ape hukamu vartae... / GG*, 920). Here the Arabic term *hukam* is used as a creative and dynamic principle of the cosmos. And Guru Amardasa explicates this point from the microcosmic viewpoint. He says that male and female principles are latently present in the micro-body (*siva sakti dehu mahi pae... /* GG, 1056). Sikh ontology does not recognise manifest gender dominated dichotomy from the ultimate standpoint. Then a question arises: Who is our primordial Mother (*kat ki mai*)? Now it is evident from the above given arguments and references that our primordial mother is infinite energy.

Instead, the Arabic term '*qudrat*' is used. It stands for cosmic creative energy. It is the matrix of all creation, including diversity of life-forms in the universe The *Qudrat* has been repeatedly used in the Guru Granth because it symbolises womb of creation. It is feminine manifestation in the ecology. In Indian tradition *shakti* as energy has also been personified as the goddess (*devi*) and is worshipped as well. The *Chandi* in the Puranic tradition was symbolised as pure and virgin goddess who fought against the demons (*asuras*) to achieve victory over evil forces. It was a mythical exposition of *shakti*. Guru Gobind Singh transformed this myth of femininity as a temporal or historical reality. She is shown fighting against evil forces in the world. The mythical concept of the goddess was demythologised and historicity of the world and human action were accepted as a temporal reality. So the mythical goddess *Chandi* in the Puranas is different from the historicised one used in the anthology of the Dasam Granth. In this script Guru Gobind Singh demythologises the personified *shakti* (goddess) as a material war weapon (sword), which destroys evil forces in the world. Similarly, other material war weapons were spiritualised. His composition, *Shastra-mala,* is devoted to the worship of war weapons. It instils martial spirit in the person who devoutly recites it with a will to translate the spirit of the words into action. In the moral struggle the goddess *Chandi* as feminine *shakti* inspires man to fortify his will power to defeat evil forces.

Sikhism argues for freedom, equality of opportunities and equality of conditions, which are justifiable ideals. Conditions are only utopian because the conditions go on changing. Like the shudras she has been underprivileged. She is to be brought at par with man. Hence, she has deeper meaning of femininity. Guru Nanak in the colophon (*sloka*) of the Japuji says air (*pavan*) as subtle energy (*shabda*) is *guru*. Water is symbolic of progenitor and the vast earth is a cosmic womb of productivity (*pavan guru pana pita mata dharti mahat* / GG, 8). The earth (*qudrat*) is a cosmic matrix of fertility and woman is a miniature mother. In the ancient world-view of India *shakti* is a living and creative principle of creation of myriad forms in the world. In Sikhism macrocosm manifests itself through microcosm. Both are real. The Sun is the primal creator of life and the earth is the producer of life forms.

In the medieval times along with the world, the manifest microforms were minimised, but in Sikhism the miniature forms regained their ontic reality. Therefore, woman as a female principle of productivity or fertility is real. She is organically related to the concerns of fertility and *shiva* as creator is juxtaposed as complementary to *shaktii.* The principle of diversification of life-forms is due to endogenous growth from within *shakti*. The combination of *shiva* and *shakti* retains dynamicity. It is a metaphysical basis of diversity of life-forms in the cosmos. It does not allow homogenising masculinity, which lays thrust on male-stream of dominance. It will destroy diversity of life and identity of the feminine. For retaining the distinct feminine identity and diversity of life *shiva* and *shakti* are the metaphysical and logical necessities. Woman is identified with productivity and diversity and man with creativity of life-forms.

(b) Genetic Dimension

Masculine and female identities are bracketed together within the conceptual constructs of the transcendent One because It transcends the gender-paradox of femininity and masculinity at phenomenal level. The female and male principles are latent at the transcendental level. The *mulmantra* (kernel tenet) of the Sikh Canon emphasises that the ontological ground of the myriad manifest forms transcends the dichotomy of gender. *Ikomkar* (=Be+ing+is) is concrete numeral symbolic of ontological One, which encompasses the phenomenal categories (cause, time, space, etc) and transcends the sex and gender dichotomy. It is unity of the ultimate Reality in which the ontological identity of the self and the Brahman neutralises are amnifested.

Mata (shakti or producer) and the father (*karta* or creator) are uniquely linked together by the innumerable functional attributes; such as, husband (*kanta, pati, bharta*), beloved (*piara, yara, mitra*) and many others. The feminine principle as cause of creation emanates manifest forms of the universe. She has been symbolised as bride yearning for union with the groom through physical, psychological, cosmological and spiritual realms. The Sikh ontology may further be split up into physical, mental, and spiritual dimensions. According to Guru Nanak human body is constituted of male's sperms and female's ova (i.e. *rakatu bindu ka ihu tano* /GG, 63). Guru Nanak asserts that the physical bodies of the males and the females are created out of fertilisation of mother's ova or female genes and father's sperms or male genes (*ma ki raktu pita binda dhara* /GG, 1022). Guru Nanak makes it more explicit that by cohabitation of father and mother human person is acquired (*mili mata pita pindu kamai* / GG, 989). It may be made clear that sex distinction is a natural biological or genetic dichotomy, but masculine and feminine genders are psycho-social cultural disparities imposed by cultural conditions in the society. This sex biased trend was condemned in Sikhism.

Male and female sexes are determined by the fertilisation of the chromosome (i.e., 'x' and 'y') in the foetus. Woman's 'x' chromosome fertilises with the male 'x' chromosome, and then female offspring will be born. And if the 'y' chromosome of male enters into the female 'x' chromosome, male offspring shall take birth. If 'y' chromosome of man is weak and 'x' chromosome of woman is dominant, the 'x' and 'x' of both shall be fertilised. It is random process. It cannot be said with certainty that the offspring of such women shall be domineering. Many things depend upon the environment, but heredity does play a significant role in some respects.

It is ridiculous that women are often blamed in the society for giving birth to girls. As a matter of fact husband is to be blamed for his weaker 'y' chromosome. Now it is scientifically clear that fertilisation of the 'x' and 'y' chromosomes are the causes of productivity and diversity of life-forms. Thus, diversity of life is a stark reality. This justifies the argument that distinctness of identities of both the sexes is to be recognised in private and public life as a scientific truth. And the awareness of gender-distinction is the outcome of psychosocial interactions in the cultural environment.

Earlier woman was suppressed, but not now in the changed conditions. Domineering women may try to do away with all relations of love and marriage. It will dissipate the harmonious relationship of married life. She will try to dominate in domestic life. So such masculine woman cannot reach the heights of life as she could otherwise achieve in a mutual friendship with her life partner. It is desirable for her to have harmonious monogamous life. The promiscuity or prostitution is to be avoided at all costs. Harmonious cohabitation is the central point of household life.

(c) Spiritual Dimension

Kabir in one of the *shabdas* says that the first primordial cause of the world is the light (*nur*) of Allah (*avali allah nuru upaia qudrati ke* (energy) *sabha bande / eka nura te sabhu jagu upajia... /* GG, 1349). Now it is self-evident that all animate and inanimate beings in the world are creations of the light (*nur*). Guru Amardasa introduces third element of light (*joti,* mind) which is non-material but it is virtually transformed subtle form energy or *shakti*. It symbolises spirit (light) (*joti / nur*) whch is symbolic of the primordial cause of creation. The

Guru applies this creative subtle cipher of *joti* on the human body. The child takes birth only when light (*joti / nur*) enters the human body. In this context, the IIIrd Guru reasserts that the human body becomes animated only when the dormant divine light (*joti*) is installed in it (*eha sarira meria hari tuma mahi joti rakhi ta tu jaga mahi aia... /* GG, 921). It means that human person cannot be animated unless the life-giving light (*joti*) is installed in it. The divine element is both transcendent and immanent in the microcosm (*pinda*) and macrocosm (*brahamanda*) respectively. It is spiritual essence of femininity for it is manifestation of *shakti*.

(iii) Social Dimension (Identity Crisis)

(a) Suppression of Woman

The prevalent denigration of the female body symbolic of cultural and religious taboos (*sutak* and *patak*) has been castigated in the Guru Granth. Before the advent of Sikh faith the status of woman was dubious and crucial because of her menstruation and child birth. Her puberty period generally starts about at the age of twelve years and the menopause ranges between 45 to 50 years. With the start of puberty period desire for union with the opposite sex is a passion for her. And with the menopause certain physiological and psychological changes take place in women. These are to be given due cognisance for her proper adjustment at home and in the public life. She was treated impure and deceitful. Sikhism accepts menstruation as a natural biological process. The very birth of man himself is due to menstruation. Without menstruation birth of child is not possible. We find in the case of eunuchs and frigid women. It is only *Akala Purakh* who is conceptualised as born without menstrual blood because He is the self-created Being (*saibhan*). Even in the Qur'an menstruation and pregnancy are not looked down upon as we find negative attitude towards it in the Indian tradition. The Qur'an says "... it is not lawful for them to hide what Allah has created in their wombs" (II, 228). Menstruation of the female is a natural biological process. Unfortunately, man has exploited it for lowering down status of woman. Far from being disdained menstrual bleeding is accepted in the Sikh Canon as an essential and natural biological phenomenon for procreation and continuity of human species. The very life itself begins with bleeding. Blood is essential for animate beings to be alive. If there is no blood in the body, there is no life. Blood is biopsychic life (*prana*) itself.

In another verse in the "Asa Ki Vara" Guru Nanak rejected the, then, prevalent superstition of *sutak,* impurity after the child's birth. After birth of a child she oozes out blood from the uterus. Blood carries germs, which may be injurious for us. Guru Nanak calls it a false belief. He argues that germs are even present in the cow-dung, wood, grains of cereals, water, etc. No doubt, physical cleanliness is hygienically necessary, but the central focus of Sikhism is on the purity of mind because real teaching of Sikhism starts from the mind, which is the essence of Reality. Impurity of mind disappears with enlightenment (*viveka*). In Sikhism the root-cause of all forms of *sutak* is to indulge in worship of literal worship of male and female idols and lower deities. Those who are blessed by His grace, they will be immunised from the primordial impurity. It is washed away by true knowledge i.e., (*nanak sutak eva na utare giana utarai dhoi* /GG, verse-17, p.72). According to Guru Nanak *sutak or patak is* attachment with the world (GG, 413). It is wrong to attach impurity to birth (*sutak*) and death (*patak*). All mankind is ruined by this superstition (... *janme sutaku mue phuni sutaku sutaka parja bigoi* / 1-41 / GG, Kabir / 331).

All such absurd ideas and beliefs are absent in the Sikh philosophy. Guru Nanak reprimands those who abhor woman on account of her menstrual periodic cycle (GG, 473). He castigates those who hate and stigmatise her for menstrual blood stained garments. Sikhism transcends the phenomenal space and creates its own conceptual space. For Guru Nanak all these are mundane concerns, which pale into insignificance at higher transcendental level. Guru Nanak argues that those who condemn her, their minds cannot be pure because they themselves are guilty of being bloodsuckers and exploiters of the oppressed subaltern masses. The realised person (*gurmukh*) of Sikhism is immunised from seductions of the world. According to Guru Nanak real purity of man and woman lies in the hearts of those who are attuned to the cosmic law (*hukam*) and their tongues recite the Divine Names (GG, 140). It was his emancipatory endeavour for restoring identity and dignity of the woman. For this purpose he articulated conceptual constructs of the Divine for the sake of the *homo sapiens*. His aim was to get recognition of complementary and dignified identity of the "second sex". Woman's estrangement from existential social realities and man's predominance over her is virulently castigated in the Sikh Canon.

From the point of view of genetics these differences are insignificant for determining racial differences among the species. The genes will determine colour of skin, length of body, physiological features, etc., but most of the differences are due to environment. Some potentialities, which are latent in man and woman, require proper conditions. If proper conditions are provided these shall be developed. If the suitable conditions are not made available to men or women, the potentialities will remain dormant. For that purpose proper education and freedom are necessary. For centuries together woman could not develop her potentialities because she was deprived of freedom of education. Man did not allow her congenial conditions to develop her potentialities. In medieval ages it was a dire necessity to emancipate her suppressed consciousness.

In certain respects she may be superior to man. For instance, a Chinese proverb says, "A man thinks he knows, but a woman knows better." It means that man is more rational and intellectual whereas woman has better intuitive understanding of the problems. Perhaps, it is because of the fact that she has been confined to the domestic emotional environment. She was deprived of education and was not allowed to mix up with other persons in the society. This point needs further probe to find out clear-cut scientific evidence that man is more rational as compared to woman. It is also not justifiable that man's physical strength gives him edge in sexual power over woman. Her meek, sublime, and less aggressive nature are not causes of her weakness. This has much to do with socialisation into passive role. She has been trained since her early childhood to be submissive even though she may be equal or stronger in strength to a boy. She needs freedom to develop her potentialities. Differences of gender and natural aptitude need to be evinced through education.

Sikhism pleaded in defence of woman as a rational being capable of getting education for discharging duties of a civilised citizen. Even the recent research in human genetics has eroded the old myth of gender and racial differences and superiority of man. Oppression of woman springs from the make-belief that men are rational and women are emotional. Or men are more logical and women are more intuitive. A French phrase says that when man and woman climb up stair cases to go to the roof, woman reaches earlier. It means that woman goes up without thinking and man slows down his speed with thinking. This belief is common in the history of philosophy both in the East and the West. In the patriarchal concoction of such biased male concepts and beliefs is possible. It may be pertinent to point out that reason does peep into the heart of reality. It is intuition which realises it. The realm of intuition is higher than that of reason. Hence it would be morally unjust to condemn and subjugate her on account of emotionality, which is fount of sublime values and virtues of men and women. Rather, she should be proud of her exclusive feminine traits.

For the sake of argument, if we accept that men and women are guaranteed equal legal and political rights and equality of their rational nature, there is no guarantee that her subordination shall be eradicated. The solution of this problem lies in change of hearts of the males. She needs friendship, equal treatment and grant for freedom and goodwill. The Gurus also advocated in defence of woman as a rational being capable of getting education for discharging the duties of a civilised citizen. The aim of the Sikh movement was to remove all impediments, which led to her subordination.

(b) Feminine Identity Crisis

Besides, there are other intertwined relevant vital issues related with the problematic of feminism. For instance, there is a need to create balance of relationship between men and women and to do away with gender and the sexual denigration of the masculine linguistic constructs, which smack of prejudices of man against the opposite sex. Such issues are related with the status of the fair sex, which were relegated to the periphery in the medieval social life. In Sikhism woman is equal or partial helpmate in the household and other specialised fields of life. She is distinct as well as complementary of man. Our problem is not only to restore equality of woman, but to create an environment of equity. She is also to regain harmonious and interdependent status at home and in the public life. It has philosophical dimensions and endogenous grounding as well.

The modern liberation movements are male-centred and woman has been denied of her divinity of life. She has been treated as soulless robot. There is no justification in it. She is not only a body for sex gratification. She is body, mind, and soul. She has been groaning for centuries together for regaining her lost soul. Guru Nanak reiterates this idea in one of his hymn. When the human soul is attuned to her divine husband, she enjoys the bliss of ambrosia (*amrit*) of seven oceans (*seja suhavi sang pira kai sata sar amritbhare* / GG, 436). She has been trying to create new civil consciousness for restoring her freedom, self-dignity and status. She is an eternal dynamic divinity for preserving and rebuilding egalitarian social structure. In short, femininity and ecology *vis-à-vis* femininity and ethnicity are virtually synonymous concepts. It follows that feminine gender and the feminine principle are essential ingredients for the upsurge of ethnicity. Ontology, cosmology, gender, ecology and ethnicity share a common philosophical ground for diversity of life forms. It is also upheld in the "Maru Sohale" in the Guru Granth. The Gurus say when spiritual unity of Akala Purakh was in an unmanifest (*nirguna*) state, there was no manifest diversity of male and female or any other life forms. When it manifested Itself, there appeared diversity of life on the earth. And when life came into existence, it was diversified into pairs of males, females and pairs of other species. The latent sexes became explicit (cf. GG, 1035). So heterogeneity of life is its metaphysical basis. Thus, homogeneity and denial of feminine identity would be unnatural and unethical. Female infanticide, child-marriage, abortion (i.e., female foetus infanticide), polyandry and *sati* are signs of threat to diversity and survival of human life on the earth.

The Sikh movement strongly reacted against the male based ideologies of liberation and emancipation, ecological destruction, and women's subjugation. Mutual male-female relationships need to be restructured in the light of granting equal opportunities to both sexes for participating in meritocratic competitions and symbolic rewards. Patriarchal and matriarchal thinking are to be changed into neutralised love-based interdependent thinking.

Middle-class and lower caste women were deprived of education in the medieval India. She could not rival man in all branches of creativity and intellectual activity. She could excel in painting and music, and military training. For instance, Minakshi goddess, princess of Madurai excelled in military training. This kind of discrimination creates male hegemony of the upper strata of the society and gives impetus to social inequalities and creates hierarchical social structure. The ideal of egalitarian society is crucified. Besides, the subordination of woman is due to her weaker physique, which has been condemned to utter dependence on man. Man has cleverly exploited her natural recessionary physical constitution to the maximum extent of female inferiority and subservience. Lording over woman is painful as it ends in dominance and subjugation. Loving is pleasurable as it develops in love and freedom. Feminist vision is to realise equality in mind, utterance and actual social life. This was the vision of Guru Nanak. Unfortunately, we are living in a patriarchal social and political structure to the disadvantage of woman. It needs to be remedied.

Men are culturally socialised to masculine values; like, competition, aggressiveness, independence, and excessive rationality. On the contrary, women are socialised to feminine values; like, submissiveness, co-operation, emotionality, subordination, and self-sacrifice. Under such circumstances it is difficult to realise equality of woman. Equality is an abstract ideal that is difficult to be substantiated. It is not similarity or identity, we are to aspire for woman's emancipation. However, we can plead for equality of opportunity for power to or love to others for harmony. The underlying motive of man has been his will to lord over the female folks. In the Nietzschean terms it expresses man's "will-to-power" and control over resources of material means of production and to have strings of political power in his hands. It was a dextrous device of man to have a strong hold over political power and social relationships. Thus, subordination of woman facilitated to strengthen patriarchy in the past. It deprived woman of empowerment and decision making bodies.

When man's age advances his physical strength is weakened. And after satisfying his bodily needs (*pravriti*) his intellectual and spiritual needs (*nivriti*) gain supremacy over material or bodily needs. Sikhism being an idealistic system in which material values don't take precedence over spiritual values. In Sikhism both bodily and spiritual needs go side by side from birth to death and renunciation and household life go together *(viche grisata udasa rahai*/*2-7*/ GG, Guru Ramdasa-494). In this context Guru Arjunadeva has made a very significant statement that one can attain inner freedom (*moksha)* while discharging responsibilities of a householder (*hasandia khelandia painandia khavandia vichai hovai mukati*/ GG, 522). It implies that biological or bodily needs are spiritualised by bracketing them together into a social continuum. It implies that husband-wife relationship of biological necessity or conjugal relationship is transformed into spiritual love of two souls. Both are co-travellers on the spiritual path to self-realisation. In true friendship both are equal co-partners. Their ontological essence is identical though they are diversified sexes at biological level with the fertilisation of sperms and ova. In the existential context emphasis is laid on complementarity, co-operation, peace, friendship, interdependence, mutual help and freedom. It is immoral that man exploits social and political power to subjugate the female folks. Man also exploits woman emotionally and intellectually. It helps him to create hegemony over the woman. It should have been exploited for sublime human values and virtues.

On the contrary, man has articulated great male dominated cultural and religious traditions. He has dominated the cultural, literary, sculptural and other human concerns. In religion he has articulated a male God. All these fields have been controlled unfairly by males' greed for supremacy and dominance to the extent of ignoring the significant sublime aptitudes and roles of woman. Sikhism conspicuously highlighted this continued neglect of woman's sublime identity in the medieval ages. It tried to restore her spiritual identity of antiquity.

The feminine divinity (*devi*) was subordinated to the male deities (*devtas*). Man created inequality for her in the conceptualised space of male dominated ideologies. It also created inequalities and tensions in the societal relationships between male and female. The Sikh Gurus have gone to the extent of identifying this issue as a dire necessity for deconstruction and reconstruction of the lopsided male dominated ideologies and theories, which were in vogue in the medieval times. In the medieval and tribal societies she has been treated as a commercialised saleable market commodity for the purpose of sex gratification and servitude in the household and in the public life. She has been treated as a soulless toy like object for man's sexual luxury. Here spiritual identity of woman is glossed over. When Guru Amardasa started *manji* (diocese) sytsem to preach Sikh tenets some women were made in-charge of the religious centres of Sikh teaching. There had never been a *jathedar* of the 'Ákala Takht'. Similarly there were not women presidents of the SGPC, excepting Bibi Jagir Kaur. I don't see any genuine reason in her elevation, but political exigency is apparent in it. Here I want to point out that Sikhs in practice have ignored the scriptural injunctions for the sake of power politics. The gurus lived above all these.

(c) Sex Roles and Functions

In order to grasp the concept of feminine identity, we are required to reformulate the relation of the fair sex to the consuming market economy including a critique of charitable and unpaid work, free feeding and nursing children. Woman's traditional responsibility for child-care is culturally determined and not biologically inevitable except breast-feeding which is now an optional obligation. The idea of reproductive issue is outside the scope of market economics. Males have been blindly continuing their domineering practice without realising that male folks represent only one half of humanity and other half has been disgracefully deprived of her identity. At this critical juncture Sikhism came forward with its iconoclastic innovations. It broached the basic issues governing the relationship between the *homo sapiens*. In order to fuse two genealogies (male and female) man has always been keen to take refuge in the transcendent articulated conceptual space of male God. He is not emasculate personal God, but a self-created (*sabhan*) transcendent Being. He is beyond sex and gender dichotomies.

In medieval ages woman was deprived of her divine identity. Thus, religion as a social force has relegated *shudras* and the women to stomach this inhuman degrading humility under the false pretext of prevalent tradition. In the medieval society discriminatory attitude of man towards the fair sex prevailed in the Indian society. To tide over the oppressive feminine dilemma the supremacy of masculine God had to be neutralised. The feudal and priestly classes were insensitive to the inhuman predicament of religious oppression of the female gender. The medieval socio-political scenario degenerated into imperial and despotic pernicious conditions. It adversely affected the subaltern man and woman in the social environment.

I think that woman should not claim for equality in all walks of life for the simple reason that she can't be equal in all the fields of specialisation because of pregnancy, child-care and child-rearing, household work, and other routine household activities at home. She may be having different genetic potentials. Hence we need to demarcate identities of each sex on the basis of their potentialities and not to plead for her equality with man. In fact, woman's claim should be according to her might and aptitudes or merits. We have to make a rational analysis into cultural praxis of the *homo sapiens* as is needed in the existential context of psycho-socio-cultural paradigmatic perspectives.

It may result in sexual division of roles and functions in the household and sharing of common responsibilities in all walks of life. It is bound to cause tension or more inharmonious relationships between the couples. Males will develop feminine habits and values and *vice versa.* It will tend to homogenise their lifestyles and will pose new problems of independence versus dependence.

The ideal person of Sikhism (*gurmuki*) is an androgynous model who attains the full human potential at social and spiritual levels. Plato in the *Symposiom* has suggested that writers and thinkers need to be androgynous to tap all the skills necessary for successful insight. Both man and woman need to be equally active and independent and complementary with equal sense of control over themselves for creative and productive activities or a meaningful involvement in the society. Stereotyped sex roles will be successfully borne by boy and girl, husband and wife, and mother and father. More emphasis shall be on congenial socialisation and harmony. The ideal man of Sikhism transcends gender distinctions. Bisexual love develops into spiritual love. He lives beyond body and sex. As a result of it, Sikhism outrightly rejects subordination and subjugation or sex harassment or abuse. It is possible, "only when man and woman both live above body and mind as freed souls, they represent the culture of lived freedom. Lived freedom is freed also of sex differences. It condemns male for treating woman as commercialised object and defile being. She was not treated as free human "person". Her soul remained in a state of suspended animation in the male dominated social structure. She has lost her beauty and divine identity, and has not yet regained her soul.

(d) Sex and Genealogy

In the medieval Indian patriarchal social structure girl was denied of all claims including female genealogy in her parental house and in her in-law's family. She was rooted out from her parental home and was transplanted into the genealogy of her husband. For this reason she has been considered as gift/property for/of her in-laws' (*paraya dhana*). This idea can be traced from economics. The oppression of women arose with the concept of property, which was envisaged by Plato in the *Republic*. It was mainly because women could reproduce boys and girls as property for the family. The capitalists and the feudal lords articulated male domineering ideologies and theories, which were founded on the idea of private property. For instance, man as worker is paid for his wages and woman serves without payment at home. In this way, the capitalists exploited two persons. This is the materialist approach towards woman. The idealists would transcend the feminine and socialist ideologies and would brace both by transcending sex and gender differences. They would advocate freedom of soul replete with spiritual love.

She has been called sparrow in our folk songs. She is to fly away from her parental home to her in-law's house. With the influence of Indian caste system, sub-castes have stealthily penetrated into the Sikh tradition as well. At her parental home she has the title of her father's caste (sub-caste) and at her in-law's house she is obliged to embrace her husband's caste (sub-caste). She is often coerced to suffix her husband's caste, and bear and rear his children. According to Sikhism no caste or sub-caste is to be suffixed to the bride's name. It will indicate descendants of her husband. Sikhism does not believe in casteism. She is only to suffix with the word '*kaur*' meaning 'princess'. The Sikh Canon and the tradition do not permit to make use of prefix or suffix. If she uses prefix (Ms 'x') as wife of some body, it deprives her distinct identity. Her real husband is the Akala Purakh.

Both men and women are females before Akala Purakh. In her parent's house she is called Miss 'x' (father' sub-caste) and in her law's house she is Ms 'y' (husband's sub-caste). In both the cases her identity is eclipsed. Some men suffix name of their villages to their names. This will not improve upon the situation. Again his wife shall be called wife of a husband who has suffixed name of his village to his name. Therefore, Sikhism in principle does not permit either suffix or prefix to the name of either sex. It only allows '*singh*' for men and '*kaur*' to women. 'Singh' signifies fearlessness and '*kaur*' as princesses recognises her dignified status. I have come across some Sikh women who do not use sub-castes of their husbands. It seems to be justified. With this suffix her dignity and status are restored. In practice the Sikh women have started using sub-castes suffixed to their names.

Owing to the Western impact the identity of woman is negated. Psychologically the husband transfers his maternal relationship to his wife. Even identity of the mother-in-law would not figure in her husband's house. Hence, woman's genealogical identity is coalesced into a single masculine genealogy. Then a question arises: Where is her identity? It is a pathetic phenomenon! Sikhism reacted sharply against this gross injustice and callous cruelty.

Woman is forced to bear children within the husband's genealogy. Her sacrifice for the child is natural and mandatory to the husband's genealogy. So much so being an embodiment of self-sacrifice she is to bear a babe at the risk of her life even. There is no legal protection to her life against this horrible peril. After marriage she has a strong desire for a male child as a safeguard for her security, protection, and dignity in her husband's family and the society at large.

Paradoxically the mother cult of fertility or productivity (e.g., *sanji*) is built up on the matrix of patriarchal genealogy of son's mother. It is detrimental to the daughter's identity. In some cases she may dominate her emasculate husband behind the curtain but in the open social life she has usually been relegated to the social periphery. Sikhism came with a bold claim to guarantee equality of opportunities, conditions, and rights as well as social justice to both the sexes. In true Platonic or worldly love no gender should dominate because bearing and producing children is no coercion for either one. It is a moral and social obligation to continue genealogy. Due to Western culture in the cosmopolitan cities the concept of 'dink family' (double income and no kids) is coming up in the world over where the couples prefer to live alone without a child or at least one male child. Not to speak of the Western societies even in India such couples are living. I know some women who have retained their identities by using subcastes of their fathers. This can be called a "dink family." It will create new social problems for the coming generations owing to scarcity of brides. Due to declining sex rate of female foetus infanticide the problem is on the increase. In this regard science has been misused to the disadvantage of woman.

Production of children is a natural biological by-product of conjugal cohabitation. Contraceptives and abortions are artificial precautionary measures against unlawful extramarital relationships. The institution of *devadasis* (devotees of gods) in the South and in Maharashtra came in vogue. The first born girl was offered to gods in a temple. With the passage of time the institution was corrupted to the extent that these girls turned into temple harlots meant for priests and kings and debauched rich persons. During Muslim period legally married wives were kept in safer places (e.g., *imambadas* of Samana, Lucknow, etc.) and the keeps or concubines were kept along with them in the battlefield. These are instances of sex abuses. These are also indirect methods of disowning responsibilities of the foundlings for sexuality.

On the other hand, the poetic compositions of the "Caritropakhian" and the "Hikaitan" in the anthology of the Dasam Granth serve stern warnings against traps of woman. These love stories are replete with sex exploitations by men and women. In the times of Guru Gobind Singh the institution of prostitution was in vogue. These are eye-openers for us to be on our guard and keep her away from the vulgarities of sex indulgences. Stories of ideal examples of Platonic love are also given in the above anthology. These tales have been taken from the world literature; such as, *Alif-Lela*, *Ahilia-Gautam*, *PancHa Tantra*, *Katha Sarita Sagar*, *Yusaf-Julekhan*, etc. (THE Qur'an; *surah*-12)). Such exploitation and abuse of sex takes away man and woman from their targets of real purpose of life. Sikhism has a positive attitude of sex life, but it advises complete self-control on it both in theory and praxis. Production of limited number of children is a moral obligation of the married couples for continuity of human race. It will be a full check on over population, which is a problem of modern India.

Indian culture advocates self-restraint in such cases. In general, people look down upon sex as something unclean or indecent as a sign of psychic and moral perversions. Indian culture looks upon sex life as a sacred phenomenon provided it is used under self-control (*sanjam*). The Ramayana opens with a curse on the hunter who separated the two birds (*kraunca*) lost in ecstasy of sex union. Sex is not a disease or a perversion, but a natural need of body. In the ancient India the householder's life was affirmed. Sikhism reaffirms it. *Gurbani* calls it heaven (*baikuntha*). But in the medieval ages the ascetic and renunciatory trends were current in Indian society. It was also a global phenomenon. A house without wife and children is like a graveyard without soul.

The author of the *Kamasutra* presents stirring of human heart and passionate serenity for attaining spiritual freedom (*moksha*). There is no mention of *moksha* in the text. Unfortunately the text has not been interpreted from the correct positive hermeneutical perspective. In the Jungian sense their arbitrary shadows of suppression and repression of sex should not haunt their conscious or unconscious selves.

As a natural phenomenon lovemaking is also present in lower species. We may not be able to understand and appreciate their expressions. Lovemaking in lower species is not long lasting for want of persistent memory and higher creative faculty which men have. Man can create linguistic tools, symbols to interpret significance or meanings, but lower animals lack all these. Lower animals and other species are superior to man in one respect. Their lovemaking is often seasonal and occasional, but man indiscriminately continues it throughout the year. Psychologists would say that excessive sexual indulgence is perversion of human mind. Indian culture and Sikhism advocate strict control over it. Some systems advocate annihilation of sex and others preach for over indulgence in it. But Sikhism advocates for strict self-control over it. It propounds that sex is to be used as a stepping stone for realising higher spiritual values of life. To purge self from the dross of the flesh is not to destroy it. Vulgarity of sex is to be refined and sanctified into its sublimated form of love. It is to transform sex into its very sublime essence freed from vulgarities of the flesh and abuses of sexuality. The highest value of feminism is pleasure freed from the dross of vulgar flesh sexuality. Love is bliss of true friendship of two souls. Their personal identities are at once distinctly identified. Two souls are unified into one complete unity. In religious tradition physical pleasure of sex is transformed into spiritual love of souls. Love of the self is of the inmost core of the self. It is love of soul to soul and the highest self.

(e) Critique of Celibacy

The traces of promiscuity were present in the pre-Vedic tribal and nomadic stage of human civilisation. The institution of marriage was well established in the age of the Rigveda. It was obligatory for girls and women to get married. Without wife man was not eligible for sacrificial rites (*Taittiriya Brahmana*-II:2, 26). In the medieval ages sexuality and promiscuity dominated the social life. Sikhism revivifies monogamous marriage as a necessity for girls and women. It was a reaction against asceticism and celibacy, which were practised in Buddhism and Jainism. The Siddhas have gone to the extreme that semen (*bindu*) is to be preserved for attaining the highest state of consciousness.

Kabir in the Sikh Canon criticised the practice of asceticism and celibacy. He argues that if with the preservation of semen one can transcend the world, why does not a eunuch attain the highest state of consciousness (i.e., *bindu rakhi jo tariai bhai / khusrai kiu na parama gati pai* (3-4)/ GG, 324). Guru Nanak has viewed this problem from a different angle. Those who preserve their semen, are called recluses (*jati*). According to Sikhism even those cannot be emancipated from the vicious cycle of birth and death without grace of true guru's *shabda* (i.e., *iki bindu jatan kari rakhade se jati kahavahi / binu gura sabda na chutahi bhrami avaihi javahi /6-14/* (GG, 419). Guru Nanak is of the view that sex should be controlled. Along with it one is to control one's mind with true guru's *shabda* (i.e., *bindu na rakhia sabda na bhakhia /62/* GG, 945). The underlying idea in this statement is that human body is consecrated by the sacrament of marriage. It is true both in the cases of man and woman.

For continuity of human progenies there is a need to have restructured legalised heterosexuality for the sublimation of genital reproduction of children. Law or state should have least interference in determining the roles and functions at home and in the family. She has an inherent urge to satisfy her natural need of maternal affection. As a result of it, she also has a moral duty towards her offspring. For woman this, is the justifiable way out through which she can achieve recognition of her dignified distinct sexuality. In spite of this, the feminine identity needs to be restructured in preference to phallic, male homosexuality or lesbian perverted gratification of sex, and extramarital sexual intercourse. The condition will revert to its natural 'polymorphously perverse sexuality'. It will result in effeminised man and masculinised woman. All these are unnatural means of sex gratification. Their identities shall be neutralised into non-productive hermaphrodites.

Householder's life (*grahasta*) is preferred to celibacy and world-renunciation. In the married life both man and woman are equal partners. It is enjoined upon them to be loyal and steadfast to each other. Husband is required to be loyal to his wife. For this reason monogamy or one-to-one relationship is enjoined upon male and female in the Sikh Canon. In support of monogamy Guru Nanak says grabbing of other's property, exploiting of other's wife and indulgence in backbiting are poisonous and troublesome (i.e., *par dara par nari ratu ninda bikhu khai dukhu paia* / GG, 1255). Practices of female infanticides and *sati* are prohibited. The documents on the Sikh codes of moral conduct (*Rahit Namas*) prohibit every Sikh from having conjugal relationships with any woman other than his own wife. To ensure equal status to woman, the Scripture makes no distinction between the sexes in matters of initiation, instruction or participation in the sacred *sangat*, and recital of the verses from the Scripture. Woman has been granted equal right for vote in the election of the SGPC elections, which control the Sikh shrines *(gurudwaras)*.

And other extreme is celibacy (*brahamacharya).* It is a contradiction in terms. It imposes shadows of repression and suppression as well as negative conditions of bondage. Kant would assert that with the observance of celibacy production of progenies will come to standstill and human race will be annihilated. In a male dominated society lesbianism may be conceived a viable alternative for combating the heterosexual ideology that perpetuates male supremacy. This kind of feminist separatist viewpoint has the danger of homosexuality and gay or lesbian perverted practices. It will be another form of celibacy. Both the sexes shall cancel each other. It will present a lopsided picture of humanity as such. It will suffer from the same fallacy of celibacy and will make us digress from the sublime goal of human life *(moksha)*. The ideology of heterosexuality is natural, which needs to be properly channelled to keep social equilibrium between man and woman.

Reproduction does not perpetuate male supremacy and inferior status of woman or problem of the identity crisis. For this reason Indian view of marriage is positive. Nature made males and females for procreation and continuity of human race and other species. This sacred purpose of nature should be continued for posterity. For this reason sex and marriage are necessary and natural phenomena. Both should be judiciously regulated under controlled conditions. This is the logical justification of family life in Sikhism. House is preserver of human species and is a nursery of human values and virtues.

Kantian definition of marriage as 'the tying together of two persons of different sexes to a life long reciprocal possession of their sexual qualities' is defective. Marriage is not sheer breeding or preserving human race, but it is a sacred union also for discharging social and moral responsibilities towards others. In Sikhism, sexual satiety is a physiological ladder for reaching out to the apogee of spiritual bliss and freedom of the spirit. True love is a cementing force of two opposite sexes. It unites two souls. Love takes us up to the higher space of spiritual freedom where one attains eternal bliss. This is possible in this life while discharging all social and householder's obligations with disinterested involvement. This was the crux of Indian concept of renunciation (*sannyasa*) which was reinterpreted by Guru Nanak in the context of changed social conditions in the fifteen and sixteen centuries. According to Sikhism this is the essence of realisation of purpose or meaning of human life without suppressing either man or woman.

No doubt, each sex has some degree of madness, but in a male dominated society the entire draconian patriarchal bias of madness is laid on the female sex. Her sexuality is looked down upon as filthy and her suppressed sexual feelings are associated with anxiety and inferiority phobia, disgust and haunting fear of castration and lesbian perverted thinking. These psychotic phenomena are prevalent in most male dominated societies world over. The patriarchal system has deprived woman of her fine and creative niceties. She must take back her feminine sublime creativity and noble virtues of which she is the fountainhead.

As a result of her social insecurity and inferiority complex she tries to keep her person with chic. It is an interesting global phenomenon that man in social and religious traditions has deceitfully eulogised beauty of the fair sex for exploiting her, but the feminine beauty has also been condemned by him as a trap for the male folks. It is strange that man simultaneously praises and condemns her. It poses a serious dilemma for us.

(f) Pardah (Veil)

The chain of argument may further be carried forth to retain and regain divine identity of woman. Man defines his fitness by reference to the infinite male God. God has been posited for man's very existence. To supplement his physical fitness he has articulated the transcendent unique male God. God has been created after the image of man. He is called our father. The recognised identity of woman is her motherhood through which son (Christ) of God is conceptualised a living flesh. It implies that for creation female is essential.

Pardah (veil), a Persian word, means a tent like gown (*burqa*) which is used by the grown-up women to cover their faces from the evil gazes of males. In India *pardah* only among royal or aristocratic families observed it as a symbol of prestige. It was not a universally accepted social practice. Common female folks did not adopt it. There was widespread use of veil in Northern India in the wake of Muslim invasions. Third Guru Amardasa (CE 1474-1574) did not allow any woman to see him in veil because he hated this hide-bound tradition. Bhai Santokh Singh, a Sikh chronicler, has recorded the Sikh tradition in his chronicle, *Gurpratapa Surya Granth* (*rasa*-1, *ansu*-33). Sarupdasa Bhalla records this story (*sakhi*) in his chronicle *Mahama Prakasha.*

Guru Amardasa did not allow Rajput hill chiefs' wives to see him veiled in the *sangat.* Woman has not been enslaved to veil. The mystic poet of Sikhism Professor Puran Singh writes, "The third Guru while giving audience to a Hindu queen of Mandi state when she came all veiled to Him said, "You O mad woman, have come to see the Guru and you cover your face from Him".[2]

The underlying idea of condemnation of oriental veil is to encroach upon her freedom and to curve her "noble self-restrain behind the oriental veils.... Veils often symbolise the beauty and mystery of the concealed and the veiled is more sacred than the unveiled. But if veils accentuate this sex difference or unveiling does the same, both are unholy".[3]

During the Muslim period, the evils of *pardah* (veil), *harem* and *zananah*, confinement of females to the interior apartments, which were used to prohibit the strangers in seclusion became a permanent feature in India after the advent of the Muslim invaders. Even in the Qur'an veil is recommended. Covering of body is a form of *purdah* (*Q*. XXIV; 30-1). Among Muslims ladies veil (*burqa*), the garment covering the face and body from head to feet with an enmeshed opening in front of the eyes, veil her face from all males except her father, brother, and husband. Woman is required to cast down her look and cover her private parts and not to display ornaments. It was a preventive measure to guard off amorous and devilish designs of man. This Qur'anic injunction was a reaction against the pre-Islamic tribal Arabic society.

The Sikh Scriptures and different traditions do not adhere to this practice. There is no direct reference of veil as a social institution in the Sikh Canon. However, Guru Arjunadeva has used the term *'parda'* seven times in the Guru Granth, which has mystical significance identical to *maya*, which conceals ontic reality. Reality is transparent to the realised man (*brahamgiani*), but ignorant person does not discern it (i.e., *ghata ghati vasahi janahi thora / hai koi sajanu parda tora* /3-1/ GG, 562). He used it in the stereological sense in which Valmikah used in the Ramayana (*kanda* VI; A-116) for high character. In the epic Rama explains to Vibhishan that real veil of woman is to guard against persons of bad character (*rakshas*). High walls of house cannot conceal her from the evil eyes of man. It is only her high character, which can shield her from evil eyes.

Mira Bai the mystic princess of Chittor (Rajasthan) never put on veil (*parda*) in the holy assembly of the male saints. For the violation of the prevalent tradition she had to drink a cup of poison. She had full faith in the Bhagavata tradition which holds that all men and women are symbolised as females (*gopis*=cow girls). It is not an erotic love. It has its deeper semiotic significance that signifies yearning of *gopis* for union with Lord Krishna. They pivot round the masculine personality of Krishna. All the *gopies* passionately yearn for union with Krishna.

(g) Remarriage and Sati

I have been arguing that sex is a means of realising the highest goal of human life. For this purpose the institution of marriage is a social legitimacy and license for sexual intercourse. It is a device to condition and develop sex instinct. It is present even in the lower species. At human level sex life without a desire for progeny would be a kind of prostitution. Sterility and frigidity may be treated as exceptions due to physiological defects in man and woman. It may lead to divorce or adultery in both the cases. In normal circumstances mutual relationship between husband and wife is preferably a desire for male child. Without child family is like a graveyard. With the birth of a child relationship between husband and wife is strengthened because welfare of child is common responsibility of man and woman. Male child is preferred because he is more useful to man and girl is economically a burden on the parents. Because of this female infanticides were common among poor people. In present India rapes have increased because of insecurity of girls. It has taken the worse form of group-raping. The Parliament has to make a law against exploitation of females.

During the Muslim period the Hindu females were considered to be a greater liability for the male folks. It economically weakened men. As a consequence of it, they had not only to feed the females, but also to protect their honour and chastity in crises. The Hindu populace was coerced to adopt the practice of female infanticide and early child marriage. The state of the widows was most pitiable. Though there was no ban in the Hindu scriptures (*shastras*) against remarriage of the widow, yet the tradition did not grant her honour and respect in the society. Polygamy was permitted only to man and woman was not allowed to remarry even after her husband's death. Self-immotation was enjoined upon the widows to immolate themselves alive on the funeral pyres of their husbands. In the context of Indian culture the feasible solution was found in the rite of the *sati* to emancipate her from the condemned state of widowhood. It was out of a sense of duty and love she was forced to make supreme sacrifice in the presence of all and sundry. The priests and other people indoctrinated the collective psyche that self-sacrifice would bring great reward to her in the next rebirth. She used to make supreme sacrifice of her life with a false hope that she would be revered as a martyred goddess (*sati mata*) till posterity. However, a concession was granted to a widow in certain exceptional cases when she was pregnant or having orphan infants, but she was practically ostracised and had to observe rigorous self-discipline. It was a morbid form of rite.

On the contrary, the myth of Savitri who remains fidel and steadfast to her husband (Satyavana) takes him back from the god of death (*jamraja*) to life. This is a make-belief and expression of steadfast love for her husband. And Sita in the Ramayana was pining away in Lanka (*Sundarakanda*-LXV,18) resolved to die, but for the timely love-ring of Rama delivered by Hanumana changed her resolution (*vikalp*); new hope of life was enlightened in her. In the Sikh Canon this concept has been reinterpreted. The real husband of woman is Akala Purakha. If she realises Him, she is a married woman (*suhagan*). In Sikhism real marriage is not of male and female, but of the human souls (*atman*) with the Akala Purakh. The worldly marriage is a stepping stone for higher spiritual marriage.

It was in the Muslim period this concept of *sati* digressed from its original significance and was distorted with a view to evading Muslim plunderers. The Indian populace lacked strong will power to confront them and they could not save honour of their spouses and maiden girls. Women and girls of India were forcibly taken away as booty and were sold off in the bazaars of Ghazani. They were sexually exploited and were kept as keeps. It is a historical fact that Sikhs in the period after Guru Gobind Singh's demise used to free captured women and girls and they were safely returned to their parents. They did not want that they should go in the hands of invaders who would have exploited them. The weak willed Indian masses resorted to this escapist method of the rite of *sati.*

Sikhism is polemic to such immoral *sati* practice (*pratha)* in the society. Sikh Gurus left no stone unturned to fortify will power of the Indian masses to confront evil of *sati* in the existential social conditions. According to the Guru Granth, true *sati* is separated from her supreme Creator (*kanta*). She always yearns for meeting her transcendental One. Kabir also reiterates this idea. He has clarified meaning of the term that a woman cannot become *sati* without observing virtuous life (i.e., *binu sata sati hoi kaisai nari* /GG, 328). And Guru Amardasa revives the ancient ideal of *sati.* He says that those are real *satis* who live life of high character of purity "*sila santokhi*" (GG, 787). They are not true *satis* who burn themselves on the funeral pyres along with their husbands. The reminiscences of *sati* are still existent in our Indian society. The widow is, often, burnt along with her husband's remains in the same pyre. Among the Muslims tombs are constructed along with graves either of wife or husband. It was more practised by the *kshatriyas*. This tradition of *sati* in Rajasthan among kshatrioyas is called *jauhar,* heroic death. True *sati* is one who suffers from the pangs of separation from her primordial divine lover.

In true love both constitute a beautiful life of creativity of spirit. Love (*prema*) is higher than sexual propagation or procreation of species. Through true love spiritual unity is realised. True love is a journey of souls through limbo of human fascination and consummation in oneness of two souls. It carries the flame to enlightenment (*nirvana* or *mukti*). It sees through the secrets of life as such and purpose of human life. The moth (*parwana*) destroys its physical self by plunging into the flame (*shama*) and realises its real self. But in Sikhism the bodily self is not destroyed. It is from within the human body reality is realised.

With the advent of Sikh movement, a powerful liberating force appeared in the Indian society for restoring dignity and honour of the woman. The Sikh Gurus' teachings were significant for them. For the Gurus divinity equally manifests in all. There is no discrimination on the basis of sex or birth. Both sexes are expected to enjoy themselves respect in the society. Guru Nanak was virulently against condemnation of the women folks on the basis of sex or gender. In his critique of the prevalent gender discrimination in the Indian society, Guru Nanak observes that she should not be looked down upon because she is woman. The derogatory word "*bhanda*" (condemned one) was often used for her. In the Indian society she was dubbed as a condemned *persona non grata* in the society. She was stigmatised as the agent of sin and evil for man, and was downgraded to the status of the shudras in the social life. She lures man for the sin of sex. As a safeguard against it, celibacy and asceticism were practised among religious persons. The Indian concept of renunciation (*sannyasa*) seems to have been misinterpreted. It was interpreted as actual withdrawal from the societal responsibilities. It was a negative interpretation. Guru Nanak, on the other hand, gave it positive significance. For him *sannyasa* is inner renunciation but outwardly it advocates disinterested active involvement in the worldly affairs. His positive attitude about the world reaffirms sex life. The household life was given honourable status in the Sikh faith. Hence, both celibacy and asceticism are escape mechanisms, which are suicidal for humankind and negate identities of man and woman.

Guru Nanak had a positive attitude towards woman. In the holy assembly (*sangat*) and free kitchen in the *gurdwara* (*guru ka langar*) she enjoys respect and equal status. In this context, verses from Guru Nanak's long poetic the "Asa Ki Vara" are recited in the holy assembly. Guru Nanak voiced in favour of the female folks. "Of woman are we born, bow before her, and yearn for marriage with her. We seek her friendship to live with her. When she dies, we go in for remarriage have binding conjugal relationship with her. Then why do we to condemn her who gives birth to kings? A woman gives birth to another woman. Without her no birth is possible. Hence she is to be praised.../ (GG, 473). No-one is born without woman only God is self-born. She, therefore, deserves all respect.

(h) Restoration of Feminine Identity

Man's psyche dyed in male supremacy has created male God to suppress woman's distinct identity. Earlier abstraction was the transcendent male-gods to lord over female folks. This process comprises the origins of patriarchy. The bias against the women remains as one of the above given parameters. Woman is, often, asked such absurd questions: Are you a virgin? Are you maid? Who is your husband? Have you got children? How many children do you have? Do you have happy family life? These are fantastic queries! In addition to these uncalled for questions it is expected of her to be chaste, pious and steadfast. For example, Sita in the Ramayana had to undergo fire-test (*agni-pariksha*) to establish her chastity. On the contrary, in a male dominated society all man's sins are blotted out and forgiven. Man puts a stop to woman's free thinking. Alas! the male dominated society does not exonerate her for her so-called marital sin. There are some essential social functions and obligations which she is expected to own. All these questions should be put to the males as well. *Ipso facto*, our basic question is that: How to retain distinct and complementary identities of both the sexes?

She has been coerced to accept the prevalent man's predominant form of patriarchal beliefs. Creation of progenies could not be possible without the female. In the Indian culture cosmic divine energy (*shakti*) is a primordial efficient and material cause of creativity of the myriad forms of life in the world. *Shakti* has been personified as the primal mother of fertility. Guru Nanak says that by union with the eternal (*shiva*) she (*shakti*) gives birth to three regents, who perform functions of creator, preserver, and judge. They hold obedience to her in carrying out their respective assigned functions (*eka mai jugati viai tini cele parvanu / iku sansari iku bhandari iku lae divanu/* / GG, p.7). The divine energy has been personified as a goddess of the female cult. In Shaivism and Vaishnavism Shiva-Shakti and Vishnu-Lakshmi are complementary to each other. Both male (*shiva*) and female (*shakti*) glued together cause procreation of the progenies. Both are to be harmonised to keep equilibrium in nature and society. The underlying idea of the Sikh advocacy of the feminine movement was to guarantee recognition of her status in the society.

With regard to the female identity there has been regression to siren goddess who fights against male god or gods in the battlefield. Today the yearning of the female is to get recognition of her distinct and complementary identity in the society. In addition to it, we must respect her progression of life and growth in life-form. Cosmic creation must enter into the female womb for progressive procreation. If complementary identities of man and woman are not accepted, there is least possibility of improvement in the diversity of human life. The universe or macrocosm (*brahmana*) is an epitome of the male/female microcosm (*pinda*). We must thereby enter into womb of woman to take birth in the world.

In the medieval ages she had been spurned around the globe. The Sikh Gurus tried to remove woman's alienation from the social life. Another significant contribution of Sikhism to the religious philosophies of the world over is the feminine infinite matrix. The Sikh Scriptures have given respectable status to the female folks in the society and the feminine nobility. Spiritual ontic unity of the One (*Ik*) which is kernel of the Sikh faith encompasses the paradox of the dormant creative energy (*shakti*) and the male creative principle (*shiva*). It transcends the dichotomy of sex and gender, but both male and female are equally revered in the Sikh Scriptures as mother and father, sister and brother, husband and wife and so on.

The Vedas are revered as most sacred and revealed scriptures (*shrutis*). In the Vedic tradition the emphasis is mainly on eternity of the sacred *shabda*. In order to retain sacredness of the Vedas their pronunciation was given priority over significance or meaning. Women were deprived of education in the medieval times. Women and shudras were not allowed to receive spiritual knowledge of the sacred scriptures. The elite class of the Brahmans considered that the shudras and the women were incapable of reciting correctly the sacred shudras or *mantras* of the Vedas. They were, therefore, deprived of reciting and even listening to the sacred *mantras* of the Vedas. They were also debarred from receiving religious instructions or initiation. Mostly in the mythological literature the woman has been presented as celibate and emasculate *shakti,* which could successfully destroy the evil forces, demons (*asuras*). Thus, the feminine *shakti* has been made strong willed to eradicate atrocities in the society. Despite all these factors, male divinity (God) has been posited by man to lord over his female partner. In this way woman's identity was marginalised. Her identity, as a divine *shakti* coupled with male principle, was personified as a dynamic principle of creation of the universe, but she was not made subservient to man. In the Indian philosophy and mythology, *shakti* is inseparable from Brahman or *shiva*. The metaphor of half-woman and half-man (*ardhanari-ardhanara*) had been misinterpreted. Its semiotic interpretation within the gamut of dynamicity of the world is complementarity and interdependence of both the sexes. Either one separated from the other is sterile and non-productive. By separating each other their diversity and dynamic nature shall be negated. They will be separate static and sterile elements. God as creator (*karta pụrakha*) shall become non-productive hermaphrodite. Transcendental God is potentially capable of actualising diversity of life at phenomenal level. If femininity is not postulated, then it will not be possible to have continuity of human race. Therefore, social dimension is the metaphysical necessity of the dynamic Being.

Coming down to the brass tacks of the above given arguments, I have been reasoning out to establish that woman should be given dignified status and equity in the society. She has been victim of inhuman social discrimination in the past. Sikhism tried to take her out of the quagmire of social injustice with a view to restoring her distinct dignity and identity. This ideal was envisaged in the Sikh Scriptures. This is also the underlying idea of the ancient India and the modern movement of feminism. In recent years the problem of feminism has drawn attention of the scholars world over. Philosophy is to embed thought about justice for man and woman in the concrete existential societal situations of the medieval and the modern India. And the contemporary feminist movement is also continuation of the clarion revolt of Sikhism against the femine-centric prejudices. The Sikh philosophy is a rebellious upsurge against masculine biases and atrocities. It tried to restore identity, dignity, and status of woman in the society. It had an impact on social and political thought of Indian society and polity. When men are suppressed, it is called a tragedy, and when women are oppressed it is overlooked as a tradition. Thus, the Sikh attitude is a critique of false and biased assumption of the male superiority. The critique of such ideology of the gender discrimination is a singular landmark in the field of humanity at large, and femininity in particular.

Notes

1. Puran Singh, *The Sprit Born People*. Punjabi University, Patiala, 1990, p. 34.
2. Ibid., p. 33.
3. Ibid., p. 34.

11

Contributions of Sikhism

(i) Sikhism Harbinger of Indian Culture

It is said that "structures of inequalities are obstructions for goals of democracy". This idea of equalities of all human beings was recognised in the modern time. M.K. Gandhi, Ambedkar and others reinterpreted Indian philosophy and culture. Earlier Bhaktas and Gurus, from Guru Nanak to Guru Gobind Singh, emphasised on fresh outlook of subaltern perspective and egalitarian ideology. They were the real subaltern trendsetters for the present India. Collective responsibility, communitarian solidarity, and dissolution of idolised hero-worship and charismatic personalities, incarnations of God are the contributions of the medieval saints/ gurus. They drove a nail into the coffins of the medieval despotism and feudalism. They also endeavoured to do away with casteism and recognised status and identity of the women folks. Equality, liberty, and voluntarism were preached for restoring justice. These were the singular aspects of the medieval pious dignitaries' contributions.

In addition to these the undisputed singular contributions of the spiritual celebrities are revival of Indian culture and human values, critique of 'otherworldliness' and reaffirmation of the mundane world. They reaffirmed 'historical time' and man's historical action. Restoration of dynamic philosophy of life for discharging moral and other responsibilities are highlighted. Synthesis of theory and praxis is the quintessence of the living religions. The medieval religious teachers emphasised this aspect of Guru Nanak in one of his hymns says that truth is high, but truthful living is higher than it (see, GG, p. 62). Guru Nanak and other Gurus preached and practised this ideal in their life spans. There was innovation of new social and human values.

One of the most significant contributions of the Gurus was to revive the heroic culture of India. This is the philosophy of voluntarism, which the Gita propounds. The Gurus were staunch voluntarists. They glorified human will and identified with the cosmic will to discharge *nishkama karmas*. Fortification of will was the undercurrent of the medieval religious literature. In the modern times, M.K. Gandhi is the advocate of it. This is revisiting the ancient heroic culture of India.

Indian culture presents 'simultaneity of the non-contemporaneous'. Its philosophical interpretation is that Indian culture has been passing through zigzagged epochs of retrogression and progression. Her intrinsic values did not get lost in the arid deserts of time. Similarly, other cultures, which migrated to India, carried forth their traditions to India. Hence, these are contemporaneous in the present cultural milieu of India. This concept is bedrock of Indian culture's complex nature. It is composite, plural and multiple culture at one and the same time. It emanates from Indian philosophy, which is unity-in-diversity. Unity is the anchor and diversities are its manifestations as rays are manifestations of the sun.

Indian Philosophy embraces the eternal and the phenomenon, and reconciles theory and praxis. We, therefore, are to rediscover distinct identity of Indian culture. The fundamental issue of this work is restoration of identity of Indian philosophy and culture. I, therefore, propose to concentrate on some current cultural crises that India is facing. These are cultural crisis of religious plurality, caste division, linguistic problems, and bigotry, terrorism, national integration, and the diasporas' cultural identity.

Every interpretation, either of the sacred scripture or the tradition, is in flux. The scriptures propound eternal dynamic truth. The message of the scriptures is eternal for posterity.

The tradition stems from the scripture and the historical exigencies. We can safely infer that interpreter has to be vigilant and better equipped to make us understand candidly the ciphers in the 'sacred texts'. The reader should have developed intuitive insight for understanding the objective truth in the texts.

Culture is a reservoir of ideals of the people. Ideology is articulation of new social order, beliefs, values, norms, and the alike. It imposes checks and constraints on instinctive actions of man and social groups and their inter-group relationships. The cultural elements refine beast in man. It is a means of refinement of collective psyche of human beings. It is a mirror of the belief systems. It mirrors collective memory and oral traditions, collective beliefs, and ethos. It represents ethnic gods and their mutual habitats. The gods of the ethnic cultures live on common mountains. The Kailash *parvat* is rendezvous of Shiva and Baikuntha is the abode of Vishnu in seclusion. The havens of the Indian gods are the Kailash Mountain (*parvat*) and the Greek gods live on the Olympic Mountain. Thus, culture is a process of putting old wine in new bottles. Ideology constantly refines or reformulates beliefs, values, and norms. These are the functional ways of cultural life.

The Bhakti cult made a radical departure from the morbid and outdated traditions of the past and introduced new socially oriented healthy trends. It ushered in the trend of reaffirmation of social realities and historicity of human action. From the existential standpoint, it projects man as a concrete unit in the society struggling for human freedom. It tried to make man perfect as an emancipator of humanity and guarantor of social and political justice.

At the very outset some philosophical questions come to my mind. What is the ideology of democracy? How does it originate, develop, and culminate? What was the purpose of creation of the ideology? How is the Khalsa-panth of Guru Gobind Singh culmination of democratic ideology? What is its relevance in the present scenario? We are concerned here with ideology of collective will of democracy.

The genesis of democratic ideology is attributed to transfer from nomadic and pastoral life to the settled life in small tribal social groups knitted together with kinship ties. Since the societal relations are dynamic, so ideologies are always in flux. The Indian society in the medieval ages was on the crossroads of transition when the Bhakti cult was set in. It made radical departures from the morbid and outdated traditions of the past and introduced new socially oriented ones. From the existential standpoint it projected man as a concrete unit in the society struggling for human freedom. The Bhaktas and the Gurus strived to make man perfect as an emancipator of humanity and guarantor of social and political justice. They laid the foundation of modern democratic structure of the Indian polity. They left no stone unturned to do away with existing inequalities in the Indian society.

They ushered in democratic insurgence to make divinity to descend on the earth to emancipate the downtrodden and wretched sons of the Indian soil from the eternal fire of suffering inflicted by the feudal lords and the tyrant Sultans and the Mughal Emperors. They innovated the noble moral, social and political human values. The movement fortified will of the wretched folks of the land. They strived to eradicate evil and tyranny from India. It was a revolt against exploitation of power by the despotic kings and the feudal lords. The devotional movement was a logical and existential process of demythologising and historicising the new ideals and values. The spirited khalsa of Guru Gobind Singh is a 'knight of the Akala Purakh' in the world.

The Akala Purakh is not a transcendental Being but the Divine is in the hearts of the khalsa. In the creation of the khalsa we find the principles of democracy realised in history and translated into a living reality. The fundamental goal of democracy is to achieve social and political autonomy of the self for discharging all kinds of responsibilities while living in the society. It reflects affirmation of societal reality and historical human action.

The Bhakti movement initiated as a social rejuvenation for the achievement of the highest horizon of spirituality and emancipation of mankind. In the beginning it was more of spirituality and less of polity. It was a bold revolt of conscience against brutality of the Central Asian invaders and shameless effeminacy of the indigenous priestly class and the feudal exploiters. They strangulated human values. It was a movement of resurrection of sense of sensitivity for the welfare of humanity irrespective of any rank, sex, religion, caste, race, ethnicity, and other discriminatory practices. It was a path-breaking bold resistance for waging perpetual war against tyranny, atrocities, and injustice in the society. It was a moral commitment to the amelioration of the marginalised masses and solemn resolution for bearing historical responsibilities.

The purpose of human life has been projected as an emancipation of human suffering and homecoming voyage to eternity. Its philosophy of voluntarism came as an alarming crusade for the oppressed masses of India. The Sikh Gurus tried to put to 'use' their ideals into practice. They left no stone unturned to translate their ideals into living realities. Sikhism deals with concrete social life in history from the existential viewpoint. It was reconstruction of the medieval society that was overwhelmingly dominated by feudalism, despotism, and Brahmanical rituals of the priestly class. It rebelled against them and set in the subaltern trends of the democratic social order. The major stumbling block on the path of democracy is inequalities which manifests in different social institutions. The exponents of the Bhakti cult made all efforts to eradicate inequalities in the society.

Continuing the Indian cyclic view of time, the cyclic and realistic concept of historicity does not anticipate viability of the end of ideology or history. Escapist attitude of withdrawal from the social realities has no room in the Bhakti movement. So long as the *homo sapiens* survive on this planet, they will always be entangled in the existential predicaments. They need ideologies for tiding over their day-to-day ordeals. For this purpose the creative mind articulates ideals and values that are formulated as ideal social structures or ideologies. These ideologies are not abstract concepts, which have nothing to do with truth and social life. These ideologies dig out the dormant being in man for unfolding best in man in history. Truthfulness of ideologies is tested in the existential social situations. If they are successful in the societal relationships, these will be true ideologies. For making true ideologies it enjoins upon us to continuously reformulate them in accordance with the changing social conditions. The ideologue is required to peep into the uniqueness of every social situation. He is to be simultaneously in the empirical world and steadfastly attuned to eternity.

It is argued that in the modern industrial and consumerist society whether there is going to be an end of ideology. In this context, it can be argued that so long as man is on this planet ideology can't come to an end. Even if man withdraws from the world, he has to envisage some ideology in the other-world. The social phenomena are instantaneously changing and man is always confronted with conflicts with the changing environment. He wants to adjust to his social ecology. It is possible only if one articulates some ideal space beyond the empirical world. It is nothing but an ideal or value structure that guides one to transcend from the existential conflicts. The ideology is a structure that guides for securing the ideal social order and peace in the society. It should picture macro-reality. We are to be on our guard that while carrying over our cultural heritage of religion, art, poetry and other elements the malignant impact of materialistic Western cultural values should be relegated to the background. The Western ideologies should not overshadow our Indian culture. However, we can carry forth our ancient material culture, but it should be sanctified and spiritualised. In short, ideology is a set of principles that determine the whole gamut of societal relations. It should be of this-world and eternity tampered with dynamic spiritual continuum.

It is, often, argued that in the modern age of globalisation, industrialisation and consumerism man's inner free self has been enslaved, but we should not be pessimist and disheartened in this unfortunate situation. It is a cry of the day to restore human freedom of all and sundry. If the super-powers swallow up the smaller cultures, the hidden design for dominance over others shall be a great danger to them. This is the underlying motive behind this global problem. The sham is reminiscent of the age old children's fable of 'wolf and lamb' in which the wolf who wants to eat up the hapless continues cooking up all kinds of excuses one after the other till he actually manages to gobble up the lamb. If the super-powers are not checkmated a neo-colonial world order is in the offing.

The world opinion is the only remedy to stop this gangrenous trend. Therefore, in the modern age emphasis is on shifting from the dominance of super-culture to the subaltern one, which is based on equality of the genders, and dissolution of the charismatic religious personality and hero-worship. The present is an age without static ideologies and hero-worship. In the changing social conditions there is always a need of a new ideology, which requires continuous hermeneutical restructuring. It is to articulate an ideal space, which is to be realised in the course of history.

On a viable civil society Leo Tolstoy's "The Kingdom of God is Within You" wanted to find God's own envisaged "Kingdom" of simple peasants in life. Gandhi suggested smashing the superstructure of "exchange values" and advocated bread labour to create fraternal relations among grass root community. He also wished to fuse the rulers and the ruled by smashing the centralised state machinery. It is due to this disgust and atrocious regimentation of modern states, that political discourse stressed the role of autonomous civil societies and a consensual face-to-face plebiscite style of life, so does Gandhi. In avoiding exchange values, differentiation of skills and enterprises, it must be realised that life in such a civil society would be hardly create of self-identity. In such a civil society modern technology, scholarship, arts and refined consumer products world will not be there. It won't fascinate us for various people having always bartered their freedom for security running after industrial tinsel from their free state. It tells history of slavery. There is no reason that the utopias such as those of Thomas More, Plato, Quakers, Tolstoy would ever be realised. None of them would be concretised. Man cannot give up his addiction to his artificial environment of comforts, discriminations and hubris of power in general. Saints are on sound footing of "golden means" for adhering to "rule of law". The social contract model, over the last five hundred years, from the works of political thinkers has been dominating mind of the people.

Guru Nanak envisioned an ideal democratic social structure of the *sacha-khanda* and Guru Gobind Singh further restructured the existent social order and brought into being the militant civil social order (Khalsa-panth) that represented synthesis of the indigenous, the Semitic, the Vedic and other religious traditions of the medieval, global cultural milieus. As a religious genius, he was the creator of history and crusader of humanity. His role in the history was that of the emancipator and crusader for justice against tyranny and evil. It was restoration of human freedom and self-respect. This innovative endeavour was to introduce altruistic and humanitarian values, that were imperatives for restructuring the social order. In the times of Guru Nanak, the religious dignitaries were cowardly withdrawing from the existential historical responsibilities. In such a state of suppression and oppression, Guru Nanak was deeply concerned with secular and historical duties.

The elect (*pancha*) in the Sikh tradition is the select social group of the enlightened persons. No sacred book is of least help to man in the existential situations, but one's conscience is the only decisive source of human action. The *sangat* of the five persons represents the collective commitment and the five beloved ones are the purified ones (*nirmala*). They are embodiments of collective will and responsibility. They are the stepping stones of modern democracy and are beyond the sectarian barriers. They are representatives of the divine will and are the moving figures of eternity. They are the baptised persons and mirror the total social unity. They are committed to restoring justice and serving humanity. In a critical juncture of conflicting values, he prefers higher values. For instance, if a tiger is standing before an enemy, it should be killed to save the enemy. Here the higher value is preferred to the lower one. Sikhism is a radical philosophy of conscience that is committed to the common people. It was a protest against the medieval Indian feudalism. It brought into focus the medieval otherworldliness and reiterated values of the mundane world and restoration of the voluntarist life in the social context.

In this way the medieval feudalism and the absolute autocratic monarchy were brushed aside with the initiation of the Khalsa-Panth. Instead, the temporal power was spiritualised. It was a departure to transform the existing social structure of the medieval hierarchical social structure into the egalitarian social order. It transformed the despotic temporal kingship into the spiritual democratic militant society of the Khalsa-panth. Thus, the Sikh movement bridges between the medieval autocracy or feudalism and the modern democratic subaltern trends. Guru Gobind Singh did not abolish the institution of monarchy. He rather divinised the institution of monarchy and created the divine monarchy of the Akala Purakh, and transformed its pure secular and democratic characters into the secular-cum-spiritual monarchy. The movement was an epitome of democratic spirit and amelioration of human sufferings.

(ii) Reinterpretation of Non-Violence (*Ahinsa*)

Some exponents of the Indian metaphysics offer lopsided perspectives of human condition in the existential situations. Perhaps, for this reason, the medieval Bhaktas and the Gurus reinterpreted the Buddhist and the Jaina concept of non-violence. It sets in a trend of active resistance to atrocities committed by the native rulers In Sikhism, violence is interpreted as if it is used for restoring peace and justice in society. The use of sword for upholding truth is justified. Therefore, killing the evildoer is given precedence over other considerations. If all rational arguments fail, it is proper to wield the sword because it is the last resort for restoring peace, social equilibrium, and justice in society. It is revisiting the concept of the Mahabharata. When Krishna could not succeed in reconciling the dispute of the Kauravas and the Pandavas, war was inevitable. Sword becomes a necessary weapon for eradicating evil in the society.

Non-violence is also a form of martyrdom. If the martyr remains non-violent, he wants to prick conscience of the tyrant. He arouses the tyrant's conscience and makes him feel guilty for his sin. Guru Tegh Bahadur's stoic endurance of tortures might have haunted Aurangzeb's guilty conscience. He expressed his sense of guilt in two letters that he had written to his son asking him that no canopy (*chhatri)* should be built on his tomb. He did not want that there should be any barrier between him and God. He wanted that all elements of dust should be dropped between him and Allah. He wanted to make a confession of his guilt before God. It was a sacrifice of his ego seeking forgiveness. Socrates willfully swallowed the cup of hemlock and remained non-violent. This kind of martyrdom is witness to conscience that is a mirror of truth. In this state of eternal equanimity, the physical pain does not disturb the martyr's mind. When Christ was nailed to death on the cross, he remained non-violent and uttered: "Father, forgive them for they know not what they do!" His non-violent sacrifice on the crucifix made him eternal. Similarly, Guru Tegh Bahadur laid down his life for the freedom of conscience of the Kashmiri Pandits. Martyrdom of the Guru was the outcome of his fortified will power. His martyrdom short-circuited the tyranny of Aurangzeb. The Mughal rule collapsed in a short time. Thus, witness of inner conscience is a higher value than convictional faith and the theologian's belief. This is true form of euthanasia and martyrdom.

The *khanda-pauhul* is a process of making one transcend from absurdity of death through corrective violence (ahimsa) of the sword. For Guru Gobind Singh the highest form of non-violence is love for the Akala Purakh and humanity. Thus, for eradicating evil and tyranny the sword is the necessity in the Sikh faith. It is praxis of justice through grace of the sword. This is how the tenth mentor reinterpreted the most vital concept of the ahimsa of the khalsa as a graced weapon. It is the weapon for upholding the righteous order (*dharma*) in the society. *Dharma* and *karma* are the interlocked concepts. Both are the bases of the dynamic philosophy of the Sikh voluntarism.

Death is an eternal truth. One who is born is bound to die. Once man realizes this truth, he transcends the fear of death. He can be free to discharge his voluntary actions. For this purpose, the Guru Granth is an eternal guide to humanity in critical situations. It is a perennial source of inspiration for the Sikhs, who have implicit faith in the Sikh Canon. If they do not have faith in it, the Scripture does not help them. Guru Gobind Singh ordained at Nanded in October 1708 that the Guru Granth should be revered as the living guru. He passed over the charismatic personality of personal guruship to the *shabda-guru*.

The Gurus were convinced that nobody could be Akala. One is required to transcend the material causality and be in the higher realm of autonomy of the self. The will of individual gets absorbed into the historical time and is attuned to the cosmic time (*Mahakala*). This creative cognitive-will (*chita-sankalp*) in man arouses the desire to overcome the human suffering and evil in the society. Inherent freedom of man prompts him to go beyond the spatio-temporal limits. It also arouses the desire for continuity after death. This is the crux of the Sikh voluntarism to be active in the world, but having no attachment with the world. This was reinterpretation of the concept of self-transcendence in Indian culture. It resulted in restoration of the social realities and historicity of the human action. With the creation of the khalsa, the caste system and other discriminatory social practices were dispensed with in the Khalsa-panth. The hereditary hierarchical social structure of the Hindu *vararan-asharama-dharma* was replaced with the egalitarian social structure of the Khalsa-order.

The struggle initiated by the first Guru culminated in CE 1699 with the creation of the khalsa as a *sant-sipahi* (saint-soldier) and the Khalsa-panth (militant civil society) by the tenth mentor, Guru Gobind Singh. The Gurus propounded universal human values, spread the message of a catholic and tolerant attitude towards other sacred scriptures, and respect for the lifestyles of other religious traditions. The Gurus articulated a space for the synthesis of plurality and diversity or identity-in-diversity in the global society consisting of free inhabitants seeking to realize the eternal values of fraternity, social equality and dynamic world-view. Restoration of freedom and self-respect of all men and women was the avowed aim of the Sikh Gurus.

Guru Nanak's concept of time is existential. The foundation of the Gita is the mythical construct of time that motivates the person to disinterested action. The central message of the Gita is the epitome of the Vedic lore. With the passage of epochs, we find a wide gap between theory and practice in the existential situations. In the medieval times, it was at its zenith. This was the main concern of Guru Nanak to restore lived time in the practical life. This concept has a close affinity with the Semitic concept of time. Prophet Zoroaster has the similar viewpoint of time. The Semitic and the Zoroastrian traditions have no significance of the otherworld and the mythical world. Guru Nanak had a coeval existential problem to reconcile the Semitic and the Indic views.

Lived and the mystic's time (*waqt*) are identical. The lived time of a mystic is contrasted with the measurable time of the scientists, which continues to unending successions. Measured time is qualitatively distinct from the lived time of the mystic. The latter does not constitute continuously fleeting moments, but stills eternity in *sahj*—mystical experience. In a sense, the mystical experience is ecstasy or rupture. It is the pinnacle of time. Ordinary experience is contingent and ecstatic one is eternal and necessary. The illumined self lives in it. The meaning and significance of the world is transmuted. Because of it, it is difficult to express ecstatic or intuitive experience. The transcendental moments are interiorised and they manifest qualities of the inward lived time. The creative mind integrates triad of past, present and future into the '*now*'. However, the mystical ecstasy can be partially expressed through signs, metaphors, similes and other linguistic constructs. This has the religious glow of spirituality. It makes one oblivious of the ghost of death. Atheist existentialists and materialists do not recognise the mystical experience. They deny creativity of man. Death is the key to understand temporal experience, which is rooted in ecstasy. Hence, trans-temporal 'moment' is rooted in time. Therefore, Guru Nanak's concept of time merges into eternity. The divine providence takes man trapped in time to eternity, freedom, and authentic self. The free consciousness is authenticity of the self.

Authentic existence of man is culmination of the temporal existence in eternity. Man has the potentiality to expand his temporal self and merges into eternity. It brings in the issue of immortality of the self. It is impossible to stop physical death. It is an absolute certainty. It can be postponed but it cannot be put to an end. It has been a wild goose chase for victory over the physical death. Thus, human existence has been a ceaseless striving to overcome the spectre of death. Indian religious traditions do not declare that human existence is a total failure. Guru Nanak, in particular, tries to wriggle out of this crisis and catastrophic predicament. He comes forth with an existential solution. Man stretches out his inner time (*waqt*) into eternity and lives in it. This is the lived time of freedom.

Then a question arises: Is it an end of time? Our reply to it is that it is not end of time. It is also not abnegation of the self-identity of man. Man continues living detached life in time without having the fear of death. Man can dissolve this contradiction by overcoming the fear of death.

Time is man himself because he is in time and lives through it until his last breath. Time and activily go together Consciousness is the central temporal process. Human experience of time puts together past, present, and future into 'eternal present'. Man lives in time because the world is constantly in a flux and so is the consciousness. Lived time is a conscious temporality. Temporality constitutes core of human reality in existential time. It means that man lives through time. This is the existential view of time. Every point-instant is real for Guru Nanak. Man lives through grades of existential experiences and growth or decline in lived time. Sikhism projects man as a concrete microscopic unit in the existential situations. Lived time is the embodiment (*dharmasala*) of his self-disclosure.

Restoration of the historical sense is one of the singular contributions of the Gurus to the cultural history of medieval India. The Gurus have themselves enshrined the Sikh doctrinal world-view in the Guru Granth that is the fountainhead of the Sikh faith. It is the canonised recension. An authentic text is necessary to find out ciphers in the text. It helps the interpreter to work out coherent syntax of the text for discerning the meanings. The Sikh tradition derives the meanings from the Guru Granth. The life-events of the Gurus have contributed to the Sikh tradition. It enjoins upon us to understand the scripture in its proper perspective. The doctrines of the scripture and the tradition should go hand in hand. Like Goethe's interpretation of the "living nature," *qudrat* in the Sikh Canon is a historical world-picture of the Akala Purakh. Goethe calls the living nature an organism. The morphology of the organism of history and life, and all that bears the sign of direction and destiny is physiognomic. In culture, history, and religion we are concerned with direction and destiny of man and the nature. History is a continuous progression from uncivilised society to the civilised social order.

Guru Nanak envisages the ideology of the social order (*sacha-khanda*) to the creation of the Khalsa-panth is a historical progression from the possible to the actual. It unfolds the realm of actuality. Unfortunately, the present scenario of the khalsa ideology in praxis is cut off from the inner vision of the supreme truth. The *karma* manifests in three phases of thought, utterance, and deed (*mana, bacha,* and *karma*). It culminates in *nishkama karma* when the self attains absolute freedom in the state of *mukti*. The optimal synthesis of theory and practice is the central theme of the scripture. We do not find dichotomy in the preaching and practice in the Gurus. The Gurus represent quintessence of the doctrinal aspect of the Guru Granth. The Gurus demythologise the mythical Indic and the Semitic ideologies, prevalent in the medieval ages. Guru Nanak was seized of secular and historical realities of his time. He raised a voice of revolt against atrocities of the despots. It shows Guru Nanak's historical sense of responsibility towards the amelioration of the subaltern. He identifies himself with their agonies. His hymns advocate his crusade for freedom and self-dignity. It sets aside the medieval monarchic and the feudal despotic authoritarianism. He does not tolerate exploitation of the poor by the feudal drones. These are the kernel issues addressed by the Sikh movement against the medieval philosophies and cruel practices prevalent on the land.

Under such circumstances the poor, the children, and the women had to withstand the worst of destruction. The cultural concept of honourable death for the sake of a noble cause was the innovation of the Gurus. This is possible only if one has a historical sense and is alive to the societal and historical duties. The Punjabis were tolerating humiliation at the hands of the alien invaders. They were mostly menial workers and tillers of the land. Brahmins through rituals, ruled over the peasantry. Moneylenders too exploited them. Landowners dominated the power. It was virtually anarchy without a just and strong central seat of power. The feudal lords had the reins of power in their hands. On the contrary, the Rajputs and the Marathas had the real sense of history. They had been engaged in skirmishes and battles for their dignity.

If man is a self-creative being, he perpetually creates and changes himself and the world around him. It is not necessary that it shall be a repetitive phenomenon. Like Nietzschean philosophy, the Sikh philosophy, too, explodes the Greek myth of the 'eternal return or recurrence'. We cannot catch up the transitory moments, which do not return to the same or identical recurrences. Time cannot be stilled. The moment we try to still it, it slips away from us. The Siddhas and the *sannyasis* tried to arrest it, but failed. Hence, every moment is *distinct* and unique. The Gurus and the Bhaktas at once lived in the historical time and eternity. It implies that history does not repeat itself. The ideal man in Sikhism is required to swim with the tide of temporality like a lotus in the water.

The Sikh-world-view is built on the foundation of the historical time. The Sikh world-view is the creation of the genius of Guru Nanak. Other contributors to the Sikh Canon supplemented it with their hymns. Guru Nanak, Guru Amardasa, and Guru Arjunadeva schematised it. The contents of the Guru Granth are eternal, but the Scripture itself was created. When it was created, it became eternal because of eternal values expounded in it. In the Sikh tradition, the scripture becomes eternal because it is true for all the times to come. It is not of an age, but of all the ages. It presents the view that man has an inherent tendency of self-transcendence because of his creative nature.

Sikhism is critical of the gangrenous and corrupt medieval religious practices sanctioned by the traditions. It bitterly condemns the rulers on the ground that they themselves subsumed or usurped all the temporal powers in their own persons. They became both *de facto* and *de jure* rulers. So much so, they concentrated all powers in their own hands. They claimed to be 'God incarnates', and relegated God to the peripheral status. This was the blatant exploitation of their worldly power. The Dasam Granth takes up this substantive problem in the autobiographical poetic composition, "Bachitra Natika" (wonderful cosmic drama), which is a creative work. The intention of the author is to expose false religious practices current in the society. The anthology does not deal only with his life events, but also depicts different *avtaras*, both in the Hindu and the Buddhist traditions, who appeared on the canvass of history in the four mythical ages (*yugas*) from the *satyayuga* (pure truth) to the *kaliyuga* (dark age). The khalsa of Guru Gobind Singh treads on the canvass of history and leaves his footprints for the coming generations.

The Sikh onto-theology is different in nature and tone from previous ones. The Sikh revelation is not the progressive self-disclosure of the Akala Purakh as is found in the Semitic traditions. In the Sikh view revelation is the outcome of ecstasy (*sahaj*) and absorption in the Akala Purakh (Numinous). The revelation of the Guru Granth embodies the ideological identity of monism, inclusive of all possible multiplicities of the creation, but it is subject to variations in attributes, which are hermeneutical coeval reactions of the contemporary contributors to the Guru Granth. We find that all the contributors to the

Sikh Canon have an identical monist ideology, but attributes of the Numinous have diversity of expressions in the context of their respective cultural milieus. Bhaktas' and Sufis' hymns, outside the Sikh Canon, has different tenor and are to be interpreted within the context of the Sikh tradition. When these hymns are incorporated in the Guru Granth, their meanings are transformed within the philosophical context of the Sikh Canon. That is to say, the bigger footprint covers the smaller footprint. Similarly, the context of the Guru Granth is wider because it covers the Indian and the Semitic cultural contexts. It does not reject the other revelations, but subsumes them in the wider circle. Thus, the Guru Granth encompasses the Semitic revelation as well as the *shruti* of the Vedic lore.

In India, the primacy of the otherworld over the secular world gained ground in the early medieval period. In the beginning, Islam was the religion of this-world, but later it developed the otherworldly tendency. Before Guru Nanak, asceticism was practised in both Indias and Islamic traditions in pursuit of salvation. The emphasis was laid on giving up one's home, which caused hardship to one's family. The ideal of the otherworld adopted the extreme form of negation of one's own existence. The concept of the otherworld was common in India and the Islamic countries. Guru Nanak bitterly condemns it in his hymns. The Guru Granth offers its critique. The Scripture advocates wrestling with the oddities of the world for the sake of the subaltern folks.

In the Semitic traditions –book, prophet, and revelation are central. Revelation, being a horizontal progression, is self-disclosure of reality in historical time. The historical time is accepted because the Semitic revelation progresses and narrows down the gap between the self and the Numinous. Complete identity between the self and the personal Deity is not achieved.

Guru Nanak and other Gurus continue playing a pivotal role until Guru Gobind Singh elevated the Guru Granth to the status of the supreme Divine. The Gurus' charismatic personality as central linchpin was replaced by the *shabda-guru*. The Guru's charismatic personality disappears. The Guru Granth mirrors the Akala Purakh. It is an embodiment of the

Numinous. On the contrary, the Semitic traditions do not do away with the prophet's charismatic personality. Revelation is progression in the linear time and historical realm. Sikhism interprets history in the Semitic sense. In the Semitic religions, personal God is central and in the Vedantic, tradition monism is the reigning ideology. The Guru Granth represents the restructured Indic ideology (monism).

When we say that the Guru Granth constitutes an epiphany of the *shabda-guru* (*etenal verbum*), it means that the scripture alone is a living contemporary sacred scripture (*pragat guran ki deha*). The Guru Granth is a living spirituality on the earth. Then a question arises in our minds: What is spirituality? The quintessence of revealed religion emphasises on love for sentient and insentient beings because it postulates immanent in everything. The Divine is present in every plant, animal, and person. Perceiving this unity is the essence of spirituality. Religion is a *modus operandi* for realising it. Love for humanity necessarily follows from the spiritual unity of the Numinous. Thus, spirituality is the fount of all creation, which is within the all-inclusive spirituality.

On the other hand, in the Indic traditions revelation of spirituality is not presented in historical time because time in Indian thought is illusory. It is only in the Sikh tradition that historical time as reality is accepted. Sikhism reconciles the cyclic concept of the time of the Indian and the Greek traditions with the linear concept of time, enshrined in the Semitic traditions and the Holy Scriptures. It is interesting to note that the revelation in the Guru Granth is not progressive like the Semitic traditions. The ideology of the Guru Granth is its kernel, but the interpretations differ. The revelation in the Guru Granth has an ideological identity of monism but the contributors to the Scripture capture the contemporaneous fluid social realities. They were critical of the morbid social and political conditions prevalent in the medieval society. The medieval Indian culture was in turmoil. The social and religious institutions were static and had lost their contact with the existential reality.

Indian revelation is an outcome of the esoteric discipline of the recluse (*rishi*), the bhaktas and the gurus. Therefore, the Guru Granth is a treasure-trove of medieval ecstasies of the bhaktas and the Sufis who had identical monistic ideologies. The hymns of the contributors of the Guru Granth were modified by Guru Amardas and Guru Arjundev to cohere with the central theme. Their ideologies are subsumed within the concrete ideology of the Guru Granth.

Select Bibliography

Alberuni, *India (11th cent.), trans.* by Edward Sachau. Delhi: D.K. Publisher, 2003.

Arjundeva, Guru (edit), *Shabadath: Shri Guru Granth Sahib* (Pbi). And annotated). Amritsar: SGPC, 1969.

Bhagavadgita, The. Gorakhpur: Gita Press, 1966.

Bhattacharyya, K.C., "Swaraj" in *Indian Philosophical Quarterly* (Pune): Vol. XI, October 1984.

Eckermann, *Conversations with Goethe*. London: J.M. Dent, 1946.

Fanon, Frantz, *The Wretched of the Earth*. NY: Penguin, 1982.

Freire, Paulo, *Cultural Action for Freedom*. London: Penguin, 1974.

—————, *Pedagogy of the Oppressed*. NY: Herder & Herder, 1972.

Ganapathy, T.N., *The Philosophy of the Tamil Siddhas*. Delhi: ICPR, 1993.

Gibb, H.A., *Ibn Battuta –Travels in Asia-Africa*. New Delhi: D.K. Publishers, 2004.

Gokal Chand, *Transformation of Sikhism* Patiala: Punjabi University, n.d.

Hamidullah, Muhmmad. *Introduction to Islam*. New Delhi: Kitab Bhavan, 2003.

Jha, D. N., *Ancient India: In Historical Outline*. New Delhi: Manohar 2004.

Jhanji, Rekha (edit.), *Essays in Honour of Dharmendra Goel: Knowledge, Culture, and Action*. Delhi: Ajanta Books International, 1994.

Kosambi, D.D., *The Culture and Civilization of Ancient India in Historical Outline*. Delhi: Vikas, 1994.

Majumdar, R.C., *An Advanced History of India*. London: Macmillan, 1951.

Padam, Piara Singh, *Guru Kian Sakhian*. Amritsar; Singh Brothers, 1999.

Padam, Piara Singh, Char Sahibzade. Amritsar: Singh Brothers,1998.

Panneerselvam, P., "The Philosophy of the Tamil Siddhas", *JICPR (Special* Issue) edited by R.C. Pradhan. New Delhi: ICPR, 2202.

Rajagopalachari, C., *Mahabharata*. Bombay: Bhartiya Vidya Bhavan, 1990.

——————, *Ramayana*. Bombay: Bhartiya Vidya Bhavan, 1989.

Randhir Singh, Bhai (compl.), *and Shabadârth: Dasam Granth, 3 Vols.* (Pbi. and annotated) Patiala: Punjabi University, 1973, 1982, and 1988.

Sarvarkar, V.D., *The Indian War of Independence,* Parts I-II. Bombay: Pœnix, n.d.

Singh, Nirbhai, *Philosophy of Sikhism (Reality and its Manifestations).* New Delhi: Atlantic, 1990.

——————, *Bhagata Nâmadeva in The Guru Grantha*. Patiala: Punjabi University, 1981.

——————, The *Sikh Vision of Heroic Life and Death.* Amritsar: Singh Brothers, 2006.

——————, *The Philosophical Perspective on Sikh View of Martyrdom.* Amritsar: Singh Brothers, 2007.

——————, Philosophical Contributions of Bhaktas and Gurus to Indian Culture. Delhi: Gyan Publishing House, 2010.

Singh, Puran, *The Spirit Born People*. Punjabi University Patiala, 1990.

Spengler, Oswald, *The Decline of the West, 2 Vols.* London: George Allen & Unwin. n.d.

Staniley Wollpert, *Gandhi and His Passion*. Delhi: OUP, 2001.

Tara Chand, *Influence of Islam on Indian Culture.* Allahabad: The Indian Press, 1963.

Thapar, Romila, *Early India (From the Origin to AD 1300).* New Delhi: Penguin, 2002.

Tolstoy, Leo, *The Kingdom of God and Peace Essays.* New Delhi: Rupa, 2001.

Weininger, Otto, *Sex and Character*. London: William Heinemann, 1975.

Wittgenstein, Ludwig, *Lectures and Conversations on Aesthetics, Psychology and Religion.* Oxford: Basil Blackwell, n.d.

Wittgenstein, Ludwig, *Philosophical Investigations.* Oxford: Basil Blackwell, 1972.

————, *Tractatus Logico-Philosophicus.* London: Rutledge & Kegan Paul, 1963.

————, *Culture and Value* edited by G.H. Von Wright. Oxford; Basil Blackwell, 1980.

Yardi, M.R., *Jñâneúvari.* Pune: Bharatiya Vidya Bhavan, 1995.

General Index

Philosophical Index